THE
GREEN
AND THE
BLACK

The Complete Story of the
Shale Revolution,
the Fight over Fracking, and
the Future of Energy

GARY SERNOVITZ

ST. MARTIN'S PRESS ⚏ NEW YORK

www.stmartins.com

The Library of Congress Cataloging-in-Publication Data is available upon request.

ISBN 978-1-250-08066-0 (hardcover)
ISBN 978-1-4668-9257-6 (e-book)

Our books may be purchased in bulk for promotional, educational, or business use. Please contact your local bookseller or the Macmillan Corporate and Premium Sales Department at 1-800-221-7945, extension 5442, or by e-mail at MacmillanSpecialMarkets@macmillan.com.

First Edition: February 2016

10 9 8 7 6 5 4 3 2 1

To Molly,
Every word is ours

CONTENTS

PART V: THE NATIONAL PERSPECTIVE

INTRODUCTION

I HAD NEVER BEEN TO NORTHEAST HARBOR, MAINE, BEFORE, BUT I FELT like I was home. The July weather was obscenely perfect. My lungs and mind had been liberated from a strangling Manhattan summer by days in the spruce and pine of Acadia National Park. I was there for the wedding of an old friend. The gathered were people I had known for fifteen years. Or they were people who felt wonderfully, immediately knowable: they were from the same colleges, from the same opinions, from everywhere but now living in the same neighborhoods of San Francisco, Washington, Boston, New York.

I hugged the mother of the groom, both of us giddy with the privilege of the salt air, the absorbing greens, most of all the occasion itself. Eventually—one can hug for only so long—we had to make small talk. She asked me if I was still writing. I am expert at handling that awkwardness. I mumbled something nonsensical and sort of untrue: "Always." It had been nine years since my second novel had been published.

Then she asked me if I was still working in investments and oil and whatnot.

That was easier to answer, I thought. "Yes."

"Well," she said, "I hope you don't frack."

I would not bring clouds into Northeast Harbor, into that celebration of love. I smiled too widely and asked too loudly, "But tell me, Jean, how are *you*?"

I WORK IN THE OIL INDUSTRY. I live in New York. For many years, without much problem, I kept those worlds separate, body and mind. But in 2010, the hydraulic fracturing—fracking—of gas wells infiltrated that hypothalamus of the metropolitan brain: it appeared on HBO. And ten months after the anti-fracking documentary *Gasland* debuted, a *New York Times* investigative reporting series attacked shale gas development, impact by impact. At the same time, inside the oil and gas business, we were beginning to understand that the advances in fracking and horizontal drilling techniques were swelling into something more than just ways to extract oil and gas from disconnected plays in Texas or North Dakota. The technological improvements, the volume of drilling, and the well-to-well leaps in productivity were aggregating into a gusher of American oil and gas production and an unforeseen energy renaissance. Looking back, the more stunning absurdity of the mother of the groom's question was not that amid the canapés we were discussing seventy-year-old, once obscure oil and gas well stimulation techniques. It was that the question in 2011 was only about the local impact of fracking. For as we talked, unknown to us both, fracking and related technologies had already begun to reshape the economy, environment, energy, and balance of power of the world.

Now the questions on the shale revolution—and all of its effects—from friends, family, investors, and strangers are constant. I am often their most proximate oilman. Doesn't fracking cause taps to light on fire? Doesn't it cause earthquakes? Isn't the boom just about gas? Isn't the boom hype? Hasn't the boom busted? Isn't it increasing carbon emissions? Isn't it decreasing carbon emissions? Aren't we now energy independent? Isn't Russia toast?

The people grilling me sense that fracking is important. But the shale revolution has erupted so quickly and has changed so continuously that the questions often seem to refer to issues inhabiting different timescales. Some are about problems, like *Gasland*'s lit faucets, that have been addressed, or were never exactly problems to begin with. The answers to other questions, such as the shales' long-term impact on commodity prices or greenhouse gas emissions, demand forecasts that we've only started to develop.

The questions also tend to be narrow. They focus on fracking's threat to water wells, or gas prices' influence on America's competitiveness, or the value of oil company bonds. But people rarely seem to wonder how all the questions interact. To me—at bottom, this is the reason for this book—the understanding of the shale revolution, one of the most unexpected and consequential changes of the last decade, resembles the classic blind men and the elephant problem. In the Indian fable, each blind man touches only part of an elephant and extrapolates from the part he feels what the whole elephant must be: a snake, a fan, a wall, the trunk of a tree.

When the U.S. oil industry was just beginning to adapt long-standing horizontal drilling and fracking techniques to unlock previously inaccessible reservoirs of gas and then oil, Americans couldn't have been expected to see the whole elephant. Seeing it was hard enough for us who worked in the energy sector. But too much has changed, the effects are too pervasive, and the elephant has stormed into the room. For the first time in forty years, we now live in a country of abundant—maybe too abundant—oil and gas. As a result, executives are trying to anticipate whether cheaper American energy will persist when deciding whether to build a factory in Shenzhen or South Carolina. College trustees are weighing the morality of investing in fossil fuels, and their investment offices are fretting over how to do so in an upended world. Commuters are anxiously hoping that the lower gasoline prices that came for Christmas 2014 will last forever. Communities are debating whether fracking is a danger to their groundwater or a savior to their hometowns. And policymakers outside the United States are contemplating their own national direction: to run away from or copy, if they can, the American boom.

Seeing the whole elephant doesn't make any of those decisions simple. The future is not linear; cause bumps into effect and knocks into cause. The boom puts values—about neighborliness, property rights, sacrifice, our responsibility to the planet's inhabitants today and to generations to come—to the test and in conflict. But too many people, I've found, are trying to answer the thorny questions sprouting from the boom with limited information. They hear only from people whose livelihoods depend on advocating or opposing the shale revolution. They hear only from the green or the black, environmentalists or the oil industry, lining up on the usual sides.

I WAS NOT BORN the son of a wildcatter in the West Texas scrub. For twenty-two years, I couldn't tell you what a wildcatter was or what Texas was like, save my unshakable knowledge that everyone there still wore cowboy hats. Maybe I also knew it was hot. In college I studied European history and was gripped by a dream of an academic career, until a summer of silence in the British Library previewed a lifetime of the same. In my first job out of college, at Goldman Sachs, I was assigned to the oil industry team in the equity research department because, well, that's where an opening was. Three years later, I announced that I was completely and irreversibly done with Wall Street and quit to write novels. For six years I lived in the East Village, stretched a jar of pasta sauce over as many noodles as it could go, and tried to will myself to be F. Scott Fitzgerald. Two novels were published. I was not declared the new Fitzgerald. And then, fettuccine money dwindling, I found out that I was apparently neither completely nor irreversibly done with Wall Street. Since 2004, I have worked at an oil-and-gas-industry-focused private equity firm, for much of that time as a managing director. We invest in small oil and gas producing and oilfield service companies. We also directly buy, operate—and, yes, frack—oil and gas fields.

(Oil, to make it clear, is crude oil. This is what comes from the ground and is converted in refineries to gasoline, diesel, jet fuel, and the rest. Gas is natural gas, the methane mainly that also comes from underground reservoirs and is delivered as a fuel to your stovetop and, in many cases, your local power plant. When people refer to the oil industry, they almost always mean the oil *and* gas industry. To occasion more confusion, gas is also a nickname for gasoline. When I refer to gas, though, it is to natural gas.)

When I started in the oil business, few Americans outside of it paid much attention. People recognized that oil companies existed, and few of those companies were ever popular. But the oil industry operated in the flyover beer belly of America, in the background of cosmopolitan consciousness. Climate change concerns, two years before the Kyoto Protocol, were still at their dawn. Also, the oil industry was dull: in 1995, companies like Exxon and Shell were old-line corporations like Chrysler or U.S. Steel, glamorous only to Rich Uncle Pennybags, the Monopoly man.

Then, around a decade ago, the oil and gas business emerged from hiding in plain sight. Advanced fracking and related tools launched a boom in U.S. shale reservoirs, of all places. We knew that America could conquer the world with iPhones and LeBron and #hashtag, but could that hillbilly-meets-Bond-villain industry really be a story of America, once again, on top?

It has been. Small technological tweaks, entrepreneurial orneriness, and—always a key ingredient—the right amount of desperation launched a revolution that allowed small oil and gas companies to extract hydrocarbons from shale rock and other low permeability, or "tight," reservoirs. Revolution is not too ambitious a word. In 2007, the country was rushing to build liquefied natural gas—LNG—import terminals before a cold, murderous winter arrived when we couldn't heat our homes. Energy experts debated what exactly our oil-constrained future would look like: a peaked-oil, Mad Max apocalypse as we battled each other and Tina Turner for the last drop of crude, or "just" a milder scenario, with the economy brought down by shortages and skyrocketing prices, 1970s-style, but without the benefits of sideburns or disco.

The trend lines have now turned sharp corners. From 2007 to 2014, U.S. shale gas production increased tenfold,[1] and the United States is now building LNG terminals to *export* gas. For two decades, until 2005, onshore oil production in the Lower 48 states declined every single year, falling by half. Since 2007, it has risen 123 percent. It's 1980 again.[2] Not only is the United States now the largest producer of oil and gas in the world, supplying 13 percent of the world's oil and 21 percent of its gas, fracked onshore U.S. wells have met effectively all of the world's incremental demand for oil over the last several years.[3] Indeed, in the past five years, the new, fracked supply of U.S. oil and gas has swamped demand, crashing natural gas prices in 2009 and leaving the industry speechless in

2014 with an almost 60 percent decline in oil prices in four breakneck months. Even stranger, this U.S. shale renaissance has happened in left-for-dead places like West Texas (oil country, for sure, but granddad's black-and-white oil country) and in places I had forgotten ever had oil or gas. North Dakota now has double the oil production per capita of Kuwait. Eight years ago, it produced less oil than Italy.[4]

And suddenly, the separate gardens I inhabited were growing together, vines leaping over walls. My Houston friends, who have long needled me as a Democrat-donating, yoga-practicing, skinny-pants-wearing New York City cliché—practically Obama himself in bald, less impressive form—would ask me to defend what "my" *New York Times* was saying about fracking now. And when I would have dinner with friends in New York, I would be eager to talk about books, politics, romantic intrigues of declining volume and spice as we entered our forties—really anything but my work. And my friends wanted to talk about fracking, even if they weren't totally sure what fracking was.

You don't do *that*, they would ask again and again, leaning back, like a child not sure she really wants to know what daddy did with Lady Hopalot, her sick pet bunny.

Yep, I would answer. We frack. You can't be in the business and not.

SURGING AMERICAN OIL AND GAS volumes and lower oil and gas prices are turning many elements of America and the world upside down. The fear of future price spikes has evaporated like the fear of smallpox, scrambling America's foreign policy toward antagonists like Iran and often antagonistic allies like Saudi Arabia. The shale revolution cut by 53 percent—$221 billion less—America's annual net bill for importing oil, gas, and petroleum products.[5] And it is having multiplier effects. With prices of its feedstock cheaper, the chemical industry has invested $138 billion "and counting" in new U.S. projects,[6] perhaps stoking an American manufacturing revival. While the upstream and midstream oil and gas industry accounted for only 0.35 percent of the American work-force at the start of 2004, it created 6.4 percent of new jobs over the next ten years—over 400,000 in total, when good jobs were hard to find.[7]

Miraculously, the United States achieved these benefits without directly aggravating climate change. The opposite was true: cheap natural gas displaced 200 million tons of coal consumed by Americans each year, all of it twice as polluting as gas.[8] From 2007 to 2012, largely thanks to natural gas, U.S. annual carbon dioxide emissions fell by a world-leading 725 million metric tons, equivalent to the total emissions from Germany.[9]

But the environmental implications of the U.S. shale revolution are not wholly good. Methane might or might not be an issue, as I discuss later. On the local level, the boom isn't an invisible economic phenomenon, like cloud computing. Drilling and fracking are loud, messy activities that bring pollution and disruption to communities. Capturing the boom's benefits while sometimes sacrificing the land and quiet of those communities might be the right thing to do for the country. It is not, however, fair.

More alarming, oil, gas, and coal still account for 86 percent of the primary energy consumed in the world.[10] We used to think we would reduce our emissions from fossil fuels because we would have no choice: demand would soon exceed our capacity to produce the fuels, especially oil, at reasonable prices. Alternative energies or radically transformed fuel efficiency would be necessary. But with oil and gas cheaper and more abundant after the shale revolution, we are now more likely to continue to consume fossil fuels. Americans are now buying fewer fuel efficient cars and trucks.[11] And while U.S. carbon emissions are down, global emissions in 2013 were 31 percent higher than a decade before.[12] And the world continues to get hotter by the year.

"OF COURSE SOCIAL OR POLITICAL collisions will take place," the philosopher Isaiah Berlin argued, "the mere conflict of positive values alone makes this unavoidable. Yet they can, I believe, be minimized by promoting and preserving an uneasy equilibrium, which is constantly threatened and in constant need of repair."[13] When people downplay the potential *or* perils of the American oil and gas renaissance to our collective future, when they try to promote a too easy equilibrium, I get frustrated and yappy.

The boom is the Internet of oil, a spark from and to existing technologies that led to an industrial change of such magnitude and speed that we have woken up, after a short nap, in a once impossible world. Yet public understanding of the changes brought by the shale revolution has severely—dangerously, I believe—lagged behind understanding the Internet. This has cleared the way for hype, scaremongering, bad policy—real rips in the equilibrium that need repairing. It has prevented us from seeing the positive values in collision or candidly discussing the urgent moral, technical, and environmental challenges before us. Because of that partial understanding, we risk losing some of the benefits of America's energy revolution. Fracking has been banned in the state where I live, by the governor I voted for. It has been outlawed in other cities, too. The Internet of oil won't be unplugged, but it will have outages.

This book ends with an uneasy but *precise* equilibrium. Along the way, it presents the whole story and the essential facts. I spend my days and too many nights discussing oil and gas with my colleagues, oil company executives, and (most central to my paycheck) institutional investors who look to us to invest their capital and help them understand what the shale revolution means to them, as fiduciaries and citizens. Those conversations, the crucible of this book, have convinced me that explaining the shale revolution should rest on two near paradoxical premises. First, I believe that each of five primary perspectives on the boom—industrial, local, financial, global, and national—must inform the others. Second, I believe that each perspective must be isolated to be studied up close, to understand it in full and not to retreat from its practical and ethical challenges. Each section of this book thus takes on a different point of view: the industrial perspective of how the old iron laws of the oil and gas business were broken; the local perspective of what drilling and fracking mean to the communities where it is happening; the financial perspective of how individuals and companies made money, by disruption and luck; the global perspective, of how the shale revolution is helping and hindering the fight against climate change; and the national perspective of how the revolution could be altering America's economy and relationships in the world.

So where do I stand? Upton Sinclair wrote, eighty years ago: "It is difficult to get a man to understand something, when his salary depends on his not understanding it."[14] But what is difficult is not impossible, and everything challenging gets better with practice. My practice consists of two decades of defending my views in New York on Monday and Houston on Tuesday, and trying to listen closely, open-mindedly to what all the sides say. I have come to understand, as salary-dependent as I am, the objections to fracking and the shale revolution. Oil and gas drilling is loud, dirty, and complicated. Its accidents have real victims. Not all companies will follow all the necessary regulations. And the shale revolution, by enabling a period of ample oil and gas, is causing the world to double down on fossil fuels. There is good evidence that this is a fatal mistake.

Yet when I see a billboard like the one put up by Yoko Ono and Sean Lennon asking New York City drivers to "Imagine there's no fracking,"[15] I cringe. That's because I imagine it. If the U.S. shale revolution hadn't happened, oil and gas prices would probably be triple what they are today, the United States might, like Europe, still be feebly climbing out of the global recession, our trade balance would be weaker, the dollar in the pits, American coal consumption and carbon emissions would be increasing, the Canadian oil sands would be the dominant source of new North American oil, poor people throughout the world would have less access to energy, the power of Putin and Middle Eastern monarchies would be dangerously magnified, and thriving Iran would be in a much better position to laugh off attempts to limit its quest for nuclear bombs.

The shale revolution is a testament to American engineering, rowdiness, and cocky refusal to give up. It came so suddenly, from such small adaptations to how the oil business was usually done, and from such seemingly unnatural places—rural Pennsylvania and North Dakota rather than Silicon Valley—that it is hard to measure how fundamentally it has already reshaped our prospects.

The shale revolution also urgently poses a hard question: is there any way to retain all of its world-changing, world-improving benefits without any of its global or local costs? I wish there were a simple answer. When the planet is at stake, answers never seem to be unambiguous enough. This book's mission is to explain the shale revolution, and its ambiguities, to allow us to make the best available decisions, ones beyond and more precise than either-or. To do so, we must start first with a total understanding, to know the green *and* the black, all the realities and possibilities of this once unimaginable shift. This is a book about where we have shockingly, excitingly, frighteningly found ourselves. Where we go from here, well, that's up to us.

Part I

THE INDUSTRIAL PERSPECTIVE

1. ROBBING THE MINT

I MAY NOT HAVE LEARNED ABOUT THE RESOURCE TRIANGLE ON MY FIRST day in the oil business in 1995, but it couldn't have been long after. The world, I was taught before I was taught much else, operates according to clear rules: the distribution of oil and natural gas follows a triangle shape. On the top is the good stuff: the gushers, oil almost as light as gasoline, natural gas rich with methane. The triangle gets broader with a greater volume of increasingly poorer reservoirs—less permeable, in smaller fields, the oil and gas of lower quality. Like a Life in the Middle Ages Triangle or a Contemporary Novel Triangle, the distribution is straightforward: the crappier it gets, the more of it you get.

The triangle has another feature, though: the crappier it gets, the more of it you get, the more costly to extract it gets. A century and a half of oil business experience had confirmed this.

By the mid-2000s, we were still living, as we had always lived, by the iron laws of the Resource Triangle. In the best case, we were supposed to find tomorrow's oil and gas at the bottom of the triangle, in increasingly hostile and expensive places. In the worst case, we were supposed to start running out of it altogether, just about now.

For most people outside the oil business, the industry remains the same: oil guys stick holes in the ground somewhere and oil comes up somehow and then whamo, presto, gasoline ends up at a BP station, where one distracts oneself from the price by studying real demonstrations of human ingenuity like the variety of Dr Peppers available today. But the consumers' unimpressed boredom may be the boom's most conspicuous achievement.

Oil and gas today is plentiful and cheap because there has been a revolution in many of the industry's basic premises. Laughably tiny incremental adaptations led to a stampede of industrial creativity. And my first lesson, that easiest lesson involving a triangle, came almost completely undone.

WHEN I WAS ASSIGNED to the oil group at Goldman Sachs in 1995, it was not the most enviable position in the equity research department. The action was in covering Intel or Seagate Technology, then dominating the cutting-edge world of disk drives. I suspect I was assigned to the backwaters because I came to the firm armed with all the stock market savvy a History degree could provide. My last summer of college had been spent researching British working-class attitudes toward imperialism, circa 1902, a topic that didn't even excite the British. Before that, I stocked nails at a hardware store. The senior Goldman Sachs analyst I worked for, I would later learn, hired me because I reminded him of his "somewhat lost" son.

The oil and gas business that year was at the end of a decade of price stagnation, except for the brief oil price spike around the first Gulf War. Nothing felt particularly new. The maturity didn't mean that there weren't new wells in new places, or innovation. After you drill into an oil or gas reservoir and bring it onto production, it can continue producing for years, sometimes decades. However, a well's daily produced volume declines every year as the reduction in the number of molecules in the reservoir (some, after all, are now powering someone's car) causes a decrease in the pressure expelling the oil or gas. While there is technical controversy over how much oil and gas production declines each year from the world's existing fields, the "observed" decline rate is an estimated 4 to 5 percent per year with the actual "natural" decline rate, if oil companies completely abandoned investing in those fields, at an estimated 8 to 9 percent per year.[1]

Field declines force the industry to remain dynamic. To supply the exact same amount of oil and gas, the industry must constantly develop new fields to make up for the declining production from old ones. For com-

panies that own drilling rigs and the like, this is the most wonderful feature in the natural order of the universe. (It's as if you ran a construction
company and your dearest fantasy came true: 4 to 5 percent of the world's
buildings disappeared every January 1, needing to be replaced.) Field declines are supportive of reasonable oil and gas prices, too: even if there is
no growth in demand—and global oil demand usually grows only 1 to
2 percent per year[2]—prices have to be stable and high enough for companies to make a profit, or hope that they can make a profit, from new wells.

At all times, the oil and gas industry needs to find new sources of
hydrocarbons. In 1995, the cliché that would dominate the first dozen or
so years of my career was already in use: we were at the end of the era of
easy oil and gas. The easiest oil and gas, at the tip of the Resource Triangle, are the fields in which if you drill a well, the pressure of the earth
spouts the oil into the sky, and 100 years later Daniel Day-Lewis wins an
Oscar for being you. There are massive older fields still producing easy
oil and gas today. People are still fighting over Kirkuk in Iraq, first discovered in 1927. The Ghawar field in Saudi Arabia, the biggest in history,
has been in production since 1951 and still makes 5 million barrels of oil
per day[3]—about 5.3 percent of what the world needs.[4]

But these tip-of-the-triangle fields have already been found. The last
giant million-barrel-per-day-plus fields discovered were Prudhoe Bay
in Alaska in 1968 and Cantarell in Mexico eight years later.[5] While some
large fields have been discovered over the last thirty years (albeit at an increasingly diminishing rate), the industry in which I learned the business
was focused on developing oil and gas fields that weren't easy: ones in
inconvenient locations, collected in smaller pools, trapped in complicated
geology, or containing heavier oil that requires more effort to refine (such
as the Canadian oil sands).

The biggest thrills in my early career were the helicopter rides to a
Texaco platform in the North Sea, and to a Brazilian one off the coast of
Rio, where I watched, fascinated, the fishing boats tied companionably to
the platform legs. The industry's innovators, big companies like Mobil and
Chevron, were doing the hard stuff: drilling in deeper waters offshore,
developing fields in sketchy kleptocracies, orchestrating "pipeline politics" to get oil and gas to market, or doing triple-axel flips by developing

complicated fields and international pipeline systems from places like Kazakhstan. Or in Kazakhstan itself, where the giant Kashagan field, for which the first seismic surveys were conducted in 1993, has still failed to launch.[6] If you think that your twenty-one-year-old still living in your basement is frustrating, take comfort that at least he didn't cost $50 billion to raise.

Yes, the oil business innovated, but it was almost dutiful. Gone were the glamorous days of the 1960s and 1970s when the Sauds and Vens took operatorship of their national oil companies away from companies like Exxon and Shell, nationalizing "our" reserves and forcing the industry into new areas like Alaska and the North Sea. By 1995, even the two key recent innovations to help the industry find the harder oil and gas were already becoming routine: deepwater drilling and three-dimensional seismic surveying that let companies better map potential reservoirs underground. The oil industry then was like a star quarterback at the end of his career, still able to get the ball into the end zone but without the acrobatics or pep of his prime. And maybe the oil industry didn't need to be forever young: in 1995, the oil consumption growth rate had been only 1.4 percent per year for a decade.[7] In 1998, oil prices collapsed from oversupply.

The ultimate sign of the industry's maturity was that it did what every industry does when business growth doesn't lead to much profit growth: it caught synergy fever. Within three years, starting in 1998, major oil companies merged, forming a class of "supermajors."

Was there any excitement in the oil and gas business? Well, Enron was the rage.

ELSEWHERE, IN 1995, the employees of Mitchell Energy, a midsized Texas natural gas producer, were getting fed up with the Barnett Shale, a natural gas play outside Fort Worth. (In the oil industry, a play is a geological zone or concept in a specific area.) They'd been at it for fourteen years, with little to show for their efforts. The rock in the Barnett would not give up commercial amounts of gas, no matter what they did. Nick Steinsberger, a thirty-four-year-old petroleum engineer who joined the company that year, was told, "We might drill for a couple more years and then give up."[8] Had that surrender happened, company founder George Mitchell's eventual triumph in the Barnett Shale would not be the Concord and Lexington of the shale revolution. The near surrenders, though, help burnish Mitchell's legend. The best way to be seen as a visionary and not a crank is to be successful. But to be a visionary, and not just an average orthopedist-in-Scarsdale success, requires a decade—and preferably decades—in which people see you as a crank. And by 1995, George Mitchell was in his fourteenth year of increasing skepticism of his pursuit of the Barnett.[9]

In hindsight, of course (and it is always of course, with hindsight), Mitchell seemed destined to become the Henry Ford of the shales. He was the son of hardworking immigrants: his Greek immigrant father had let his own name be changed to Mike Mitchell under the sensible theory that Savvas Paraskevopoulos is not easy to say.[10] By fate or by the pedestrian fact that his father's cousin owned a shoeshine stand in Houston, George Mitchell was born in Texas. After growing up in Galveston, Mitchell studied at Texas A&M, which produces oilmen and oilwomen with only slightly less fervor than it produces football obsessives.

Mitchell majored in petroleum engineering at A&M, but after many geology courses seemed to have developed the soul of a geologist. That self-image explains a lot to us in the business. There are three basic disciplines in the American oil industry: geology, engineering, and land. (There is a fourth category of oil company workers, the finance and accounting side, but the rest of the business thinks of us as the Ringo of the enterprise: technically necessary but hardly central to the band.) We in the business think of land folks, who go by the name landmen—even, awkwardly, if they are women—as the smooth talkers of the business. Their job is to convince ranchers or farmers to let a company drill on their land. Landmen also have the less glamorous task of making sure all the leases and legal titles are in order. But acknowledging that dull reality deprives the rest of us from thinking of landmen as hustling, drunk, or likely both.

Engineers are the proud realists of the oil business, designing and managing the drilling and completing of wells, analyzing the volumes and likelihood of producing reserves in the first place, making sure wells produce as much as they can, and daily classifying (with precise formulas) every nonengineer in the business as either useless, totally useless, totally useless and counterproductive, or just insane.

The last crack is directed as often as not at geologists, the industry's dreamers, always with an idea (often a nutty one) about some massive deposit. Engineers habitually scoff that oil and gas in the ground won't do much good if you can't produce it, but geologists are right: there is a tremendous amount of oil and gas in the ground. Modern humans have lived for 200,000 years, a mere 13 seconds to the day of the 1.3 billion years there has been multicellular life on earth. The plants, animals, and fungi on earth for the 23 hours, 59 minutes, and 47 seconds before us didn't pack up their bodies and fly to Mars but died here, often in ancient seas, their living matter sometimes decomposing into molecules on sea floors. Over tens of millions of years, geological movements buried these seas—and the plant and marine organism corpses in them. Once buried, the pressure of the earth from above and the heat of the earth from below cooked the organic molecules into coal, oil, and natural gas.

Layer upon layer of varying rock types underlie every inch of the earth. People picture those layers like a Rothko painting, in calming horizons. But underground strata are jumbled, intricate, and faulted with de Kooning–style disorder, from many causes: volcanoes, the clash of continents, the erosion of gigantic mountain chains. Geologists describe the resulting "depositional environment" so vividly and excitably, as if they are describing a thousand-room palace filled with diamond curtains and chocolate furniture, that the rest of us are forced to remind them that their wonderland is underground rock.

The buried organisms have been cooked into hydrocarbons—molecules with both hydrogen and carbon in them—at various depths in that depositional environment, given how long and chaotic the earth's geological history has been. Many of the cooked hydrocarbons have remained in place, but other molecules have moved upward, in paths of least resistance, to lower-pressure areas through natural cracks and fissures in the earth. They were pushed up, effectively, from the heavy weight of the earth—the overburden—above them. You can reenact this by jumping on a wet sponge. Water even at the bottom of the sponge will shoot up into the air, which has much lower pressure than the ceiling of the apartment below. If your downstairs neighbors complain, explain that you're their overburden.

The sponge analogy is helpful in another regard. Oil and gas reservoirs are not buried tanks filled with liquids or gases that you puncture and drain. Oil and gas molecules are contained within the pore spaces of rocks. Some rare rocks have large pore spaces, more like a dried sponge. But most types of underground rocks have such low "porosity" that the pores are invisible to the naked eye—and sometimes even the average microscope.

The other key measure of a rock for petroleum geologists is permeability: how easy it is for oil and gas molecules to travel through and between the pores of the rock. If you were an oil molecule and the rock around you were a hotel, porosity is the size of your room. Permeability, measured in units called darcies (named after a French engineer, not the emotionally impermeable Mr. Darcy), is how easy it is to move through the halls and stairwells connecting the rooms and floors. Some rocks, like in the Ghawar field, have gorgeous carpeted passageways, making the journey to the surface a joy. Other rocks are like Alcatraz.

By the time George Mitchell, in 1981, embarked on the project that would make him more than an ordinary oilman, his business was already flourishing. Building on initial finds from his wildcatter days in the 1950s, Mitchell ran an eponymous publicly traded company, albeit a relatively small one. Mitchell Energy's economic engine was a collection of gas fields in North Texas that supplied about 10 percent of Chicago's gas.[11] That wasn't all that kept Mitchell busy. He had ten children. He founded The Woodlands, a real estate development—now a full-fledged community of over 100,000 people—twenty-seven miles north of downtown Houston. (ExxonMobil moved many of its workers to a complex near The Woodlands in 2014. It's as if the Yankees had decided to move their stadium to a town built by the coach of the Trenton Thunder.)

Mitchell's contract to supply gas to Chicago was a yoked ox, financially powerful but perennially dangerous, as the company was obligated to supply guaranteed volumes with gas from depleting fields. One of the strategies his company came up with was drilling in the Barnett Shale. Mitchell didn't discover the Barnett. For decades, others had drilled through it. Well logging tools, which let them know the characteristics of various strata underground, had revealed the presence of gas in the shale.

The problem was that the Barnett Shale, located 5,000 to 8,000 feet below the surface in its most productive areas, was an exceptionally low permeability source rock. Oil and gas is found at all sorts of depths and geological structures, but it's not made everywhere. It's made in the kitchen: usually deeply buried source rocks, either black shales or black limestones called marls, in which temperature and pressure cook the dead organic matter into oil and gas. This process happens continuously: "self-sourcing" rocks are still cooking oil and gas today. One of the most astonishing geological lessons of the shale revolution is that there is much more oil and gas still in place in source rocks than we had ever imagined.

As the concentration of oil or gas builds in source rocks, pressure expands within them and expels some of that oil or gas. If your room in the rock hotel started producing people, and you found yourself with all ten of George Mitchell's children on your bed, you would want to find a way to get out.

The earth has escape routes: natural fractures and faults and other permeable conduits. Oil and gas will gravitate upward as much as it can, pushed by the pressure of the overburden. Sometimes—"up through the ground come a-bubblin' crude"—it will gravitate all the way to the surface, allowing a Sumerian to seal his pots or Jed Clampett to move to Beverly Hills. The migration of a lot of oil and gas, however, is halted by what geologists call traps, impermeable seal rocks that prevent the molecules from moving any further. Imagine that your overcrowded room drove you up the floors of the hotel as you sought fresh air on the roof deck. You desperately took elevators, climbed stairs, made progress—until you found the last available stairwell was bricked up. You are in a trap.

The whole history of the oil business, the history I was taught, was about the production of oil and gas from conventional trapped reservoirs: oil and gas pressured upward from the source rock into buried reefs, shoals, channels, and bar sands. Every oil and gas reservoir has to have a source rock somewhere, just as every baby has parents. The industry's conventional wisdom was that it was pointless to drill into the source rock because it was either too deep (and too expensive) to drill or the porosity and permeability were absurdly low. If you wanted oil or gas from source rock, geologists would joke, all you had to do—all you could do—was wait. It would eventually migrate up in a few hundred thousand years.

And yet drilling into source rock was what Mitchell and his employees were trying to do. It wasn't completely delusional. There was, in theory, a lot of gas in the Barnett. And the oil business, since the beginning, has found ways to stimulate oil and gas in tight, low permeability rocks that won't flow naturally to a wellbore. There are discrete stages in getting oil and gas from the ground, as I detail in Chapter 5. Stimulation activities, including fracking, are part of the completion stage that occurs after drilling. They create escape routes for hydrocarbon molecules, making artificial fractures and channels in a reservoir by which the hotel guests can get to the roof deck and sip champagne under the stars.

The guiding principle in the history of well stimulation has been an all-American theory of why-the-hell-not. In 1866, only seven years after the modern oil industry began, Civil War veterans dropped dynamite torpedoes down wells to fracture reservoirs.[12] Over the next century, in lockstep with the ever increasing sophistication of humans to kill other humans, stimulation techniques evolved to include acid, nitroglycerin, napalm, and—in a few 1950s experiments that were more *Dr. Strangelove* than Tom and Jerry—nuclear bombs.[13] In the 1940s, companies started using water, pumped at high pressure, to break up the rock and create fractures. What became known as hydraulic fracturing was much safer and more effective than dynamite.

The road from the first frack jobs in the 1940s to the Kitty Hawk of the shale revolution, a Mitchell Energy well in North Texas called the S. H. Griffin #4, is a long and—for frack junkies, at least—interesting one. Mitchell himself had fracked in shallower zones above the Barnett Shale as early as the 1950s.[14] The second part of this book dives into the environmental controversies over fracking and what fracking actually is. But in the industrial history of the shale revolution, there are two important things to note. First, shale gas drilling was not some new invention, like Pringles, in which some tidy fellow at Procter & Gamble came upon the idea to reshape potato chips to fit into a tube—and the world was never the same. It was more like the iPhone, in which a lot of strands of existing and newer technologies came together. (Recent studies of creativity highlight the depressing finding that big breakthroughs, upon closer inspection, are almost always smaller and less breakthroughy than first thought.) Mitchell Energy started its search for ways to stimulate the Barnett Shale in 1981. For the next seventeen years, as engineers at the company experimented with different reservoir stimulation techniques, so did hundreds of other companies in hundreds of other oil and gas fields. The U.S. federal government, too, sponsored basic research and field experiments to extract gas from "unconventional" reservoirs like shales.

The second thing to know about Mitchell's advance is that the successes and failures over those seventeen years were not all binary outcomes; there was no fifty-game losing streak that ended with a stomping victory. In fields with traps sealing in the reservoir, results are often a win or a loss: you have either a producer or a duster—a dry hole. There are, however, other oil and gas reservoirs in which the outcomes are more subtle. The questions are not whether there are hydrocarbons or not, but how much, and can you produce enough of them to make money. In an ongoing source rock like the Barnett Shale, there is no doubt that there is gas underground. But as a friend likes to remind others in our business, what we do is no different than making widgets. It's all about the margin: a well that costs $5 million to drill and recovers only $1 million worth of gas is just as bad as a duster. The S. H. Griffin #4 well was not the first well ever to produce gas from the Barnett Shale. It was the first widget to make money.

Mitchell's engineers and geologists experimented in the Barnett the same way people in the oil business are still experimenting with shale reservoirs: well by well. In fracking, there are two essential components: fluid that hydraulically cracks the rock and sand or ceramic particles—proppants (pronounced "PROP-intz" not "prop pants," as if they were stunt trousers)—that keep the new fractures propped open. Without proppants, the overburden of the earth, pushing down, would reclose the fracks.

Shale deposits in different areas, even ones close by, react sometimes unpredictably to different types of frack fluid and different sizes and strengths of proppants. You have to try stuff to see what works. Nick Steinsberger suggested a series of new ways to frack—called "completion designs" in the business—because they were cheaper and, well, nothing else had succeeded. Operators in Kansas had been using "slickwater" fracks for decades. A buddy of Steinsberger explained that he was using them for another type of rock in another part of Texas.[15] Steinsberger's adaptation of those frack techniques to the Barnett was somewhere between a Hail Mary and a hunch.[16]

Steinsberger's first attempt, Askey B-4, suffered a mechanical failure. But when the second attempt, the S. H. Griffin #4 well, produced 1.5 million cubic feet of gas per day, the Mitchell team finally had a profitable well. There was only a slight exhale inside the company. As a geologist who worked at Mitchell at the time told me, "It was not until we had fifteen-plus rigs in the field drilling the Barnett Shale coupled with the increase in production that everyone finally believed it was the real thing."[17]

The profitability of the S. H. Griffin #4 was, to some extent, due to the increased probability of success at anything after a larger number of attempts. Yet what really allowed the S. H. Griffin #4 to come to be was that Steinsberger worked for a company led by a stubborn optimist with plenty of money and a corporate structure that permitted him to do whatever the hell he wanted to. Mitchell Energy, which was never an energy giant, spent $250 million on the Barnett Shale over seventeen years with very little to show for it. Any sane company would have shut down trying in the fifth year. And if it was engineers like Steinsberger to the rescue—and engineers smile that they are always to the rescue—with a fracking technique that finally worked, that technique was comprised of proppant, water, *and* a creative, entrepreneurially relentless American business culture that celebrated audacity.

Whatever the cause, finally being able to commercially produce hydrocarbons from source rock was a signal event in the history of the oil business. Slick Willie Sutton robbed banks because that's where the money is. But this was no longer robbing banks. It was robbing the mint.

2. PEAKERS, BUNKERS, IMPORTS, AND YURTS

AND THE GLOBAL INDUSTRY YAWNED.

In 1998, the year of the S. H. Griffin #4, the year I coincidentally quit Goldman Sachs, I was completely unaware of the well. Frankly, it wouldn't have mattered had I known about it: my future was in fiction, not fracking. But after six years of two published novels and trying (and failing) to impress people with my command of the lesser works of John Updike, I started working in 2004 at an oil-and-gas-focused private equity firm founded by two friends from Goldman Sachs. I still work there, where my primary job is to convince institutional investors to entrust us with some of their money to make new investments in small companies or to buy mature oil and gas properties. While my wife's description to strangers of what I do—"he writes funny e-mails all day"—may omit a task or two of my role as a titan of energy finance, my daily life is not as a Wolf of Oily Wall Street. Indeed, my career has had such a dearth of skullduggery, hanky-panky, double-dealing, diamond-booted glamour, or crazy jackpot deals that Leonardo DiCaprio would refuse to play me, despite our uncanny physical resemblance. I spend most of my time out of the office in conference rooms at foundations, endowments, pension funds, and other investors talking to them about what we do—and how the oil and gas business is changing.

In my six years away from the business, it felt like nothing had changed at all. Yes, Mitchell Energy had discovered how to produce from the

Barnett Shale, and in 2001, Devon Energy bought the company for $3.5 billion.[1] But as exciting as that must have been if you were a public shareholder of Mitchell Energy or, even better, George Mitchell (who became a billionaire), gas from the Barnett Shale still made up less than 2 percent of total U.S. gas production in 2004.[2] We considered it, along with a few other oddball oil and gas fields, an unconventional resource, just another tight reservoir. We didn't rub our hands greedily with strategies to empty the mint.

I look back flabbergasted that I didn't think of that high-cost play as any more or less interesting than others, such as drilling for small fields in the Gulf of Mexico. It would take a second phase of the boom for me to see the shale revolution as a national phenomenon, and another phase after that for it to reshape the world. In the meantime came four years of increasingly grave doubts as to whether the oil and gas business was capable of meeting its most basic task: supplying the country and the world with fuel.

IN 2004, WE CONSIDERED the Barnett local news even though operators had begun to succeed in combining Mitchell Energy's six-year-old fracking recipe with horizontal drilling, the second of three major innovations of the boom. (Oryx Energy had drilled horizontally in the Barnett in the mid-1990s but, like Moses unable to enter the promised land, never made any good wells because it lacked the right completion techniques.[3]) A shale reservoir like the Barnett might only be 300 feet thick, buried 7,000 feet below the surface. The well commuting downward toward it produces from nothing, a straw in cement. Even once the vertical well reaches its targeted depth and is fracked, it extracts gas only from a few feet from the fractures themselves, cracks thinner than a human hair. Those cracks extend a couple of hundred feet in all directions from the end of the wellbore, in an area the size of a small arena. This was why production from the S. H. Griffin #4, as historic as it was, was still relatively low.

Horizontal drilling, however, allows a company to drill along an underground highway collecting gas from one arena after the next. Horizontal drilling was not designed for U.S. shales. It wasn't, by 2004, even all that new. It was only the latest variant of directional drilling, which had been around since the 1930s but had become standard in offshore wells in the 1970s. In offshore wells then (and now), operators wanted to limit the area from which they had to drill, to forgo the construction of a pricey platform or the need to move a rig. Given the large conventional fields that companies were targeting at the time, they could also be somewhat casual about how their well got to the reservoir. This was good because the imprecise technology then available led to a lot of artful rambling and stopping and starting to figure out where the heck the well actually was. It was only with the advent of measurement while drilling—MWD—technology in the 1980s that oil companies, through accelerometers, magnetometers, and other tools near the drill bit, could receive prompt well location information at the surface miles away. (They did this through pulses sent through drilling mud, like Morse code from the underworld.) Oil companies, finally able both to get from here to there and to know where they were during the process, could at last start coloring within the lines.

I have found that horizontal drilling is one of the more difficult things for people to visualize. People can intuit how fracking works: if I aim water from a high-pressure hose at a brick wall, anarchy ensues. But it is harder to picture how to drill a well two miles deep and then turn it horizontal, especially when drilling is done with thirty-foot sections of hard steel pipe. The steel isn't being bent by Underground Superman, nor is there some gadget that shoots a pipe horizontally from a vertical well. A well becomes horizontal after it curves over great distances. While wells vary, a typical shale well will turn from vertical to horizontal over 500 to 800 vertical feet.

Imagine a drill pipe as a pencil: it would take 300 pencils attached end to end, the height of a seventeen-story building, to get to a typical shale reservoir vertically, 9,000 feet deep. If you're going horizontal, you first guide the pencils straight down, each new pencil driving the whole drill string deeper, for fourteen floors. Over the three lowest floors, you communicate to a motor on the bottommost pencil to angle that pencil 2 to 4 degrees closer to horizontal from the direction of the previous one. You repeat this action, with each new pencil at a gently different angle. Over forty to fifty pencils or so, in a sweet good night, the pencil string goes from being upright to lying on its side. Reality is messier than pencils, of course. In an oil or gas well, the move from vertical to horizontal is not always a calm slumber. There is considerable "tortuosity" and variance in each angle of repose as the well responds to rock.[4]

No new play is ever ignored for long in the oil business. At my firm, we talked about the Barnett, but it seemed neither big nor repeatable enough to matter much beyond a few counties in North Texas. When I returned to the oil industry in 2004, our two existential challenges were, indeed, as they ever were. First, the industry had to find incremental sources of oil, and it was primarily doing so with some "hard" strategies in deepwater locations, smaller deposits, challenging countries, tricky reservoirs, and older fields that could be subjected to enhanced recovery techniques. Second, the industry needed to find enough natural gas to supply America's needs.

While U.S. gas consumption was growing just 1 percent or so annually in the 1990s and 2000s, and while there was plenty of gas in the world, it was not in convenient locations or easy to import, except by pipelines from Canada.[5] You can pump oil onto oceangoing tankers, and away you go. For natural gas, you have to construct multibillion-dollar liquefaction plants to freeze it into liquid form—the gas would take up 600 times the space if you didn't—and then build multibillion-dollar regasification plants to turn the LNG back into gas people can use. A global LNG business had been in existence since 1964. LNG was first exported from Alaska in 1969. There were even a few small LNG regasification plants built in the continental United States in the energy-scarred 1970s.[6] But like velour suits, they were mothballed as a fad of the era.

No country or gas consumer wants to import LNG if they can get gas more cheaply by pipeline or from domestic sources. So, with production from existing U.S. gas fields naturally declining as always, 2004 was another year in a multi-decade game of Where Will the Next Source of U.S. Gas Come From? In the 1990s, there was Canada, the shales of that era. Then came a line of other contenders: coalbed methane, new basins in the Rockies, smaller fields in the shallow-water Gulf. The enthusiasm for these sources overlapped, or rose and fell in mini-cycles. The Barnett was thought of as a lesser round in the same old game.

While there were exceptions, the two quests—the one for new sources of oil and gas for the entire world, and the one for new sources of gas for the United States—were generally handled by different types of companies, cousin industries operating in parallel. The global quest for new sources was driven by big state-owned national oil companies, like Saudi Aramco, and big international oil companies, like Shell—supertanker enterprises that moved slowly but with force. The U.S. gas quest was pursued almost wholly by independent exploration and production (E&P) companies solely focused on the upstream—oil and gas extraction—segment of the business.

E&P companies were, and are, a diverse group of businesses that come in every size, from large public companies (some with projects internationally) to minuscule businesses with a long-faced hound dog standing in for an actual third employee. E&P companies also come in every personality. Some are geologist-driven dreamers, out for the big score, descendants of the old-time wildcatters. Some are grind-it-out businesses focused on improving margins on older fields. Some are shady promoters, barely companies at all.

Despite the diversity of personalities, the U.S. E&P industry collectively operated (and still operates) on the principle that if there is a cubic foot of gas or an ounce of oil that can be produced profitably—or for some, even if there's a hey-you-never-know chance that it can be produced profitably—someone will try. By 2005, there were 100 operators in the Barnett alone. Production had risen sixfold since 2000.[7] That year, half of all the drilling rigs in the world were operating in the United States even though the country produced just 12 percent of the world's hydrocarbons.[8] And 86 percent of the rigs drilling in the United States were drilling for gas.[9]

IF I HADN'T MISSED MUCH in my six years away from the business, the manageable stroll of the industry in 2004—meeting gently increasing demand despite the end of easy oil and gas—was turning onto a much steeper path. For the next four years of my life, my job wasn't about Mitchell Energy's fracking breakthrough. My job was explaining to investors how we were navigating through steadily and, in the final flourish, almost unbelievably rising prices.

But, still, the dynamics were understood by the industry's existing rules. In the previous forty years, oil price spikes came primarily from supply shocks: the two notorious ones in the 1970s with the Arab oil embargo and the Iranian Revolution, and some lesser ones, around the two Gulf Wars. Leading oil industry chronicler Dan Yergin called what happened from 2002 to the middle of 2008 a "demand shock," only the second modern one after a similarly scorching period of consumption in the late 1960s and early 1970s.[10]

The 2002–2008 demand shock was a global phenomenon but also a Chinese one. China's oil consumption during that period rose by over half and accounted for 36 percent of increased global demand.[11] (It had started importing oil only in 1993.)[12] On the face of it, though, global demand still increased during that time by a less-than-frightening-seeming 2 percent per year, compared to 1.2 percent from the five-year period that preceded it.[13]

However, it is important to remember that the oil industry, like many, faces a battle between the exponential and the arithmetic. Oil demand tends to increase as a percentage of the year before, with population and economic growth. (Your car will be driven more if you get a job or if your daughter gets her license.) But a 2 percent increase in demand in 2004 calls for many more physical barrels to be produced than a 2 percent increase in 1984, when less oil was consumed. And from 2002 to 2007, the world consumed 1.7 million barrels per day more on average than the year before. (A barrel is forty-two gallons.) From 1997 to 2002, the increase had been about half that level.[14]

The problem is that oil supply doesn't increase exponentially. Existing wells and fields will help the industry find the new necessary ones only if there is a lot of "well control." In an area with high well control, a new well drilled near an existing one will be similar in its results and characteristics. A Big Mac at the new McDonald's will taste like all the other Big Macs in town. An area with low well control means that when you're drilling a new well, results from a neighboring well reveal little. The new McDonald's Big Macs could taste like cod. The "post-easy" era of oil and gas meant, essentially, that oil companies were operating in many areas without much well control. Each new field was a new invention. Seismic and other technologies were mitigating higher-risk exploration a bit, but even if you found a field in a remote place, the development of it would be fraught.

The savior—at least to those of us who make a living selling oil—was classical economics. As known since the days of Adam Smith, the price of a commodity should follow its cost of production. And so with new supply coming primarily from harder, more costly places, oil prices should— and did—rise. In some areas, like the North Sea, for example, this meant that we could afford to strike relatively small deposits of oil even in only one out of every three or four exploration wells. The high price received for the oil in the successes would pay for the dusters. In other areas, with fields with lower-quality oil or with soaring drilling costs, projects that were losers if companies got only $30 per barrel would open up when oil was $75.

The expectation in the industry was guided by the Resource Triangle: each year, we would need to develop more high-cost barrels. The rise in oil prices at first made sense. But when they eventually, unexpectedly quadrupled from $27 per barrel in 2002, based on the monthly closing price, to an average of $113 per barrel in the first half of 2008,[15] people who do not find higher oil prices to be a blessing (those people including my father and pretty much everyone else on the planet) started to wonder. Was this "classical economics"? Were shadowy speculators the cause? Were oil companies manipulating the market? Was I, my dad asked, manipulating the market? Or—the question most surprising to me—was peak oil finally here?

THE PEAK OIL CONCEPT was derived from the work of a formidable geologist, M. King Hubbert. It was no surprise that Hubbert—cantankerous, abrasive, arrogant—chose to go by his royal middle name. He was also part of a uniform-wearing North American movement called Technocracy, whose members saluted their leader, the Great Engineer, when he walked into the room.[16] But Hubbert is not remembered (luckily for him) for his leader saluting of the 1930s but for his oil production modeling twenty years later. Hubbert argued that no matter what you did, no matter how many enhanced oil recovery techniques you tried, eventually you couldn't increase oil production anymore in any basin. Production, following a bell-shape curve, would start to decline when about half the oil that could be produced was produced. The top of Hubbert's production curve became known as Hubbert's Peak.

Peak oil theories derived from Hubbert's work were buds off the old Malthusian pessimism: when demand for anything increases exponentially and supply increases arithmetically, we're screwed. For a while, according to the theories, the global industry could still increase production by opening up new basins around the world. Eventually, though, like an alcoholic facing an emptied liquor cabinet, there would be no more basins or countries to tap. The whole world would be unable to increase production. The debate, among the peakers, was not if peak oil would happen in any one place—it had happened in lots of them, including the continental United States—but what year it would happen for the planet. Some, by the mid-2000s, claimed that it was already here.

I never bought into peak oil theories. I had confidence that innovation would increase recoveries from existing oilfields—someday. Peak oil was also a pet theory of environmental radicals and ultraconservative survivalists, and I had an unshakable belief that anytime the far left and far right agree on anything (the meaningless of bourgeois existence, the 1939 divisibility of Poland) they are wrong. I also had a distaste for the smug, nihilistic, almost gleeful of-course-I-wouldn't-wish-ill-on-anyone-*but* rhetoric of the peakers. Their predictions of The End seemed too tied up in a need to prove that awful modern civilization, with its oil addiction and carbon spewing and nylon panty hose and television entertainment programs, was finally being presented with the bill. Some peakers were preparing themselves for the end, depending on their political leanings, in bunker or yurt.

In July 2008, *GQ* published "World Without Oil, Amen," a fascinating peaker case study (by a writer I know and respect, his yurty peakedness aside). The article dripped with skepticism for anyone who doubted peak oil, musing on the possibility of independent thought by an oil company employee. It ended with a visit to the Canadian oil sands, an "unconventional" source of oil then thought of as the only long-term hope for North American onshore oil production. Its only drawbacks, the article argued, were being "unconventionally expensive" and "unconventionally destructive."[17]

The article annoyed me. But my gut dislike wasn't an argument. My argument was likely the same as most everyone in the oil business: technology would save us. But if you asked me to name that technology, I would have hummed the *Star Trek* theme to distract you. I had no idea. The peakers' evidence also seemed more concrete than my hope: continental U.S. oil production, as in many places, was already skiing down Hubbert's Peak. From 1986 to 2005, it fell by half. Total U.S. production declines were more moderate, only because of new basins in Alaska and the deepwater Gulf of Mexico.[18]

As a believer in what economists call price signals, disliking peak oil was also getting more difficult by the day. Oil prices were rising fast—$35 per barrel, or 57 percent, in 2007 alone. They shot up an additional 33 percent in the first five months of 2008.[19] Matt Simmons, the most famous energy investment banker at the time, wrote a book, *Twilight in the Desert*, that argued that the Saudis would peak soon, too, but were lying to hide their fate. The implications were clear. The twilight was happening in the desert, but the darkness would descend on us all. In March 2008, analysts at Goldman Sachs, where only a decade ago I was part of the team that would boldly raise our per-barrel oil price assumption from $19 to $20, warned that oil price "super-spikes" to $200 per barrel could occur by 2012.[20]

I hated peak oil theory. But I started to wonder. Was I more of a bunker guy or a yurt guy? Would I look better in a loincloth made out of deer hide or bark?

It is hard to fathom that this was eight years ago.

EXCEPT ON THE LOONIEST FRINGES, no one predicted an imminent peak in global gas production. The earth has more gas in it than oil, as oil is cooked in a more limited range of depths and prone, when too hot or pressured, to become gas. U.S. consumers also weren't ravenously consuming gas. Gas here is used primarily for heating buildings, generating power, and making stuff. In the late 2000s, a rise in power sector use was being offset by flatlining demand in the residential sector (with increasing fuel efficiency) and falling demand in the industrial sector. U.S. gas demand was only 15 percent or so greater than it had been forty years before.[21]

Yet there was also no easy solution for how to meet even stagnant demand with domestically produced gas. The hundreds of indefatigable independents, with their thousand rigs ferociously drilling, were having trouble increasing production. Gas prices were rising because we were drilling in increasingly poor reservoirs, like George Mitchell had in that (when terms like millidarcies just won't do) tight-as-a-flea's-butthole Barnett Shale. They were rising because, by 2007, 14 percent of the nation's gas came from fields in the federal waters of the Gulf of Mexico vulnerable to hurricanes.

That year, we were also importing 3.3 percent of our gas as LNG, over triple the amount at the start of the decade.[22] At strategy sessions at my firm, we cited credible studies that LNG imports would increase to 10 percent of the nation's supply by 2015. Forty-five new LNG import terminal projects had been announced. At least sixteen, we were confident, would be built. By 2008, the number of rigs drilling for gas topped 1,600, 52 percent higher than four years earlier.[23]

U.S. gas consumers' increasing reliance on LNG was comforting to us in a way. As long as an operator, whatever its strategy, could produce gas by drilling a well that made money at an equivalent price to the cost of importing it, that project was safe. There was a sense that price stability, at $8 to $9 per thousand cubic feet, was on the horizon. (Average homes in the Midwest consume about 100,000 cubic feet of gas per year; homes in California half that.)[24] What alternatives did American gas consumers have? You could get gas from tight, small, second-rate fields drilled right here in North America, or you could rely on our bizarre globalized world: someone would freeze gas in a poor and sweltering place like Trinidad, Algeria, or Nigeria and ship it over here so some other crazy bastard could thaw it out so people wouldn't freeze their keisters off in Terre Haute. In either arduous way, gas was going to be more expensive.

Average gas prices tripled from the first half of 2002 to the first half of 2008.

3. SHALEMANIA AND SCIENCE EXPERIMENTS

I MAY HAVE KNOWN WHAT SOURCE ROCK WAS FROM SOME LONG-AGO primer about how oil and gas is made. ("Once there were dinosaurs, Timmy, and now they're in your Chevrolet . . .") But when I talked to investors and colleagues from 2004 to 2008, the topics were generally the familiar ones: the global opportunities in the oil and gas business and the end—the definitive, sad, okay, excitingly price-spurring end—of easy oil and gas. From 2004 to 2008, my firm was focused on trying to invest in companies that were profiting from one of the two old goals, developing more oil and gas projects internationally or finding some reasonably rewarding, if still high-cost, gas fields in the United States. Yes, we invested in shale producers—or companies that would become them. But that wasn't our exclusive strategy. We also invested in small E&P companies exploring for conventional reservoirs in South Texas and British companies exploring in the North Sea. We partnered with companies advancing offshore pipeline welding technology and invested in the construction of advanced drilling rigs that would allow operators to go further offshore. As late as 2007, we wrote to our investors about what I thought were the four primary incremental sources of global oil supply, the BICS: Brazil, Iraq, the Canadian oil sands, and Saudi Arabia. It was a nod to the increasingly hip term BRIC, used for Brazil, Russia, India, and China. I hoped my coinage would catch on BRICishly.

It didn't, and not only because it was stupid—a transformative boom in the USA was starting, and it was the beginning of the era of the land rushes. I watched each land rush for its wild, fun frenzy. Only later did it sink in that their repercussions were more important than the show.

WHEN PEOPLE IN THE OIL business talk about Aubrey McClendon, some refer to him as the Steve Jobs of the shale revolution, the visionary who brought it all together. Some think of him as its P. T. Barnum, the character who started the circus. But everyone knows that he is the Beyoncé of the business, the only person whom everyone refers to by his first name. I don't think I've ever been in the same room as the man, but that hasn't stopped me from saying things like, "Well, that's just Aubrey being Aubrey," as if I were talking about my brother.

Aubrey—and I'm too deep into Aubreyness to stop now—was well known before the boom as the most charismatic, aggressive, brash, and self-possessed E&P company CEO. He was not the most successful oilman, though, or the most placidly consistent. With Aubrey, as everyone knows, you're not playing nickel bingo at the old folks' home. He and Chesapeake, the company he founded and ran with Tom Ward, took their lumps hard when an earlier natural gas play, the Austin Chalk, turned out to contain much less gas than Aubrey had promoted. Over 1997 and 1998, Chesapeake's stock fell by 97 percent.[1] (If you ever need to drop knowledge to an oilman, I can think of no better way to do so than referring to the time when "Aubrey busted his pick on the Chalk.")

I'm not sure why a filmmaker or novelist hasn't yet given Aubrey the full Dreiser treatment, to convey his presence, get right his appearance (rimless glasses and a mane of graying blond hair that puts him somewhere between a Viennese conductor and a Civil War–era senator), to reconcile the contradictions of an occasionally anarchic, Duke graduate, establishment WASP from a prominent political and oil family in Oklahoma City. As I write this, Aubrey is still the best show in town, watched with jealousy, admiration, contempt, and awe for his appetites for everything: vintage maps, vacation homes, OKC pride, antique boats, rare wines, money, trades, action, risk, deals. He is the apotheosis of the landman, the king of the Duke frat boys.

Aubrey did not hear about the S. H. Griffin #4 on a Tuesday afternoon in 1998 and ignite the boom on Wednesday. Devon, the company that bought Mitchell Energy, drove the technical advancement of the Barnett Shale after it acquired Mitchell's assets. Oil companies make hydrocarbon widgets, and the slow, incremental work of Devon and other companies operating in the Barnett drove down the unit costs of the widgets by making each well cheaper (by, for instance, drilling it more quickly) and getting more gas from each well they drilled (most importantly by shifting to horizontal drilling).

Aubrey's company was not Devon, its buttoned-up fellow resident of Oklahoma City. Chesapeake's role was more sociological. Imagine you're at a small-town butcher shop. You and your friends, talking to the butcher about what's available, are politely competitive as to who will get the best cut of steak. All of a sudden, *she* walks in, the town's biggest personality, wearing an even brighter Ferrari-red dress than that orange number she wore at church, and announces, "I'll have everything."

"One of everything?" the butcher asks.

"No. Everything."

That was Chesapeake, a fast follower with a strategy to dominate the leasing of any and every play that showed promise. Like most U.S. E&P companies, Chesapeake had always been focused on onshore U.S. gas. Through success in conventional plays, primarily in Oklahoma and neighboring areas, it had grown to a mid-sized competitor by the early 2000s.[2] Then Aubrey put out the word to investment bankers that he wanted to be the first call on every deal—and he'd pay the highest price to win any auction. He bought shales but seemed just as interested in other types of gas fields. All would benefit, he believed, from rising gas prices in an era of falling U.S. gas production.[3] Bankers started calling him the buyer of first resort. By 2005, Chesapeake had already spent $10 billion on properties over the prior decade, a dumbfounding amount for a company of its size.[4] In 2006, 2007, and 2008, it would buy another $15 billion worth of companies, properties, and leases.[5]

A lot of people want to buy things, but Aubrey had the core talent of promoters, charmers, and true believers in his ability to get the capital to finance his spree. In his romping, necessary guide to the boom, *The Frackers*,

Gregory Zuckerman notes that a common comparison of Aubrey is to Bill Clinton, "for his ability to make everyone he meets feel like the most special person in the room."[6] By Aubrey's charms, Chesapeake raised the necessary capital through a tangle of old-fashioned ways (issuing new stock, taking on new debt early, often, and enthusiastically) and new-fashioned ways (foreign joint venture partners, getting "carried" on capital spending by other oil companies, subsidiary preferred shares, and clever structures like volumetric production payments).

The other independents, like the other customers in the butcher shop, had varying responses. There were mini-Aubreys, who tried to buy everything, even if they didn't have the cash. There were anti-Aubreys, who left in disgust. And there were companies in the middle, who bought more than they necessarily wanted or needed or maybe could afford but were afraid Aubrey was going to leave them without any meat.

As entertaining as it can be to describe the boom's land rushes in breathless prose, I need to moderate this tale with two bits of context. First, $5 billion per year may be a lot of money, but Chesapeake's buying of land was within the old sociology of the oil business: the U.S. onshore E&P sector was still the minor leagues. Chevron, for instance, has a single deep-water Gulf of Mexico project that will cost $7.5 billion.[7] Second—and this may be the reason that I didn't recognize the boom for what it was—the U.S. oil and gas renaissance didn't happen everywhere all at once. There were a succession of scenes along the same reel: land left for dead; vertical test wells drilled; quiet, confusing buzz starts; Aubrey barrels into town; companies report big wells; Chesapeake issues press release; and a land rush for surrounding acreage and overlooked parcels begins.

Each of these stories—and there would eventually be six main gas plays and three main oil ones—was similar to the Barnett but slightly different, sequels to a superhero film. (*Shaleman VI: Guardian of the Gaslaxy*?) The fourth shale gas boom—following the original Barnett, the Fayetteville in Arkansas in 2004, and the Woodford in Oklahoma a year later—was the Haynesville in northern Louisiana in 2008. When you're in any business, you like to imagine you know everything about it before the man on the street. But when I read about a Haynesville well in *The Wall Street Journal* in July 2008, it was like my barber telling me that my cousin had gotten married. Maybe I should have known. In March of that year, Petrohawk, led by an imperious, wry, slightly less Aubreyish Aubrey named Floyd Wilson, had "revealed" the Haynesville at an investor meeting. A month later, Aubrey himself announced that Chesapeake had leased 200,000 acres.[8] But in 2008, that year of wonders, who could pay attention to every press release or new well? Gas prices were skyrocketing. The world seemed to be running out of cheap oil.

And then I saw in the *Journal* the initial production rates of the first successful horizontal Haynesville well: 17 million cubic feet per day[9]— twelve times the production of the S. H. Griffin #4 a decade earlier. That was an offshore well result, a Qatar well result, not anything that should be possible in Cajun country. It seemed like a typo, or a lie.

But more reports of more giant production rates followed, and the Haynesville in the summer of 2008 became the first superhero movie with modern digital graphics. *The New York Times* profiled landowners who were one day struggling in Shreveport and were the next day, aw shucks, rich.[10] *60 Minutes*, visiting the Haynesville boom, introduced the word "shaleionaires" to the world.

And in each new shale in each new part of the country, Chesapeake and other companies rushed in to secure land in one of two ways. They bought smaller companies, often private ones, some of whom had been working podunk conventional reservoirs in shale regions for decades. (These reservoirs were not just above the shales but *of* the shales, as the gas or oil had migrated upward from deeper shale source rock reservoirs that were considered unexploitable before modern fracking began.) Hungry companies also sent swarms of landmen into rural areas to lease acreage straight from landowners. Landmen would try to be the first to a farm, offering—this being capitalism—the lowest amount they could pay without being scooped by higher-paying competitors. (*Promised Land,* the Matt Damon anti-gas movie I think of as *Good Will Fracking*, has some technical and plotting problems but accurately captures the day-to-day hustle and moral universe of landmen.)

Crushing to my self-image as an astute observer of the business, I saw the stars but not the constellation. I didn't sneeze at reports of wells with initial production of 20 million cubic feet per day. Investors wanted to talk about those, and I had to mumble that, No, we didn't own that well you saw on *60 Minutes*. But like a guy who comes up with airtight reasons why every girl at the bar is uninterested in him (she's a snob, she hates nice guys, she's prejudiced against men who wear "interesting" sweaters), I processed shale news as same-as-it-ever-was normalcy in one of three ways.

First, I thought the shales were just one of a multitude of ways to make money in the U.S. gas business, an industry filled with diverse plays, with different costs, in different areas. There were other action movies in the theater, some starring tight gas, some coalbed methane. There were still untapped conventional reservoirs around, in plays like the Chautauqua Platform, the Central Kansas Uplift, the Palo Duro—names that, seven years later, sound comically made-up, like some map of the country with alternate states, South Virginia and Mindiana. The shales, in that diverse universe, weren't even all that economically compelling. In 2007, one analysis of the shale boom noted that five of the eight new shale basins made money only when gas prices were above $7 per thousand cubic feet—right at the border of being worth it. Month-end U.S. gas prices that year averaged $7.24.[11]

Second, I told myself that a new shale play was just a local story, like the Barnett—a sugar rush, good if you were in it, but hardly providing the basic gas supply nutrients the country needed. Americans were still going to need the frozen gas of unfrozen Algeria et al.

Finally, I reminded myself that the plays might turn out to be the hype of Petrohawk, Chesapeake, and the other barkers on the midway. "Shalemania," as the shale gas boom started to be called around 2007, was not totally a compliment. The shale plays were so new that no one knew the ultimate gas that would come from any well. Everyone recognized that successful shale gas wells oftentimes had unbelievably high initial production rates. But we knew that the production from shale gas wells declined hard, like YouTube sensations. Second-year production might be 70 percent below the first year's in places like the Haynesville.[12] Professional skeptics like Art Berman argued that the ultimate production of shales, year after declining year, would be much lower than the cheer squad would have you believe based on a few months on production. Canadians, the former supplier of incremental gas to the United States, threw charts and graphs over the border that proved that the shales were not as impressive as we imagined. Eh? (As recently as 2005–2008, America imported an average of $28 billion per year of Canadian gas. We imported half of that in 2014.[13])

The skeptics weren't totally wrong. The Haynesville is not in the Museum of Why Did We Ever Think That, like the Palo Duro, but it's known as a high-cost area today. Much of the land leased in the successive shalemanias, including some very recent ones, have been bad deals.

THE SKEPTICS, HOWEVER, MISSED what made the shale revolution unique: the well control that comes from drilling in low permeability rock turned shale wells into unprecedented engineering labs.

The ubiquity of hydrocarbons in shales is sometimes overstated. Yes, there is gas or oil everywhere in shale rock. There are also people everywhere in Tokyo, which doesn't mean that every part of Tokyo is the same. Shale rocks have different geophysical characteristics, shale deposits have different thicknesses and thermal maturities, and shale hydrocarbons come in different concentrations. Nonetheless, compared to conventional reservoirs, shale reservoirs, especially in the best areas, are marvels of well control. In the core areas of the best plays, you can count on a well drilled near a prior well to produce similar results, the special sauce of the new Big Mac just as special and just as saucy. The oil and gas business is a highly empirical one. There is science but also a great deal of tinkering. The high well control in the good areas allowed engineers to adjust variables in semi-controlled experiments—testing different proppants, fluids, well lengths—to extract the most gas they could out of the shale.

The second key factor that accelerated the boom during this period was money. The engineering labs of the shale revolution, the wells themselves, don't come cheap. Horizontal wells to extract gas from the shales cost $2 million apiece in the early days of the Barnett.[14] Now deeper, longer, and more complex, they are three to four times that amount. Luckily in the mid-2000s, America was flush with money for new wells. The stock market, bond market, and commercial banks were providing capital to

E&P companies. Private energy investors like us were willing to take risks. Beginning in 2005, we started investing in companies targeting unconventional gas, including shales. In 2007, we invested in a tight oil play in West Texas that would, over time, become a shale play more valuable than we could have ever modeled.

The third accelerating factor was gossip. Oil companies competed fiercely to lease land in the boom. Nobody wanted to wake up to read a press release that Aubrey had vacuumed up 500,000 acres in a play he or she had targeted. But once land in an area was leased, E&P companies realized that competing against their next-door neighbor wasn't going to accomplish much. And so engineers from different companies talked well strategies over burgers, as they always had. Sometimes whole companies agreed to exchange data. Engineers and geologists also attended conferences and presented papers, primarily because other attendees were much more interested than their spouses in hearing the fascinating ramifications of drilling azimuth.

The gossip had oxygen from another source. E&P companies, with a few exceptions, don't own their own drilling and fracking equipment; they rely on oilfield service companies for the products and services to get oil and gas out of the ground. One service company bulldozes the "pad" where the rig will go. A second company drills the well. A third company, oddly to an outsider, comes to the rig to guide which direction the drill bit will go. A well site can come to resemble the town saloon where everyone drives up for a poke. And folks in the always-be-closing oilfield service sector are just as human as the rest of us: they love to talk about what's going on next door. They love even more to sell what they sold next door. So whenever anyone made a breakthrough—in where a well was drilled, in how a well was fracked—oilfield service folks ensured that the news traveled fast.

And there was a lot of news. Experiments in well direction, in fracking tools, in whole new plays were happening quickly. They had to be: lease expiration was the final accelerating factor of this period. As I talk about in Chapter 7, when a landman tries to convince a farmer to sign a lease, he offers him a bonus payment per acre, a royalty, and payments for things such as using the farmer's water. The landman also negotiates the term of the lease, such that if the oil company doesn't drill for three or five years, the farmer can lease the rights to someone else. But once an oil company drills a well—or sometimes multiple wells, as negotiated—it "holds" the lease forever, as long as those wells are producing oil or gas.

So if an oil company spent $100 million in bonus payments to lease 10,000 acres of land from ten different farmers, that oil company might have to drill ten wells (in an area that might ultimately support fifty or 100 more wells) within five years or lose the $100 million. During the feverish days of any play, many companies—not just Chesapeake—would think nothing of leasing thousands, sometimes hundreds of thousands, of acres with industry results from only a few vertical test wells. The countdown to lease expiration would then begin, with companies having limited time to figure out what they had bought. Which areas made the best wells? Which didn't work at all? Where do I need to drill now or forever lose my rights to Farmer Johnson's land?

THE PHRASE "SCIENCE EXPERIMENT" became the fashionable way to describe those early wells, the trial-and-error process to discover what worked best in an undrilled area. I used it and continue to use it when an investor asks me how a company is doing. I sometimes have to admit that I don't know because the company has so far drilled only a few science experiments.

Science experiment is sometimes a sincere metaphor for a reasonable economic wager: a health food restaurant on a city's fast food row. Science experiment is also a good way to justify any project that loses money. Sorry, honey, that I put our life savings into Piña Alota, the store that sold only pineapple-themed gifts. It was a science experiment.

But to oil company engineers, all the factors encouraging drilling in the early years of the shale revolution were like the rush of falling in love, each element better than the last: risk-tolerant money, good well control, chatty service companies, your bosses telling you to drill, drill, experiment, and drill. Thus began one of the biggest play dates in the history of American petroleum engineering. What made it so fun (when it worked) and frustrating (when it didn't) were the dozens of main variables of any shale well: how thick is the rock (gas may be ubiquitous throughout a deposited shale layer, but that layer could be 300 feet thick or 100 feet), how long should you drill horizontally, what frack fluids should you use and in what sequence, and more. For no matter where you were, you could never be certain of the quality of any shale location until you drilled it. Shale layers have different stress fields that will naturally orient the direction of the fractures. Some shales are more brittle and easier to frack. Some layers, with more clay content, can be fatal to good fracks because the rock re-forms after the fluid is pumped in, closing off the pathways just made. Many areas of the Codell play in Colorado, for instance, can't be fracked because of "swelling smectite," which is what happens when clay minerals inside shale absorb water. Finally, some shales lie within a muddled geological history, with all sorts of faults and fractures that could mean a horizontal well traveling merrily along could end up in a different type of rock, with different density of gas in place than where it began.

To help shale producers meet all these challenges, the oilfield service sector hawked all sorts of fabulous-seeming toys: proppant with the strength of 100 grains of sand, "micro-seismic" services that give you X-ray vision into the fracks, perforating charges unrivaled in the history of man—or at least in the history of perforation. And so quickly, sometimes hectically, with each well that wowed the industry, with each well that fizzled, the industry collectively and independently learned how to make cheaper widgets.

Free market theorists wept from joy.

SKEPTICS WOULD MISS SOMETHING ELSE big when they wrapped the "mania" of shalemania in disapproving quotes. Shale, it turned out, was not just about natural gas. And in a trend that should by now be clear, I was also late to recognize how the U.S. shale oil renaissance would piggyback on—and eventually take over—the shale gas boom.

There were many reasons why the shale gas boom occurred first. Gas prices rose to the level where shale gas drilling was profitable well before oil prices did for equivalent oil plays, which are inherently more expensive. Also, the U.S. E&P business for decades was a gas business, not an oil business. Oil production in the continental United States, after all, had been on a slide down Hubbert's Peak for thirty years. Onshore U.S. oil was coming from tiny Roman candle plays that burst and fell before you noticed, from creaky low-volume "stripper" wells in places like West Texas where you'd have to be brave to scratch out a living in the business, or (as oilmen joked) in the People's Republic of California where you'd have to be a masochist to want to.

Oil also came late to the shale revolution because it didn't really seem possible. You intuitively understand the forms of matter when you smell cigarette smoke from a hotel room next door, traveling through the partition's pores. You'd be freaked out, though, if the smoker shoved her cigarette through the wall. Shale rock has such low permeability that in the history of industry no one thought that, even with fracking, you could extract commercial amounts of small gas molecules. (Mitchell Energy's failures for seventeen years seemed to prove the point.) Given that oil molecules are ten times larger than gas molecules and that the viscosity of liquids inhibits their movement through pore "throats," geologists and engineers thought it especially impossible for those big, viscous oil molecules to be able to squeeze through hydraulically created fractures.

There was also confusion between the shales of the boom and "oil shale," which was an effort, centered in Colorado in the 1980s, to heat shale rock underground to move it up a wellbore. It wasn't even exactly oil they heated, but kerogen, a precursor hydrocarbon that has to be retorted in a refining process to become usable. Exxon, Shell, and others spent billions on these projects but abandoned them with chasms to cross before they could be cost-effective. Even in the 2000s, we were sent oil shale business plans (usually by someone unaffiliated with a commercial enterprise but with an earthlink.com e-mail address). We read those plans, usually peak oily in their rhetoric, and snickered that oil shale would make an excellent source of fuel right around the time that civilization ended.[15]

Finally, the oil boom happened later than gas because it happened first in North Dakota. There had been an oil industry in that state since the 1950s, a low-tech, stop-and-start affair. But as recently as 2003, North Dakota production was only 49,000 barrels per day higher than it was in do-they-even-have-oil-there Illinois.[16] Conducting shale science experiments with new horizontal drilling and fracking adaptations requires a critical mass of competitors, service providers, and skilled labor. The last, especially, was not always easy to find, even in Texas. And the oil industry pitch to come to North Dakota included good money, nice people, extreme hot and extreme cold (whichever you prefer), housing in ratty motels or man camps (whichever you prefer), and no women. In 2006 and 2007, when techniques were being advanced to extract oil from the Bakken Shale underlying parts of the state, there were never more than fifty-five rigs working at any one time.[17]

But a breakthrough occurred there, too, driven by two companies: EOG Resources, led by Mark Papa, and Continental Resources, led by Harold Hamm. Papa and Hamm are carved next to Aubrey and George Mitchell on the Mount Rushmore of the shale revolution. Hamm, born in 1945, would be its Lincoln. He rose from near log cabin poverty—rural Oklahoma sharecropper parents, charismatic Christian church, shack with no electricity or running water, twelve older brothers and sisters[18]—to become the most successful of the four, as measured by money. The down-to-earth, intellectually driven, witty Papa would have to be the Jefferson. (Larry Nichols of Devon Energy is the James Madison of the boom, a founding father for sure, but not quite as shale-fixated or well known.)

Papa's EOG is still considered the "Harvard of Shale," the technical leader in the industry.[19] The triumphs of EOG and Continental fit the pattern of many of the winners of the boom, as I discuss in the third part of the book: early in exploiting some low-quality rock and patient—or confident or desperate—enough to not give up before they found the proper technique. The key to unlocking North Dakota's Bakken Shale for EOG and Continental was multi-stage fracking. In single-stage open hole fracks, the fluid and proppant are pumped down a well but don't propagate evenly to every part of the targeted reservoir. Indeed, much of the reservoir ends up not fracked at all. In North Dakota, EOG innovated and Continental helped adapt to oil shales a process first deployed in the 1990s in non-shale basins and in the mid-2000s in shale gas: they began to frack horizontal wells in stages.[20] In a multi-stage frack, an operator first perforates—blows rings of holes—in the steel casing of a well only at the well's far end. It fracks that section. It then plugs that section to make sure that the frack fluid sent down the wellbore doesn't travel past the point where it will do any good. The operator then moves on to do the exact same thing closer in, in repeated stages.[21] Multi-stage fracking is expensive and complicated, with more tools and time and labor required, but the operator is able to frack more of the reservoir, with each frack creating more powerful and longer fractures, giving more oil or gas molecules more pathways to the well. Open hole fracking had been like trying to complete a multiple choice quiz by answering all the questions at once. With multi-stage fracking, the industry figured out how to answer one question at a time.

I didn't immediately recognize the world-changing implications of those multi-stage Bakken wells. Life moves fast; news is unending. I couldn't pay deep attention to every single announcement of every great new well any more than I could contemplate—to say nothing of read—every worthwhile novel published in a month. When I first heard about the Bakken, I knew people were making money there flipping land, and I wished it were me. But I thought that the Bakken had nothing to do with global oil supply and demand. First of all, the oil there was expensive. A smart Montana engineer I know analyzed the Bakken in 2007. He proved that, at $70 per barrel, even Joe Harvard EOG was losing money on every well drilled, given the costs of all that multi-stage frack equipment. (Mark Papa would have told him that EOG was not done improving unit costs.) The Bakken was also tiny. Sure, North Dakota production in 2007 was 46 percent higher than in 2004, but it was still only 0.15 percent of world oil supply.[22] The rest of the global oil industry in 2007 was a thousand times louder and brassier than some mandolin plucking on the Plains. By 2008, prices were shrieking. China was on pace to consume all the nickel, pigs, steel, manhole covers, and—yes!—oil on earth. Even peak oil might not be untrue.

AND THEN THE GLOBAL RECESSION CAME. In other books about other economic sectors, this is the point where the author talks about "market therapy," how the stock or bond market forced him to relearn everything he thought he knew. Yet in the story of the boom, the 2008 crash paused the U.S. oil and gas renaissance for only about eighteen months.

But just because a root canal won't forever alter the way I eat doesn't mean I want to schedule one for Thursday. The crash wasn't fun. To a cresting boom, it removed one of the driving forces: capital. Debt and equity investors were staring at their flattened net worth in horror, not providing new capital. By the end of 2008, oil and gas prices were 60 to 70 percent below the otherworldly seeming prices of six months earlier. Landmen were depressed that they would lose all of their hard-won leases. The engineers' massive play date appeared over.

There were individuals and companies for whom the crash stung hard, or worse, because they had taken on too much debt. The most dramatic case happened to the most debt-loving of oilmen. In the summer of 2008, Aubrey was worth about $3 billion. Never at rest, never in doubt, he had borrowed money to buy more shares of Chesapeake in his personal account, about $200 million worth in the first half of the year alone.[23] During the crash, investors sold Chesapeake's shares mercilessly because of all the high-cost acreage it had brazenly bought when gas prices were higher. In October 2008, when Aubrey's shares in his own company were worth not much more than what he had borrowed to buy them, his bankers made a margin call, demanding to be paid back a half billion dollars.[24] To get that money, Aubrey sold more than 31 million shares, worth $1 billion at the end of 2007 and, at their 2008 peak, twice that amount. After the margin call, the worth of Aubrey's stake in Chesapeake was $32 million.[25]

The Chesapeake board, never a group to stand between Aubrey and his desires, paid him a $75 million retention bonus at the end of 2008 "because of other entrepreneurial opportunities that exist in the industry."[26] (Running another oil company? Opening a juice bar?) Without the retention bonus, his salary that year would have been $37 million.[27]

THE CRASH TESTED OUR INVESTMENTS and demanded responses. Rig hands serving companies no longer drilling needed to be laid off. Negotiations with landowners to lease their land at prices that made sense in

June 2008 but not in December 2008 were halted. (For landowners, it was as if their winning lottery ticket had fallen through the sewer grate.)

And as after any crash, fear wrestled with greed. Should we go all in? Wait for it to get really bad? Sell everything now? We congratulated our steady selves (okay, only slightly panicked selves) in contrast to the people who had really gone nuts, including a few peers who thought that they had put together all of the facts. If plunging oil prices and the election of Barack Hussein Obama weren't exactly causal—oil prices plunged first— to some on the extremes they were both symptoms of some End Times stuff. Bunkers were armed. Gold was buried.

But within a few years, they could disarm their bunkers and use their guns to shoot things for no reason at all, that favorite Texas pastime. Yes, natural gas prices remained low but—and the difference is important— oil prices by the end of 2009 had returned to where they were a year before the crash.

The crash may have even accelerated the renaissance, given the shales' relative attractiveness as places to invest. And just like that, the oil and gas sector, which had experienced a different boom through the quadrupling of oil prices and tripling of gas prices, was once again one of the most popular kids in town. Capital came into the industry even more vigorously. And it was during the next six years, in the inter-crash period between the global recession and the oil price correction of 2014, that the U.S. shale revolution transformed from a collection of plays in out-of-the-way places into the defining force of the global oil and gas industry.

4. HOW THE OIL BUSINESS REVERSED GRAVITY

FOR MOST OF US, IN MOST OF OUR LIVES, MOST OF THE THINGS WE LEARN, conveniently, confirm things we already knew. There are times, of course, when there is a severe break in one's biases. Some fact comes out and you realize that black was white, up was down, your mother was your father. But there are other times when you seem to grasp your new understanding of the world only in retrospect. You are twenty-five years old and think of yourself as a young person, a college kid, just a son. One day, you look back and realize how long you've been an adult.

For me, the moment that made me realize that I—and the industry—was operating by a new type of physics was the 2011 acquisition of Brigham Resources, a North Dakota oil producer and innovator of two-mile-long horizontal wells, by Statoil, a major international oil company. The acquisition wasn't the biggest ("only" $4.4 billion), and it wasn't even Statoil's first acquisition in the U.S. shales. It had been one of the creative financing sources for Aubrey in 2008. But it seemed unnatural: why would a company that was a leader in harsh environment offshore oil and gas development, a company that was two-thirds owned by the government of oil-rich Norway, *want* to own onshore oil fields in North Dakota? Wasn't it cold enough in Norway? Was there a plot to stoke the ethnic loyalties of Scandinavian immigrants of Minnesota and the Great Plains to form a breakaway republic dedicated to herring, blond pigtails, and pleasantness?

Four years later, the acquisition doesn't seem strange at all. When I was a child, I understood as a child.

DEVELOPMENTS IN THE INDUSTRY since 2008, such as the Brigham acquisition, form the most revolutionary part of the industrial history of the boom. Change happened, and fast. Before this period, landmen and companies made hey-you–never-know bets in the plays that would dominate the industry after the boom. But in five years, from 2009 to 2013, today's most important shales were unlocked in earnest: the gas plays of the Utica and Marcellus and the oil plays of the Bakken, Niobrara, Eagle Ford, and Permian. During this half decade, as discussed in the next chapter, fracking became notorious in New York, given Marcellus drilling's proximity; alarm over it became a sign of environmental consciousness. Also during this period, "Saudi America" energy patriotism became trendy, and support of it a sign (to others) of good sense.

But to narrate this half decade would be dull. Yes, there were head-turning bursts of local excitement. Hello, New Mexico. Welcome to the club, Ohio. It's not looking so hot, Kansas. Yet each land rush would be a familiar story: a basin left for dead by the conventional wisdom (but a basin known because someone had extracted oil and gas from above the shales at some point in the last 150 years); some post–Barnett Shale leasing with long-shot bets of $25 or $50 per acre; gutsy pioneers drilling intriguing test wells; the swarms arriving to lease and buy land at much higher values; and the separation, with each well, of the more prolific parts of a basin from the less.

Given that a playbook now existed, with the basic techniques of multistage horizontal fracking well known, this phase of the boom was also more efficient. The reigning cliché became that we were not exploring for oil or gas anymore but, hyperbolically, "manufacturing" it. I felt less awe, less bewilderment in the face of monster reported production rates of fracked wells than professional satisfaction in how the industry was unlocking another play.

The post-2008 phase of the boom was also more institutional. Volume

growth and technical advances were being driven by now giant independents like EOG, big private companies, and integrated international companies returning to the United States. We had moved, in Max Weber's
terms, from the charismatic to the bureaucratic phase of the boom.
Aubrey would find it harder to fit in.

Maybe it took the inertial force of big companies' efforts to change
the facts for me—to confront the new. Maybe it took Norwegians enter-
ing North Dakota again to get through my thick head. But at some point,
I realized that four of my—and the oil business's—fundamental truths
were no longer true.

PERHAPS MOST GLOBALLY BENEFICIAL, as I examine in the fourth part of
this book, natural gas in the United States was no longer fated to get
ever scarcer and more expensive. George Mitchell, Aubrey, and almost
all the participants in the first phase of the shale revolution had been
driven by an unshakable belief that even high-cost, junky rock was better
than importing LNG. Yet from the end of 2009, when the market crash's
effect on the oil business dissipated, to the end of 2011, the price of natural gas fell by 46 percent. Gas prices since the "gaspocalypse" have rebounded and fallen a few times—the weather causes large swings in
demand—but they have largely remained at levels about half of what
they were in 2006 and 2007.

The industry has become, if anything, too good at producing gas
cheaply. By 2014, shale gas production had risen to half of total U.S.
gas production, from 6 percent in 2007.[1] We now have an abundance of
gas, especially in the Northeast. Productivity is astounding in what were
once thought to be deep and useless shales, the Utica and Marcellus,
overlapping formations with their sweet spot in two areas: a collection of
counties in southwestern Pennsylvania, southeastern Ohio, and northern West Virginia; and two counties in northeastern Pennsylvania. In
December 2014, the Marcellus produced 16.7 billion cubic feet per day of
gas, 21 percent of U.S. production. It had supplied 2 percent five years
earlier.[2] That gain in market share is as if, in four years, Subaru sales

jumped from one in thirty-three cars sold in America to one in five, greater even than GM.[3] The country would be Burlington, Vermont.

The Marcellus's startling gain has happened with the industry hardly breaking a sweat. The rigs drilling in Pennsylvania, that swarm of locusts once thought to be racing toward Manhattan, grew from twenty at the start of 2008 to 116 in the summer of 2011. There were only fifty-four rigs in Pennsylvania at the end of 2014. Overall, the number of rigs drilling for natural gas in the United States fell below 300 in March 2015, one-sixth the level of their peak in the summer of 2008. In the Barnett, where it all began, there were only six rigs drilling. There had been seventy-eight four years earlier.[4]

And yet total U.S. production continues to climb every year because of head-turning efficiency gains. The underground gas factories in the Marcellus or Utica are allowing the industry to "make" gas so cheap it makes us laugh—and weep. The average well in the Marcellus Shale in 2013 will extract four times the gas over its lifetime as the average well in the same play in 2009 and seventeen times more than the average well in 2007.[5] New techniques like pad drilling, in which a rig drills six to seven—sometimes more—wells in multiple directions from a single location instead of moving each time a well is needed, are driving costs down even further.

For Aubrey, the rapidly declining gas price triggered the unthinkable. Chesapeake's precarious balance sheet, the mountains of leases in second-rate areas, falling gas prices, and revelations of his appetites (for instance, he had long personally participated as a direct owner in each well Chesapeake drilled) swirled into a tornado of shareholder anger that forced the company's board to ask him to resign in January 2013. It was like the E Street Band kicking out Springsteen.

The problem for Chesapeake was not that it had uniformly bad acreage: it had leased land in some of the best gas producing regions in the world. But for it, and for many other companies, its acreage was at war with itself. Wells in the Utica produced widgets so cheaply that they made those in most parts of the Barnett, once a case study of U.S. innovation, feel as cutting-edge as a desktop PC.

And so now gas producers, like a high school freshman paging through college catalogues, wait impatiently for the day when they can get out of the house, with exports. As I note in Chapter 12, increased gas use over the next decade is likely, coming from more gas-fired electricity generation and from new chemical and other factories of what optimists see as a blossoming U.S. manufacturing renaissance. But for the next five years, exports are the major hoped-for release valve for the oversupply of U.S. gas. This is taking time. Building LNG export facilities demands patience to get regulatory approval, with local approvals sometimes complicated by the anti-fracking movement and the lobbying of gas consumers. Even though the first LNG export facilities are being built on the sites of now useless import facilities, they will still take years to construct. There is no switch to convert an oven into a fridge.

The ironies are deep. Ten years ago, we calculated at what volume LNG imports would cap gas prices. We now wonder at what volume LNG exports will lift them. At the $2.89 per thousand cubic feet gas price of the end of 2014, the industry was drilling for gas in only a dozen or so counties in the entire country. There are many U.S. basins with trillions of cubic feet of gas in which companies would drill if prices were higher. An analysis by experts at ITG estimated that at $2.50 per thousand cubic feet gas prices—about where they were in early 2015—U.S. shale gas production would remain essentially flat for the next decade. At $4 per thousand cubic feet gas prices, production would be 35 percent higher.[6]

THE ABUNDANCE OF U.S. GAS will continue to be linked, and exacerbated, by another overturned truth of the energy business: that American oil production, forever peaked, was dismissibly irrelevant to global supply-demand. I've had exchanges with peak oilers since the boom. I have sympathy for them. The doubling of onshore U.S. oil production is unimaginable in their theories. It is a dead man risen, who then runs a marathon. Some gerrymander their peak oil theories by describing shale oil as "unconventional." We in the industry use the term, too. However, we are steadily abandoning it as it becomes clear that the conventions are what have changed: almost every well drilled onshore in America today would have been considered unconventional a decade ago.

There are now three big oil plays in the United States: the Bakken in North Dakota, the Eagle Ford in South Texas, and the Permian across West Texas and New Mexico. There are two other important ones, the Niobrara in Colorado and the SCOOP/STACK in Oklahoma. Some natural gas plays, like parts of the Marcellus and some sections of the Eagle Ford, also produce meaningful amounts of natural gas liquids like butane and propane, which have overlapping use with crude-derived products. The Permian, likely to become the biggest American oil source of all, is less a single play than a jamboree of shale plays and other "tight" low permeability reservoirs that respond productively to fracking. (Indeed, the "tight reservoir" revolution would be a more accurate if less felicitous name than the shale revolution.)

Everyone in the newer oil plays looks to the Bakken, which tripled production in only four years, as an indication of what success looks like. To the instant terror of people at parties, I have a weak spot for North Dakota oil production facts. If the state, which produced 12.5 percent of U.S. oil in 2014, were its own country, it would be the nineteenth largest oil producer in the world. Given that only 740,000 people live there, the state's oil revenue at $60 per barrel oil prices is $32,000 per person. This puts the Nation of North Dakota at four to five times the level of per capita oil wealth of Saudi Arabia or the UAE and closer to Qatar's combined per capita oil and gas revenue.[7]

As I'll revisit at the end of the book, the future pace of the U.S. oil boom will be determined by the price of oil. ITG, for instance, estimated that U.S. production will climb to 12 million barrels per day by 2025—a level over double what the United States produced in 2008—if oil is above $85–$90 per barrel. It will reach only 9.5 million barrels per day if oil averages $60.[8]

That 3 million barrels per day highlights an important difference: unlike the impact of shale gas, U.S. shale oil production has not yet made us totally rethink how cheaply the fuel can be produced. Even after the 2014 oil price crash, oil was 30 percent higher than it was a decade earlier. Gas prices over that time had fallen by half.[9] This goes back to chemistry: a representative Marcellus Shale gas well in southwestern Pennsylvania extracts three time the amount of energy using standard oil-to-gas conversion ratios as a representative Permian Basin oil well in New Mexico. The physical improbability of shale oil requires a lot of capital and material.

And so U.S. shale oil production sits in a strange place in today's global supply-demand balance. The ability to profitably extract oil from near impermeable source rock is a major advance. But in a study by Goldman Sachs of the breakeven costs of the 420 top global oil and gas fields in the world, most of the U.S. oil plays were in the middle ranks, below the economics of some fields in Iraq, Brazil, or even the deepwater Gulf of Mexico.[10]

However, while operators in the new U.S. plays may not be extracting the world's cheapest oil, they are extracting among its easiest. The U.S. onshore oil industry "manufactured" 19,000 wells in the big four oil basins in 2014. Each well drilled in Brazil or the Gulf of Mexico is a bespoke operation, taking time, increasing risk. With a shale oil well, you won't get a $50 million duster (or a Macondo disaster) as you can in the Gulf of Mexico. You won't have to wait seven or eight years for first production and revenue, as may happen in Brazil. You won't be vulnerable to unknown oil prices ten years from now, as you would be in the Russian Arctic. You are not going to have to worry about ISIS.

In 2012, 2013, and early 2014, the invisible hand of the oil markets "chose" the relative ease of development of U.S. shale oil. The world consumed 2.3 million more barrels per day of oil in 2013 than in 2011, and the United States supplied 2.5 million more barrels per day of oil over that time.[11] Hundreds of discrete events around the world made room for a surging U.S. oil supply: wars, sanctions, dusters, delays, faster declines in older fields. It seemed that God Blessed America. Saudi Arabia, which had traditionally ratcheted production up and down to balance the world's supply and demand, didn't have to do anything at all.

But by 2014, the boom was like a snake steadily eating its own tail: greater U.S. oil production, which had been having no impact on prices, led to even more production. Then other producers in the world started to inch up their output. When Chinese oil demand growth continued to decelerate in 2014 and when a summer of worries about extraordinary

Middle Eastern chaos subsided into an autumn of ordinary Middle Eastern chaos, the oil markets realized that the world was egregiously oversupplied.

Thanksgiving Day 2014, for me, was one of the more disturbing in memory—and it wasn't because I was encountering something called a Tofurky at the house of a vegetarian. That day, Middle Eastern OPEC countries, particularly Saudi Arabia, abandoned a twenty-five-year history of restricting production to balance a clearly oversupplied oil market. They decided to try to drive out relatively high-cost barrels that threatened the long-term market share of their cheaper barrels from fields like Ghawar. The world's high-cost barrels weren't just production from the U.S. shales—far from it. Production in places like the Canadian oil sands and the North Sea turned out to be even more vulnerable. But lower oil prices hurt all producers.

In late 2014, I spent hours every week—sometimes every day—rubbernecking at the plunging stock prices of oil companies. Some fell by 10, 20 percent in a day. In September 2014, a headline like *The Wall Street Journal*'s "Fracking Gives U.S. Energy Boom Plenty of Room to Run"[12] generated no controversy. Four months later, *Journal* headlines made puns about a "crude awakening."[13]

The history of success in forecasting oil prices is exactly the same as the history of forecasting the stock market or college football players' NFL careers: almost universally horrible. So I won't try. Conspiracy theories aside, the king of Saudi Arabia does not sit down every New Year's Day with Vladimir Putin, Lex Luthor, Donald Rumsfeld, and ExxonMobil's CEO to set prices for the next year (and decide which senators to buy). Oil prices are determined by a knotted twine ball of global trends, aggregating a billion factors: whether a Chinese pediatrician buys a Buick, whether a small British oil well can be financed, whether a Libyan militia gains ground.

Nevertheless, as I discuss in Chapter 8, the increasing volumes, the ongoing innovations, the fundamental advantages of the U.S. shale revolution have fundamentally disrupted the global business—and are shaping it. And a few things now seem true. There is "easy" oil available to meet incremental demand. Much of that easy oil will come from the United

States, with its capacity to double or more shale oil production. It is probable but not certain that other countries will eventually be able to adopt shale exploitation techniques. It is significantly less likely for an oil shock to disrupt the global economy. The price of oil will become more volatile, if a cartel no longer keeps its hand on the tiller, increasing the cost of investing in the industry. And, in a seasoned cop-out of a person who spends much of his day talking to investors, there are as many reasons to believe oil prices will stay down as go up. This outlook, more Mild Max than Mad Max, may be too benign. But the world has enjoyed long periods of relatively stable prices, including the seventeen years after the last Saudi-instigated oil price collapse, in 1986.[14]

THERE IS ONE MORE FACTOR that will affect oil prices. The cost of supply will not remain constant. This is the third major shift in my understanding of how the oil business worked: technology, for now at least, operates in the "normal" way of other industries. When *GQ*'s peaker scoffed at the oil executive's placid confidence in technology, he saw into something. We in the industry were, to some extent, bluffing. The oil business has always developed new technologies, of course; one does not have a chance of finding oil in a reservoir six miles below the sea floor by using a rowboat and an old *National Geographic*. Yet most of the key technological advances of the previous twenty-five years had been about finding hard oil and gas in small deposits or in remote, harsh locations. The technology would make sure that the world had enough oil and gas to fly, drive, and cook dinner. It wasn't going to make those activities cheaper. For once you spent hundreds of millions to find that hard oil and gas, there was not much you could do to make it less costly, except by improving well maintenance or installing better pumps.

But new ways of horizontal drilling and fracking are working in ways similar to how technology transforms other industries, in which the computing power of our phone is greater than a national lab's thirty years ago so we can harness it for the greater good of making restaurant reservations. Oil and gas production isn't benefiting from some Moore's Law, of course, where oil and gas will get shockingly, vanishingly cheaper, even if that sometimes seems to be the case in the Marcellus Shale. A lot of steel, sand, water, equipment, time, and people are still necessary to drill and complete a well three miles across vertical and horizontal distance. Yet there are opportunities to make shale oil and gas less expensive: shale wells are still extracting only about half of the gas in place and one-tenth of the oil. All our efforts with all our technologies are aimed at raising those percentages for the same dollars spent, driving down the unit costs of the widgets.

We in the industry laugh when we hear about the "breakthrough" technologies of the shale revolution. We've been fracking since the Truman administration and drilling directionally before that. But the ingenuity now dedicated to making cheaper hydrocarbon widgets is remarkable, from designing drill bits that allow us to penetrate rock much faster to manufacturing rigs that can "walk" from one well to another. For those who lament that America no longer makes anything but bond traders, for those who think that "maker" culture only exists in a bearded guy pickling compassionately farmed okra in Austin, spend some time with oil industry engineers to absorb their enthusiasm, empiricism, technical inventiveness, and fearlessness to try and err.

Those engineers will include, unthinkable a decade ago, employees of companies like Shell and Statoil. The boom has knocked down a fourth fundamental truth of the old oil world. The industry was once divided by snobbery and strategy between "leading" companies pursuing giant oil and integrated gas projects internationally and smaller U.S. companies dining on the domestic scraps. But in the most famous jumbling of that divide, ExxonMobil bought XTO, one of the largest domestic E&P companies, for $35 billion in 2010.[15] When I read about the deal, I felt like I was in the fun house. This was a colossal bet on the U.S. onshore by Big Oil incarnate, the tallest heir of John D. Rockefeller himself, a company as famous for its arrogance as for its competence, a company that did not easily admit that anything not invented at ExxonMobil had any worth at all. Yet ExxonMobil was preceded and followed by other international oil companies, in transactions that made and lost money (sometimes dramatically so) but done with the same belief that U.S. oil and gas basins were now some of the best on earth. It was like watching Meryl

Streep and Robert De Niro stake their careers on community theater productions of *Hello, Dolly!* Regularly, the strange announcements came: Japanese buying into the Permian, Malaysians buying into Western Canada, Norwegians seeing opportunity in North Dakota, as if this were 1872 and they were looking for a place to plant wheat.

IS ANY OF THIS really new, though? Doubters have facts, too. The United States now has enough natural gas to meet its own demand, but it never imported more than a fifth of what it consumed, and most of that was from Canada.[16] And while it's great for America that it now produces 13 percent of the world's oil instead of 9 percent a decade ago, the United States still imports 27 percent of the oil it needs.[17] Isn't all this just America, with its outsized need to be exceptional, changing the definition of success to be the best?

And another thing: isn't this boom a bit too recent to declare that life has changed forever? Couldn't the boom, with lower prices, be as fleeting as a paper fire? And have I no perspective on the fallibility of efforts to forecast the energy future? In 1954, the head of the Atomic Energy Commission predicted that within fifteen years nuclear power would deliver electricity that would be "too cheap to meter."[18] Had I written this book in 2007, I would have humiliated myself with the dumb thesis that the true future lay in Brazil, Saudi Arabia, Iraq, and the Canadian oil sands. I would later have had to change my name, or written a personal apology to every reader, or left the oil business altogether for a new one, like pineapple-themed gift shops. And if my four paradigm shifts of the industrial perspective on the shale revolution—the abundance of U.S. natural gas, the global importance of U.S. oil supply growth, the role of technology in continually driving down unit costs, and the return of Big Oil to the onshore United States—prove reversible, I will look just as foolish.

Nonetheless, I am convinced that the world has experienced a major shift in how it fuels itself. The Resource Triangle, that first lesson from my first week in the oil business in 1995, remains as true as ever. What has changed is the arrow accompanying it, one that points downward to the broadest base of the triangle with a foreboding legend of "higher costs." As the industry moves from the best quality reservoirs at the top of the Resource Triangle to the worse quality but more plentiful reservoirs at the bottom, the costs to develop them should go inexorably up.

The Barnett and the Bakken and all the other basins of the boom meant that the arrow no longer strictly applies. The Barnett is a worse quality reservoir, with the gas harder to extract than from a conventional gas field. But Mitchell Energy found a way to make profitable enough gas, and the industry pressed ahead to make U.S. shale gas among the cheapest in the world. The Bakken is the kind of reservoir in the midsection of the Resource Triangle, but the cost of production in its best areas is not that different today from fields closer to the top. This violates an iron law of how the oil and gas business had forever worked.

For me, the most jarring change in the last decade of the oil business is not the startling American production data, or the industry's profits, or the price collapses, or the world-scale industries built from nothing in North Dakota or Pennsylvania. For me, what is still most difficult to process is what happened to the now splintered arrow of the Resource Triangle.

The oil industry found a way to reverse gravity.

Part II

THE LOCAL PERSPECTIVE

5. THE FOX IN THE FRACK HOUSE

ONE OF THE GREAT PRIVILEGES OF THE CONTEMPORARY WORLD IS THE ability to loudly dismiss things we haven't read or seen, because, well, who has time to read or see anything? So I never felt particularly guilty, for four years, to claim that I didn't need to watch *Gasland*, Josh Fox's 2010 documentary against gas drilling, to dismiss it. The world, for one thing, had watched it for me. The mother of the groom in Maine had watched it. My own mother had watched it and came to a Sunday telephone call with a roll of questions.

Gasland came up whenever someone lectured me on my naïveté or worse. It came up when the movie first aired on HBO, and it comes up now, as still the most famous argument against shale drilling. For years, a meeting with a college endowment scheduled to be about the performance of our investments would, at a snap, become about how dangerous fracking really was. By investors' demands, I would fill out lengthy questionnaires—plead with the companies we invested with to fill out questionnaires—on how we fracked, protected water, built well pads. We had been drilling for years. This had never happened before.

And for the first time in my career, people didn't just want to talk broadly about whether the oil industry pollutes. (Frankly, they had never seemed interested enough in the business to ask even about that, except during the Macondo spill.) Everyone had become an amateur engineer, wanting to discuss the technical details of how wells were stimulated and drilled. This forced me to learn more about well construction than I ever needed to before.

And the questions always seemed to come back to *Gasland*. Like a sharp curve one can anticipate on the long road home, I developed an intuition for when someone was about to bring up the movie's most famous scene: the moment when a mustached guy lit his indoor tap on fire.

Even before there was a "shale revolution" with all its globe-changing implications, there were the fracking debates. In hindsight, this was probably inevitable. When Americans' latest new source of oil was coming from overseas, most Americans, including me, lumped the oil industry's negative environmental or social impact with sweatshops and slums—all of a piece with the hard-to-keep-up-with and harder-to-think-too-hard-about misery and unfairness of the world. Then the oil and gas industry started drilling in the continental United States with a fervor not seen in thirty years. No one in the country knew what was going to happen because none of this—gas drilling only 150 miles from the Atlantic coast, the Resource Triangle scrambled—should have been possible.

I never disputed Josh Fox's right to raise questions about the impact on local communities of the shale revolution, even before I watched the film. I deserved to be asked tough questions, to better understand how wells were made safe. We in the industry also recognized that living in a boom-struck area was not always pleasant. Our progress over the last five years to better mitigate the shale revolution's local impacts—with new tools and better processes, many dictated by more specific regulations—were spurred in part by the need to respond to activists like Fox.

Fox was right to investigate, and explain. But what had confused me about *Gasland*, before I watched it, was that Fox started the national debate on the boom's local environmental consequences with a particularly lousy argument: the primary problem with fracking is the upward migration of chemicals and gas into the groundwater used by some people to drink. This isn't the worst argument I've heard about fracking. An industry friend in West Virginia told me that, at a 2010 community meeting in Morgantown, one woman claimed that fracking had turned her son gay. But the concerns about water contamination from fracking specifically were closer to that claim than they were to much more important environmental and social local issues related to the boom.

So before I saw the documentary, Fox and his Oscar nomination–approved righteousness irritated me because they muddled the public sense of what fracking is and rendered glib the harder-to-calculate tally of how annoying, damaging, worthwhile, or risky the ever changing U.S. shale revolution is on a local level. After I saw it, *Gasland* irritated me even more.

It's actually pretty good.

FROM THE DESCRIPTION OF IT by industry friends, I had imagined that *Gasland* would be a clunky construction of invented science, like an episode of *Gilligan's Island* in which the Professor makes a radio out of a coconut. But the movie presents the issues quickly. It absorbingly balances the story of his family, his subjects, and the national transformation. Fox himself is an effective messenger: wry, amicable, with an ingratiating I'm-so-disappointed-I-can-barely-get-out-of-bed baritone. My wife said that she found him cute, which was fine. But then she said it again.

In 2008, Fox's family had the opportunity to lease the land under its northeastern Pennsylvania vacation home, which sits atop the Marcellus Shale. *Gasland* is a quest to discover the risks and implications of signing that lease. Fox captures what were almost certainly real frustrations of the time, when dealing with Pennsylvania-focused oil companies who had yet to fully process that the oil business was anyone's business but their own.

But it's not Fox's talents as a filmmaker, or even Fox, that make *Gasland* so effective—and, for me, hard to watch. It's the people he interviews in Colorado, Texas, Wyoming, and Pennsylvania, unfortunate bystanders whose lives have been rattled by what the oil business did to their water. Middle-class or poorer, they feel abandoned by the government and assaulted by a rich industry. As often as Fox intersperses their stories with his tangled chronology and off-the-mark scientific explanations, those stories emerge and haunt. Even though I knew that he was wrong about so much—about the number of chemicals used in fracking, about Dick

Cheney's omnipotence—I couldn't deny that the lives of the people in *Gasland* had been damaged by the industry in which I work.

As essential and effective as is Fox's attention paid to the industry's victims, *Gasland* suffers from the propagandist's dilemma: fitting everything into a box of good versus evil helps persuade, but the easiest arguments to convey are sometimes the easiest to dismiss. I am not going to rebut *Gasland* scene by scene. This has been done by an article in *The New York Times*,[1] and more damningly by an industry group, Energy in Depth,[2] which I think of as the Anti-Defamation League for Texans. Energy in Depth, for all its obvious biases and over-the-top mockery, persuasively details times that Fox misstated the law, misled viewers on his own background, and reeled off misinformation that could have easily been checked.

Regardless of the details, Fox's most nationally consequential decision was his obsession with fracking. (Some in the oil industry are comically sensitive about that spelling of the word, suspecting that the "k" is a way for environmentalists like Fox to make hydraulic fracturing into a cousin of you-know-fricking-what. Some—and it continues among a few—refused to shorten hydraulic fracturing at all, like an old man who goes to Wendy's and orders a hamburger sandwich. Others insisted that the shorthand should be spelled fracing or fraccing. These were supposed to be pronounced the same as fracking, even though the words looked like a European beauty treatment or an invasive medical procedure. A few folks, aware of this, leapt to frac'ing, which might be how it is spelled in Tonga. I've never once in the industry heard anyone use some environmentalist's favorite scary word, hydrofracking.)

Gasland stoked two public worries about fracking: that it causes natural gas itself to make its way into the aquifers from which some people get their drinking water; and that fracking involves injecting "known hazardous materials, unchecked, directly into or adjacent to underground drinking water supplies."[3] The movie left viewers with the impression that both happen, and all the time. Fox manufactures this impression through the most ingenious element of the documentary: he films himself on a seemingly ambling journey through "gasland," parts of the Rockies and Texas where gas drilling had been prevalent long before the Marcellus boom. Everywhere he stops, he finds terrible problems of water contamination, seemingly an unavoidable product of how drilling and fracking works. But Fox selected the most infamous national cases of water pollution from oil and gas operations. It's as if, in making a documentary extolling charter schools, he had researched the most violent, demoralized public schools in the country and then filmed himself walking into their halls and being shocked at what he finds.

Dimock, Pennsylvania; Dish, Texas; Pavillion, Wyoming; West Garfield and Weld County, Colorado: go to the Web sites of environmental organizations and industry groups like Energy in Depth where they are still arguing about what happened five or ten years ago in those places, natural gas's Grassy Knolls. The debate in all of these situations is pretty simple: environmentalists claim that polluting drinking water is what the industry has done and will continue to do; the industry claims that water contamination—and no one disputes it—came from natural causes, happened in rare and isolated cases, and is not relevant to everyday drilling. Who is right won't uncontaminate water, but the answers illuminate how dangerous fracking is.

In Fox's highlighted cases in Wyoming and Colorado, the polluted water had nothing to do with fracking at all. The famed lit tap was connected to a well that penetrated four different seams of coals.[4] (A Colorado regulatory report issued two years before *Gasland* aired claimed the methane in the well had nothing to do with oil and gas drilling.)[5] In other cases, natural gas had leaked up from old wells drilled into shallow discoveries made decades before the shale revolution. The geology of Colorado and Wyoming also features biogenic gas—gas formed by fermentation of organic material rather than molecules cooked for eons underground—and younger and more permeable rock above those biogenic reservoirs.[6] It is likely that gas in some shallow conventional reservoirs, through quirky natural fracturing, ended up in someone's water well.

Dimock is more relevant to the shale revolution because it happened as part of it, in the Marcellus. Indeed, as the most notorious case of water contamination in the history of the boom, it's illustrative of how shockingly sloppy some in the industry were in the boom's early days and of how the industry's critics have sunk the teeth of their case into what is new (fracking) rather than what is old (human stupidity).

In 2008, Cabot Oil & Gas drilled in Dimock some of the first test wells of the northeast Pennsylvania Marcellus land rush. In the early days of any shale play, operators drill vertical tests to determine the thickness of the gas bearing shale and the petrophysics of the rock. According to Pennsylvania state investigators, Cabot did a horrible job drilling these wells: it used defective steel casing lining the well in three of them and improperly cemented twenty-two others, which allowed gas to travel upward through the cement meant to seal the casing to the rock. [7] There really was no excuse. The industry by then had been cementing and casing wells the same way, safely, for ninety years. Erle Halliburton himself developed what would become the standard in 1921.[8]

Without any direct evidence, I suspect that Cabot's drilling was so awful because it was done in Pennsylvania in 2008. The company probably had access only to some of the industry's worst oilfield equipment and crews. A Pennsylvania oilfield service executive told me that at the dawn of the Marcellus boom, the oilfield hands who came up to Pennsylvania were the ones who had no choice. They couldn't get a better job in Texas or Oklahoma, closer to home, where it was warm. Even the better rig hands who came north were drilling in rock and to a depth without almost any history to guide them. From *1900* to 2007, there were six wells drilled in Susquehanna County, where Dimock is. In 2008, there were thirty-four. Over the next five years, there would be 1,066.[9] State regulators tally thirty-two investigated water contamination incidents in the county before the end of 2011. There have been nine since.[10]

Whatever the cause of Cabot's bad wells—incompetence or unpreparedness—Pennsylvania's Department of Environmental Protection found that gas had contaminated the water wells of nineteen families. The poorest of the victims, Norma Fiorentino, suffered the most, with an explosion in her water well due to a buildup of migrating gas.[11] The Pennsylvania DEP punished Cabot with a large fine, a local moratorium, and an order to provide the affected homeowners with drinking water.[12] Cabot did itself no favors in the public eye by gruffly abiding by the regulator's rulings, denying it had done anything wrong. It eventually agreed to set aside $4.1 million—at least twice the value of each family's home—to compensate the homeowners rather than build a pipeline to carry clean water to their homes.[13] Few disagree with any of those facts. The sides loudly disagree in contemptuous, fulsome detail over whether other water wells in Dimock were polluted, how much of the contamination was naturally occurring, whether Cabot's settlement was fair, and whether an EPA investigation absolved Cabot.

Yet, quietly, one debate has definitely been resolved. *Gasland* implies that Dimock is representative of what could happen at Fox's family's house, that it effectively proves that water contamination is to shale development what cancer is to smoking. However, none of the gas infecting the wells of Dimock came from the Marcellus Shale but rather from gas-bearing rock thousands of feet *above* the Marcellus Shale.[14] And the contamination happened due to screwups before fracking even began.

Other attempts to link fracking to water contamination have also failed. Eight months after *Gasland*'s HBO premiere, *New York Times* investigative reporter Ian Urbina launched a prosecutorial series against shale gas entitled "Drilling Down." In the August 2011 article, the only evidence of groundwater contamination from fracking Urbina could find was a single incident. It happened in 1982, at half the depth of the reservoirs in today's boom, in an area of West Virginia littered with abandoned wells drilled decades earlier that could serve as pathways for contaminants.[15] While Urbina's ominous label above the article, "Evidence Surfaces," hinted that there might be more cases, he didn't present them. And in June 2015, the EPA concluded in a 998-page draft report after four years of study: "We did not find evidence that these mechanisms"—belowground hydraulic fracturing activities—"have led to widespread, systemic impacts on drinking water resources in the United States."[16] The number of cases in which any aspect of shale drilling affected drinking water was "small."[17] While it modeled theoretical ways in which gas or liquids could migrate during normal fracking and mentioned a few accidents, it found no cases in deep low-permeability shales in which normally occurring fracking contaminated drinking water.[18]

People in the oil business forwarded the Obama EPA report with enthusiasm, like muskrats praising the vision of a hawk.

Many also pointed to the near empty dossiers of Urbina and the EPA, reminded folks that Americans are innocent until proven guilty, pledged allegiance to the flag, and declared the case closed. That, to me, is the wrong route to the destination. In the 2.7 million oil and gas wells drilled since 1949, there are bound to be incidents and accidents not yet discovered. And for someone who now can't use his backyard water well, the industry's I-told-you-so satisfaction that water contamination incidents have nothing to do with fracking is like his assailant crowing that an MRI proved that she hit him with a hockey stick instead of a baseball bat.

To me, the best argument against the claim that fracking directly poisons the water table is what the process of constructing an oil or gas well, and fracking it, actually is.

To keep the description of drilling and completing a modern shale well to a tolerable length, I will leave unexplained shoes, collars, kellies, whipstocks, catwalks, monkey boards, mud cakes, reamers, and dozens of other tools and sub-processes that sound straight out of wizard camp. I will leave to the imagination seismic surveys of underground reservoirs and the none-too-cinematic but determinative deskwork before drilling a well: contracting the service providers; assembling drilling rights across often multiple leaseholders; designing every aspect of the well, from the angle of the horizontal section to the type of perforation; and permitting a well with state authorities—or federal regulators, if it's on federal land— by submitting a detailed plan.

I start with the construction of a well pad, which like everything in the drilling and completion process is done by oilfield service firms under contract and direction of the oil company with the rights to the oil and gas. (Engineers in an oil company headquarters are the composers of the symphony; the "company man" at the drill site is the conductor.) To give the drilling and fracking equipment a place to work, a construction company clears trees, if there are any, and flattens a stretch of land of roughly four to five acres. In Appalachia, to construct pads, operators often cut into a steep hillside with bulldozers and other earthmoving equipment because, as my West Virginia friend likes to joke, every flat piece of land already has a house on it and every semi-flat piece has a still.

In flat, dry West Texas, it seems that all you need to construct a well pad is a good pair of boots to kick the tumbleweed aside.

A drilling contractor then transports the rig to the site, in pieces, brought by a dozen or so trucks. A modern rig's usually 142-foot mast, once elevated, towers over the countryside, a fifteen-story building when including the rig itself. Just as in your home power drill, drilling happens by both something—you, at home—pushing on the drill bit and the bit's spinning torque. Drives on the rig or downhole motors spin the drill bit to chew up the rock (and prevent everything from getting stuck), but the real work of drilling is done by the force of the drill string: connected lengths of thirty-foot pieces of steel pipe that weigh 600 pounds apiece. By the time the drill string reaches a total depth of, say, three miles in vertical and horizontal distance, it weighs about 160 tons. That is equal to 2,000 or so people standing one on top of another. Not all the weight is on the neck of the poor guy at the bottom—some of the drill string rests on the side of the hole, much of the weight is supported by the rig—but tons of weight still push on the bit.

The drill string does not come on a spool. The rig contractor's toolpusher oversees rig hands—universally, non-pejoratively known as roughnecks—who use chains and pulleys to guide and connect the drill pipe joints. (The masts of drilling rigs are tall in order to make room for a stand of three connected joints that can be lowered into the well in one piece.) Besides having the least flattering nickname at a drill site, roughnecks also have the toughest job. The near Sisyphean frustration of their occupation is that wells are not drilled in a single effort. Different bits and tools at the end of the drill string are better suited for the varying types of rocks in the layered earth. Bits also get damaged, or worn down. So the drill string is regularly "tripped": all of it is lifted out of the well and each stand disconnected before going downhole again. It's as if, before completing a marathon, you had to run all the way back to the starting line after five and ten and fifteen miles to change your shoes.

To drill a well requires mud, a liquid sludge that is a mixture of clay and treated water, diesel, or oil. The mud is pumped down the center of the well to keep the drill bit from overheating, to control pressure in the well, and to convey back up to the surface all the rock cuttings being displaced by the well itself. At the surface, the cuttings are separated using various desanders and desilters and shakers—a piece of equipment that sifts out the rocks, not abstinent furniture makers of nineteenth-century New England—with the mud reused downhole and the solids disposed of. The cuttings are usually hauled off to a "land farm," laid in roads, and mixed with microbes until the cuttings resume their existence as plain old dirt.

All this tripping of the drill string doesn't happen quickly. In the Eagle Ford Shale, which is in the middle of the pack in terms of how deep and long wells typically go, it takes about seven to ten days of twenty-four-hour operations to drill a well after the pad is constructed.[19] For pads with multiple wells on them, a rig could be operating for a couple of months. After a well reaches TD—total depth, vertically and horizontally—operators will log the well, if it's in a new area. They lower an electric wire with measuring equipment downhole and use it to perform tests, first, to make sure that the well was properly constructed and, second, to collect information on the reservoir.

Nothing has been fracked yet. All the effort that follows, including fracking, is part of the completion of the well that starts after drilling is done. The well is first cased and cemented or the wellbore would collapse upon itself, as if you pulled a toothpick out of a freshly baked cake. Specialists lower steel tubes—the casing—into a well. Then another company pumps cement through the center of the wellbore at such high pressure that the cement returns upward around the annulus, or outside, of the wellbore to cement the five-inch or so diameter casing in place.

As I explain in the next chapter, poor casing and cementing has caused groundwater pollution, as at Dimock. (Inadequate cementing—and human error—also caused BP's Macondo disaster in the Gulf of Mexico.) But casing also makes oil and gas drilling immeasurably less likely to pollute land and water. Almost no wells in the world are drilled with just one diameter of pipe and one layer of casing. In high-volume, complicated offshore wells, operators start off with casings with a diameter larger than a manhole and then drill series of increasingly smaller holes that are cased off and cemented before the well continues deeper. Drilling a well offshore is less like sticking a hole in the ground than like building a telescoping skyscraper upside down. Life onshore is simpler. In onshore shale wells, there is always one layer of "surface casing" usually drilled to about 500 feet or so that is set and cemented before the drilling process continues through the hole inside that casing. The full length of the well is eventually sealed with "production casing" and cemented into place. In some longer onshore wells, there is also a third layer of "intermediate" casing.

In the United States, as long as anyone in the business can remember, the depth to which surface casing must go has been mandated by regulators, based on historic data of where water wells have been drilled and where groundwater is, not by an operator deciding that some spot of paradise is worth protecting. (The regulators are state authorities unless the land is owned by the federal government, in which case the regulator is the Bureau of Land Management.) Surface casing must be set at least fifty feet below groundwater in Pennsylvania and Oklahoma, for instance.[20] In Texas, you have to get approval of your surface casing design and depth from the Groundwater Advisory Unit, which sounds like the punch line of a libertarian joke.[21] Regulators also dictate testing to confirm that cementing and other steps of the completion process are done right, to prevent Dimocks.

And then, finally, fracking begins. The use of the word fracking for all that came before is like referring to a four-course meal as dessert. While the description below is of the most common types of fracking today, known as multi-stage plug and perf, there are alternatives: coil tubing fracks; open hole fracks; and sliding sleeves, which are fracking tools, not a fashion accessory for the woman on the go.

Before a frack begins, oilfield service companies assemble equipment on a well pad that soon becomes as packed as an L.A. freeway at rush hour: trucks with wires to lower perforating guns; trucks with blenders for mixing proppants; trucks with hydration units for mixing frack fluids; trucks (a lot more trucks) with pumps; tanks to hold the proppant; and the water itself in tanks or in nearby man-made plastic-lined pits.

In most shale areas, the well's drilled between a mile or two vertically before nearing the targeted shale layer. It then curves, extending horizontally for another mile or two. After the well is cased and cemented, an oilfield service company lowers on a wire four or five perforating guns, three-foot steel tubes filled with small explosives, evenly across one stage of 250 feet or so. (As with a lot of these numbers, I'm describing a general case: the number of perforation clusters and the length of the stages vary quite a bit by basin, operator, and engineer.) When their charges are activated one by one by an electrical signal from the surface, shape charges from each gun-punch, high-pressure, vaporizing gas through the casing and cement and into the rock.

In a conventional reservoir, perforating the casing sometimes starts oil or gas flowing. But to get oil or gas out of an ultra–low permeability shale reservoir, you need to create fractures. And so the "pressure pumping" fleet of about twenty pumper trucks—the numbers vary, depending on the horsepower needed—begin to rumble and roar as they pull a changing mixture of water, proppants, and chemicals from various blenders and manifolds and push them through an octopus of piping into the wellhead. Each pump shoots out a mixture at anywhere from 500 to 800 gallons per minute, thirty to fifty times more powerful than a garden hose.[22] Twenty trucks pumping fluids and proppants into the same well multiply that force twenty times.

From the outside, this is all shaking and noise, as if every washing machine in town had been placed in a field and set on spin cycle. The frack crew, making sure that nothing is leaking from all the connections, is calm, focused, silent. You can't hear anyone anyway. Earplugs are mandatory. Engines and pumps thunder as if there's a helicopter overhead.

What's being pumped inside the well changes steadily. Guided by computers, a foreman in a trailer (a dip cup almost mandatory beside him) alters the mixture over the course of a frack stage lasting two hours or so:[23] first comes acid to clean out the wellbore and treat the rock; then comes chemically treated slickwater to fracture the shale; then comes crosslinked gel or more slickwater to carry in the proppant to keep those fractures open; and then comes more water to clean everything out. The first round of frack fluid cracks the rock, leaving microscopically thin fractures growing upward and outward in every direction from the wellbore, for 100 to 300 feet, like a ring of impossibly thin, leafless trees. (Some fracks are "aimed" in one direction.) In the second round, in which the frack fluid delivers the proppants, the heat from the earth and the friction of the trip downhole "melts" the heavier frack fluid, to release the proppants into the fractures.

How much gelling agent to use in each step of this process is one of the main variables of fracking, and completion engineers argue over this with the same passion other men reserve for college football rankings. How gelatinous to make the frack fluid involves trade-offs. Using more gelling agent—the agent is usually derived from guar, the same bean used to make chewing gum chewy—allows you to carry bigger and heavier manufactured proppants: millimeter-wide BB's. Proppants, fighting a mile or two of overburden, are judged by crush strength, their ability to withstand pressure. Using a ceramic proppant is like holding up the roof with a steel beam. The alternative, natural sand, is like holding up the roof with a piece of wood.

Steel beams aren't always the answer, though. A more watery frack fluid with less gelling agent can carry only smaller proppants, but as in Nick Steinsberger's famous S. H. Griffin #4 breakthrough, slickwater fracks, unlike more gelatinous ones, experience less friction going downhole. They accelerate faster, hit the rock with more force, and in effect install more roof-holding beams.

Once an individual frack stage is complete, the fracked zone is temporarily plugged. The same process is repeated for another stage across the next 250 feet—the distance, again, depends on the basin and operator—with four or five clusters of perforations, until the entire horizontal length of the wellbore is completed and you've reached the vertical well that got you to the shale in the first place. The number of frack stages averages, nationally, twenty-two.[24]

The final stage of completing a well is production testing and frack flowback. All the proppant and frack fluid does not stay in the well. Over several days, after the frack plugs are drilled out, the excess proppant and water is cleaned out, pumped to the surface, reused, treated, and disposed of. The pressure inside the wellbore then drops, or all the hallways of the individual fracks inside the shale open up. Oil, gas, natural gas liquids, and water start to flow.

BUT WHAT IS ACTUALLY GOING down the well? What is frack fluid? Broadly speaking, a frack job is made up of about 90 percent water,

9.5 percent sand or other proppant, and 0.5 percent chemicals. All together, that 100 percent is a lot of stuff. A typical multi-stage frack job today uses about 6 million pounds of sand, which weighs as much as 35,000 people.[25] It uses 4 to 8 million gallons of water—less in the Permian Basin—or enough to fill six to twelve Olympic-size swimming pools.[26]

Activists, especially of the Malthusian variety, focus on the water consumed, concerned that we are diverting resources that could be better used, especially in areas suffering from drought. (That's another reason why there has been no shale revolution in California.) While the total freshwater consumed by the oil industry is unclear, the EPA draft report concluded that the water usage averaged 44 billion gallons in 2011 and 2012.[27] (Other estimates put a steady state in typical wells today at twice that level.)[28] Forty-four billion gallons would fill a three-square-mile lake twenty-five feet deep.

The industry defends its use of water in two ways. First, an increasing amount of water used in fracking—it ranges from 5 to 20 percent in various shale plays—is now recycled from other frack jobs or produced water.[29] So that three-square-mile lake is not totally filled with "new" freshwater. In addition, 44 billion gallons of water used in shale wells in a year, including both new and recycled water, is only 0.03 percent of the total annual water consumed in America. The water used by shale drilling that supplied 48 percent of Americans' natural gas and 22 percent of their oil was equivalent to 6 percent of the water used for livestock, 0.1 percent of the water used for irrigation, and 2 percent of what Americans used to water their gardens and lawns.[30]

(I've never spoken to anyone worried that America is running out of sand, or even the effects of sand injected downhole, a surprising fact considering that there seems to be some Americans worried about everything one can possibly worry about. Nonetheless, the sand consumption statistics are staggering: the U.S. oil industry consumed about 95 billion pounds of it in 2014.[31] The Willis Tower in Chicago weighs nearly a half a billion pounds empty. The oil industry pumps, more or less, a downtown Chicago of sand into U.S. wells every year.)

In general, opponents of shale drilling are less concerned about the sand and water in frack fluid than about everything else in it. Chemicals comprise only 0.5 percent of the combined frack fluid of proppant[32] but include some stuff you wouldn't want in your coffee: xylene, toluene, methanol, hydrochloric acid, ethylene glycol (the key ingredient in antifreeze).[33] And 0.5 percent, while a small fraction, would translate into 25,000 gallons of chemicals, about enough to fill a midsized backyard pool. Environmentalists often highlight a frighteningly large number of chemicals associated with frack fluid, with headlines like one in 2015: "EPA Report Finds Nearly 700 Chemicals Used in Fracking."[34] But this would be like saying that a batch of homemade cookies had 700 ingredients just because that's the total number of items—sugar, flour, paprika, burritos, ground beef—available at the grocery store. The median number of chemicals in a frack job, according to the EPA, is 14.[35]

The industry, in the early days of the shale revolution, fed public paranoia by refusing to reveal what chemicals were used, saying that they were the "trade secrets" of oilfield service companies like Halliburton. (Public paranoia would be notched up even more when someone would point out that the secrets were being kept by "Dick Cheney's" Halliburton.) But that secrecy was self-defeating and unnecessary: my colleagues and I joked that oilfield service companies didn't want to reveal the trade secrets of their frack fluid because the real secret, once revealed, is that everyone uses pretty much the same stuff.

The industry has now matured. Many companies have started listing the components of their frack jobs on the Web site FracFocus, which may rival Actuary.org as the most boring Web site in the history of the Internet. Doing so is the law in Pennsylvania. As can be seen on FracFocus, frack jobs use off-the-shelf chemicals for workaday tasks: acids to kill bacteria, prime the rock, or prevent casing corrosion; friction reducers, including sometimes diesel fuel, to help all the frack fluids get downhole with maximum force; and various chemicals to maintain the integrity of the viscosity of the gel as it is pumped.[36]

But are the diesel and other chemicals that form a fraction of the frack fluid dangerous? The industry claims that the chemicals pose no harm: there is 180 times more water than chemicals in frack fluid, and the primary additive, guar, is edible. One Halliburton executive famously drank some frack fluid at an industry conference in 2011 and seemed no worse for it.[37] An investor soon after asked me if I would drink frack fluid. I explained that my wife hardly lets me drink Diet Coke.

The drinkability of Pinot Frackio hardly matters, though. The worry is that at some point in the process of pumping noxious chemicals into the ground, at whatever quantities, the chemicals contaminate groundwater—and people relying on it would suffer from long-term exposure, not from a single swig. Groundwater is naturally stored in underground aquifers intermixed into the sand and rock, often in pores not unlike where oil is found. (Half of American drinking water comes from groundwater, and 14 percent of Americans get their drinking water from private water wells drawing from groundwater on their own property.)[38] The depth of usable groundwater varies by season and location—the U.S. government collects data from more than 1.5 million different sites—but water wells usually pump water up from 100 to 250 feet, with 1,000 feet or so being the deepest aquifers before water gets unpotably salty.[39]

Gasland talks of fracking as underground "earthquakes" and shows cartoons of the earth being fractured practically right up to the surface. The final part of the documentary spends ten minutes trying to frighten the Most Important People on Earth, my fellow residents of Manhattan, by filming, well, frightened residents of Manhattan, including the borough president. So maybe the best way to convey the distances and realities of fracking is through a metaphor my people can understand. Imagine a map of Manhattan as a cross-section of earth and sky. Harlem is the heavens, the Battery deep underground, and 60th Street where land meets air. Place a drilling rig on 60th and Lex, right on Bloomingdale's. Install surface casing for one-tenth of a mile to 58th Street and cement it. From inside that surface casing, continue to push the drill string all the way down Lexington Avenue, starting to bend as you get to 30th Street, so that the horizontal well is drilled crosstown on 27th Street. Stop drilling at the Hudson River. Isolate a section that's about half of a crosstown avenue block, perforate in clusters, activate the pump trucks, and frack. Repeat twenty-one more times.

All the water, chemicals, and sand would frack the city from about 26th Street to 28th Street.

Bloomingdale's would get its water from . . . Bloomingdale's, with a water well drawing water from 59th Street up to 60th.

The frack fluid being injected downtown can't go much south of 26th Street or north of 28th Street, even if oil companies wanted it to. The pressure and the energy of the fluid is eventually transferred into the rock it is fracturing. If you fire a bullet into the ground, it doesn't continue to the center of the earth.

The first irony of the concerns about water contamination is that fracking deep shale is significantly less likely to damage groundwater than almost any other type of oil and gas reservoir. In the fracking of a typical shale well, human ingenuity is squaring off against physical reality: the least permeable rock in the history of the oil business and the pressure from a mile or two of overburden work together to resist the frack fluid going far. The shale revolution happened after the industry learned how to produce oil and gas from Alcatraz rocks. Those reservoirs had not been tapped in 150 years because the conventional wisdom was that the fluid and gas molecules in them could never be stimulated to flow at reasonable volumes. Accusing fracking of groundwater contamination is like accusing Alcatraz not of being inhumane but of not being good at keeping prisoners locked up. Indeed, there are some shallow gas shales in the Midwest and coalbed methane fields in the Rockies (like the ones shown in *Gasland*), in which the distances between gas producing zones and drinking water sources are much shorter than in the shales developed in the boom.[40] The shale revolution has, nationally speaking, made American water sources *safer* by rendering drilling in those types of fields almost wholly unprofitable.

Yes, strange accidents can occur in which an operator is not aware—or hasn't keep track—of an old wellbore or mine shaft, creating pathways for gas migration. This has happened at least three times in Pennsylvania.[41] And liquid and gas can escape from source rock like shales. It must, to create conventional reservoirs formed by traps. But that process takes tens of thousands—maybe hundreds of thousands of years—one molecule at a time. Indeed, if shale gas or liquids could leak upward into groundwater, the industry wouldn't need to assemble the army of trucks and sand and water. We could drill a well like it was 1865 and watch a gusher erupt.

As it is, engineers in, for instance, the Permian Basin are forced to drill completely new horizontal wells at different depths to extract oil and gas from different deposits of shale. Most individual shale deposits are only a few hundred feet thick, which was the depth of the ancient sea floors that captured the corpses of plants and animals. Engineers dream of being able to frack through multiple "horizons." Occasionally, they get excited by freaky fracks, rising 1,000 feet or so, due to the natural fracturing of some rock. (Even the tips of those fracks are still or more below groundwater.[42]) But the results of all the other frack stages now being done—an estimated 520,000 in 2014[43]—return their hopes to earth. Fracks go only a few hundred feet.[44]

The enormous effort involved to get the frack fluid and proppant to even modest heights highlights the second irony of the fears of water contamination: the loudest complaint against fracking is disproved by its greatest weakness. Fracking doesn't create massive earthquakes and send poisons and methane into water taps. That's because for all the effort summoned to smash the rock, fracking isn't all that impressive in its scope or results. By creating millimeter-thick fractures, a typical fracked oil well, for instance, produces about 1,000 barrels a day of initial production. This subsides, with natural declines, over a year or two to about 150 barrels per day. The "burst" of initial production is equivalent to about two standard five-eighths-inch-thick garden hoses being run all day. Production in a couple of years will be equivalent to the day-long running of two bathroom sinks.[45]

Critics of the U.S. oil and gas renaissance point to shale drilling's low EROI, its energy return of investment, or how much energy it takes to produce energy. They note that we are putting a lot of money and effort—and using up a lot of the energy we produce—to mine sand and secure water and build trucks to stimulate wells for not all that much oil. They have a point. Our response in the industry is what is the cheaper, more flexible alternative? The EROI for many other energy sources is also pretty sad. A 2013 study by two Stanford professors noted that until 2010, it took more electricity to produce solar panels collectively than the electricity they were generating. The professors forecast that the panels globally will have "paid back" that energy in 2020.[46]

I HAVE TWO THEORIES of why fracking-caused water contamination, of all improbable concerns, came to be the initial and most lingering local environmental argument against shale development. I call one the New York Theory, the other the Art Theory.

The New York Theory begins with the inevitable, understandable NIMBY ("Not In My Backyard") objections to shale drilling that arose when a clanking, dusty, muddy, not accident-free industrial process entered areas unprepared for it, in ways that weren't always fair. Now, we are all NIMBYs at some time or other: the liberal car driver who doesn't want a drilling rig next door is no more or less human than the law-and-order hardcase who doesn't want a jail near his daughter's school. My company has drilled wells on oil executives' ranchettes in Oklahoma, and we can tell you that some oilmen also don't welcome drilling in their backyard as a triumph for U.S. energy self-reliance. The EPA estimates that between 2000 and 2013 there were 9.3 million Americans living within a mile of a fracked well. That means 9.3 million potential NIMBYs.[47]

As I talk about in Part Three of this book, the American oil and gas renaissance saw money falling from the sky—or emerging from the earth—in unexpected places, but it did not rain money evenly and everywhere. There were clear economic winners and losers in each area's boom. Some farmers had their lives and great-great-grandchildren's lives changed forever with shale money. But many people remained Have Nots, with no economic benefit from the boom in their area. Their land wasn't prospective for good wells. They never owned the mineral rights beneath their property. They didn't have jobs into which oil money flowed.

The NIMBY cries against fracking have been particularly loud in three places: New York City; Ithaca, New York; and Boulder, Colorado. (Perhaps as a sign that the universe is laughing at a guy like me joining the oil business, the three anti-fracking capitals are my home for twenty years, my college town for four years before that, and the city I've passed through on vacation more than any other in the last two decades.) All three cities are border towns, between conflicting political and cultural points of view and now between Haves and Have Nots of oil and gas mineral rights. In Boulder, Ithaca, and places like it, concentrations of people whose livelihood may not be much connected to the local economy (e.g., college professors) abut rural areas in which people's livings are connected to the land—and now the shale revolution. Boulder County is right next door to Weld County, home of *Gasland*'s iconic lit tap. Ithaca, the home of the Park Foundation, the most influential and perhaps largest funder of anti-fracking efforts,[48] is thirty-seven miles from the border with the American Qatar, also known as Pennsylvania.

New York City's relationship to its "border" with the shale renaissance is different than in Boulder or Ithaca, where residents can see rigs when they drive not too far out of town. New York City's concerns about water contamination center on the Catskills, a region of low mountains 100 miles to its north, which sits atop the northeastern flank of the Marcellus Shale. There is gas there, even if it's in high-cost, low-quality deposits. The southern Catskills also contain some of the reservoirs from which New York City and its suburbs get, via tunnels and aqueducts, their water.

The Catskills have a double existence, economically. They are home to often struggling rural communities. And they are home to the second homes of city folks. In many places, the first economy is dependent on the second economy and other tourists. But there is no difference in the gut revulsion that causes someone to shout Not in My Backyard versus Not in My Second Backyard. A friend with a summer home in the Catskills described for me a birthday party at a neighbor's in 2013. Some of the stylish crowd made its way to the porch to drink in the brilliant summer day. All of a sudden, one woman, not known to be an environmental activist, gathered attention as she delivered an impromptu stem-winder: all they held dear would be destroyed if gas drilling came to New York state. The water would be poisoned. The area's character would change. And the governor was coming under crushing pressure from the opposition to allow this to happen.

There were NIMSBY issues at work, of course, but there were also fundamental values. To the liberals on that porch, the boom was an encroachment into their state not just of companies but of oil companies (the worst) and not just companies run by Republicans but companies run by Texas Republicans (the scariest).

It's easy to make fun, to dismiss the New York City anti-fracking movement as selfishness masquerading as environmentalism. Just don't interrupt the peace and quiet of the Frederic Edwin Church vistas I paid dearly for with drilling rigs in my landscape or roughnecks making boob jokes at the Price Chopper. My cynicism is not abated by the celebrities at the vanguard of "fractivism," owners of summer homes in the Catskills or of idylls to rest in between movie sets. Where did you develop such strong opinions on natural gas, Yoko Ono?

Josh Fox's story is a NIMSBY one, too, Pennsylvania edition. But when you listen to him or Ono or Mark Ruffalo, the Clooney of the Catskills, it's clear that they ardently believe that fracking will poison their own water sources as well as that of their poorer neighbors. They do care. And when you drive through southwestern Pennsylvania, where the Marcellus Shale is being actively developed, you can see once tree-blanketed hillsides interrupted by grassy pipeline right-of-ways or groves flattened to make parking lots for oilfield trucks. The landscape has changed. Not all losses are measured by contaminants in water.

New York's NIMSBYs may be Have Nots of mineral rights, but they have demonstrable clout with the governor, Andrew Cuomo, who probably thinks a lot about being a Have Not, too, in having not yet been the president of the United States. While Colorado anti-shale activists have failed to date in getting a frack ban initiative on the ballot—Democratic governor and former petroleum geologist John Hickenlooper steered all sides to a compromise—New York prohibited fracking in 2014 in Cuomo's administrative ruling (one that could be reversed by future governors.)[49]

The NIMSBYs also have a huge amount of cultural power. If the Marcellus Shale was under Atlanta, concerns about water contamination—maybe fracking in general—might not have risen to national notice. But Catskills summer homes are, as the cliché goes, owned by magazine editors, theatrical directors, literary agents, journalists. (Wall Street and the famous go to the Hamptons because only Wall Street and the famous can afford the Hamptons.) When the Catskills-summering media types returned to New York, they fomented a fear of gas drilling.

People in the industry ask—in general and often me—why New York–based newspapers and magazines seem to report on every trace of drilling fluid in every Pennsylvania water well, no matter how old or infinitesimal, and not report with the same vigor on all of the spills, accidents, and facts of life of every other industrial activity necessary to live our collective modern life?[50] I have spent a lot of time in New York media culture, cheerfully, among friends and admired acquaintances. From personal experience, I can tell you that the culture was already suspicious of oil companies (although a mention of what I do, in that crowd, is met more often with restrained skepticism than blunt hostility). Frankly, there have been reasons to be suspicious of oil companies over the last 150 years. Like all corporations, they rely too much on spin. There have been obfuscation and lies.

Yet when fracking became national news, the controversy wasn't a generic high school debate question: oil companies are evil, pro or con. The issues demanded an understanding of physics and geology, of how molecules move through rock. The fracking debate led me to have hours-long, patience-testing discussions with investors—and my parents—about the depth of groundwater, the distinction between casing and drill pipe, the nuances of a safely constructed well. The people I was talking to came with impressions cast first- or secondhand by *Gasland* and by a news media not terribly sophisticated about petroleum engineering or physics. No general business or political reporter had any reason to be: before the boom, U.S. onshore oil and gas drilling wasn't news, it was history. There has been sophisticated, indispensable reporting about the shale revolution since that time, but there was way too much at its start—and still too much today—in which details were presented clumsily, paraphrases of paraphrases of descriptions of scientific and industrial processes only shallowly understood.

This was frustrating to me, but it wasn't surprising. The tin ear of a lot of reporting on the shale revolution seemed consistent with metropolitan apathy about economic pursuits outside the more glamorous, more physically clean worlds of technology, media, and Wall Street (the businesses of superstar cities, the businesses in which big city reporters have friends from college). The tin ear was also part of a broader social trend. As critics like Lawrence Summers have pointed out, culture smarts trump technical smarts among the metropolitan elite today. It's okay not to know how a computer works but not okay to be ignorant of what Melville wrote. I'm guilty, too. I have no idea how a computer works. And so like many, when I read science or engineering journalism, I'm more credulous—because I'm more ignorant.

That stew of unfamiliarity, suspicion, NIMSBYism, and mechanical ignorance culminated in the "Drilling Down" series in *The New York Times* by the Javert of shale revolution, Ian Urbina. That series, along with *Gasland*, played the most important role in defining the shape of the first arguments against shale development from a local perspective. I am a daily, near reverential *Times* reader. So Urbina's series, which would have been more accurately titled "Everything Negative I Could Think to Write About Natural Gas Drilling," caused me to burn with embarrassment at its obtuseness on how regulation works, how the oil industry works, how drilling works. It was as if my mother were caught on TV declaring that multivitamins caused sterility. This wasn't just self-consciousness. Each time Urbina drilled down, my inbox would fill with e-mails from colleagues commenting on what my "friends" at the *Times* were up to now.

But why did Urbina, like Fox, focus so much of his investigation on water? Maybe a fear of poisoned water affects people instinctually. Humans are 60 percent water.[51] Damaging it is damaging us.

Or, in my New York Theory, the focus on water came because water pollution is the primary way that fracking frightens residents of Manhattan and Brooklyn. Most of us New Yorkers don't own a summer home in the Catskills (or anywhere). Local drilling nuisances, or a poisoned water source of some poor farmer, don't affect us. Yet all of us New Yorkers think that our tap water is the world's best, also the secret ingredient to our bagels. *Gasland* is explicit about the threat to that water: fracking, it claims, could pollute the New York watershed. This is about as likely to happen as every New Yorker suddenly rooting for the Red Sox. (New York City's water, to take just one reason, comes from reservoirs filled by rain and snow, mainly, not from wells extracting groundwater.) But maybe even the least possible threat is enough to generate opposition to something when you imagine that the only people benefiting are Texas oil companies you dislike.

There is a final irony to New York's leadership in the fight against fracking. It's not clear anyone would frack much in New York anyway. At today's prices, there are some good drilling locations in the southern edges of Chemung, Tioga, and Broome counties near the Pennsylvania border. But most of the New York Marcellus, economically and geologically speaking, is fourth-rate. Even if statewide and local bans had not been put in place, Ithaca and the Catskills and my pumpernickel bagels were always safe.[52]

THE NEW YORK THEORY EXPLAINS, I believe, why water contamination became a preoccupation in the early opposition to fracking. But when I'm looking for simpler reasons, I also have the Art Theory.

When Josh Fox was searching for evidence to make his case in *Gasland*, the most convenient and most filmable analogs to the risks he wanted to find were in technically unrelated examples of water contamination. Like *The Feminine Mystique* or *Atlas Shrugged*, Fox's documentary is one of those rare cultural products that have launched a movement. Second-wave feminism would have existed without *The Feminine Mystique* and libertarianism without *Atlas Shrugged*, but there is a way in which sparking works can shape movements with their big ideas—and with their idiosyncratic concerns.

The mass fears of fracking-polluted water could have been born simply because Josh Fox made some reactive, half-thought-through decisions when rushing a film to completion. And Josh Fox, from talent and luck making him the first prominent voice of the local perspective of the shale revolution, got to start the conversation any way he wanted.

But in doing so, he might have diverted the conversation away from his side's most convincing arguments.

6. WHEN FRACKING DOESN'T MEAN FRACKING ANYMORE

MY WIFE AND I DONATE TO SEVERAL ENVIRONMENTAL ORGANIZATIONS. We give for uninteresting reasons: we want to help fight climate change, minimize pollution, conserve nature. We are aware, of course, that I work in the fossil fuel business. I used to think that that dissonance made me complex; I now suspect it might mean I'm avoiding things. While we have switched our donations to organizations that reflect more our views, we used to give to groups, out of inertia from before the fracking debate, that regularly pissed me off.

In 2011, one such group invited me and probably every other donor to a workday conference call on the campaign to restrict gas drilling in New York state. Feeling uneasily like an eavesdropper, I dialed in, ready to listen to a medley of nonsense on fracking.

It took me the whole call to realize that the brain-burrowing chorus of that pop song was never going to be played.

The activist leading the call mentioned once, in a long list of worries and complaints, the potential for long-term migration of contaminants to the water supply through naturally occurring fracks, abandoned wells, or badly drilled wells. But she admitted that there was no proof that this had happened and that she understood, on this topic, the industry's point of view. Concession aside, she did not back down from the purpose of the call: to muster support for new regulations and strict restrictions on drilling in New York, if the moratorium then in place was ever lifted.

It wasn't clear if she welcomed even more restricted drilling or if the purpose of listing conditions was to erect such high obstacles that drilling wasn't practically possible, like telling a three-year-old that she can have a milkshake if she can pay for it herself. But the woman was balanced and reasonable. And her offhand, almost neutral reference to fracking still startled after the call ended. She had skimmed over what almost every popular discussion about the shale revolution had been about for two years.

And suddenly it became clear. I had been arguing against ghosts: fracking was no longer about fracking. It had come to mean more than just water and sand being pumped down a well. It had become a synecdoche—a figure of speech in which a part signals the whole, like "Hollywood" for the film industry—for the entire drilling and completion process *and* the shale revolution itself.

Our problem, in the oil business, was that we had been overly literal. We thought fracking always meant, well, fracking. So we concluded that reporters were being misleading, or dense, when we read under a headline that "fracking causes earthquakes" an article about the disposal of produced water unrelated to fracking.

But fracking is just too fun to say, and using it to mean the whole shale extraction process—and its implications—continues. In general, this has caused the green and the black to talk past each other. But for me, understanding the more enveloping use of the word fracking has finally allowed me to comprehend the debate from the local perspective of the shale revolution. It doesn't, however, make the debate easier to resolve.

Indeed, the first phase of local environmental objections to the boom was comfortingly straightforward: either fracking contaminated groundwater or it didn't. And it didn't. The broader complaints about "fracking" are more knotty. They are directed toward a mix of nuisances, risks of accidents, and unequal sacrifices. The complaints are legitimate. The risks are real. And we as a society are being asked to judge if and when the sum of these mistakes and unfair burdens outweighs the boom's economic and potential global environmental benefits—or even the right of one family to get richer. In answering these questions, confirmation biases run deep. Environmentalists list the threats to water, air, and communities, and each new threat confirms that the list is endless, with too many people being hurt. The oil industry reads lists of exaggerated, farfetched griev-ances and sees a willed adding on.

There is also no answer outside one's moral point of view. You can be clear-eyed on the facts of what the oil industry does and does not do and still conclude that the price of the shale revolution is too high, that on balance it is hurting too many people or sacrificing too much of the beauty of the country, the purity of the land, and the last vestiges of rural life to justify something as noxious as hydrocarbons.

Few Americans, I suspect, would reach this binary conclusion. (I don't.) And that conclusion doesn't erase the ethical questions that follow from it. Residents of New York state surely have the democratic right to ban fracking, concluding that the societal and environmental costs are too high. But do New Yorkers then have the moral right to use one-twentieth of the nation's consumed gas—the fourth most of any state[1]—and effec-tively outsource the local consequences to Pennsylvanians? And the big-gest question of all, perhaps: of all the corporate activities that annoy neighbors or have the potential to harm workers, bystanders, and the environment—in manufacturing, construction, food, transportation—is shale development so uniquely prone to negative local consequences that it needs to be curtailed or altogether stopped?

And is the local perspective on the shale revolution fixed? Can shale development get worse—or better?

THE OIL AND GAS BUSINESS is not a delicate one. Drilling and completing a shale well brings together heavy equipment and usually heavy men to force steel miles into the earth and then to put more steel, cement, water, sand, and chemicals downhole. The exercise extracts inflammable, un-drinkable oil and gas. Moving it, storing it, and refining it so that oil and gas just show up, like the oxygen in the air, when you light your stove or fill up your car relies on infrastructure of varying age and maintenance. Accidents happen. Annoyances occur. *Gasland* was primarily about the bad things that could happen underground. But bad things can happen on air, land, *and* water—all the armed services.

Water pollution is not the most common source of local aggravations, but it is the chief risk for people living in areas swept up in a shale boom. Many rural homes, far from municipal water systems, obtain water from private backyard wells drilled into groundwater under their land. The EPA estimates that 8.6 million people get their drinking water from sources located within a mile of a hydraulically fractured well.[2] Polluting the groundwater that feeds these wells forces people to get water trucked in. Surface water can also be polluted and run into streams and lakes, threatening everything—fish, deer, people—that drinks from those sources.

There are three main types of fluids that can pollute groundwater: chemicals before they are mixed into the flack fluid or used in other oilfield applications; frack flowback, the chemical-treated water injected into the well that returns uphole; and produced water. The last, innate to oil and gas reservoirs, contains a lot of salt and also nasties like iron, chromium, and radium, some of which are NORMs—naturally occurring radioactive material.[3] Many people's lives—many whole companies' existence—are centered on providing tools to safely handle these fluids. And all oil and oilfield service companies have intensive health, safety, and environmental (HS&E) processes and ongoing training to make sure that the fluids are optimally managed and contained.

Yet accidents occur. While industrial gravity may have been reversed in the U.S. energy renaissance, physical gravity has not been: it's more likely that you'll spill pasta sauce on your own linoleum than your downstairs neighbor's cooking will come up through the floor. So, too, the threats to groundwater come from above and from the sides, not from fracking a mile or two below. Spilled fluids and chemicals can leak onto the ground for the same reasons they can in any industry: incompetence, laziness, did-you-see-the-game-last-night-whoa-man distraction, poorly maintained equipment, and bad luck. Spills can happen because faulty or ill-installed surface valves and piping break, perhaps ruptured by pressured gas and fluid coming up from the well. Very few oilfield spills cause momentous, irreversible harm, just as the pool boy spilling chlorine might damage your hydrangeas but won't destroy your neighborhood. The EPA's 2015 draft report, for one, found no oilfield spills that leaked into groundwater (although spills can leak into rivers and streams).[4] Yet the acids, additives, and minute traces of NORMs are there, waiting for entropy.

The treatment of frack flowback and produced water is a central activity of the oilfield. An oilfield joke so aged that no one even laughs at it anymore is that we're not in the oil business but in the water hauling business. Sometimes this isn't even a joke: Chevron is selling some treated produced water to farmers in drought-stricken California to irrigate almonds, pistachios, and other crops.[5] On average across the United States, there is an estimated ten barrels of water produced for every barrel of oil and ninety-seven barrels of water for every 1,000 cubic feet of gas[6] (or about 400,000 gallons of water produced to provide enough gas used by an average Midwestern home).[7]

While the industry had developed many solutions for both flowback and produced water, none totally eliminates the possibility of environmentally harmful mistakes. The plastic linings of the open air pits that store clean water, frack flowback, or produced water can tear, especially if operators are recklessly stingy and don't construct them properly. Violent storms can cause even perfectly constructed pits to overflow. Good pits can seem like inviting "ponds" for livestock or deer to drink from, if they are not securely fenced and if birds are not actively scared away. (Birds seem to have no luck from any energy source: burned by solar, chopped up by wind, poisoned by oil and gas. No wonder they are so angry in cell phone games.)

A company can pay to send oilfield water to privately owned—or in rare cases, municipal—treatment plants, where the water is cleaned and pumped into a river. Some of those plants are oftentimes doing the same with the sewage of us pill-popping, preservative-eating, plastic-loving people. But this strategy puts the onus on those plants to have the right technology and capability to treat the produced water. In Pennsylvania, some municipal treatment plants were unprepared for the sixfold increase in water from the Marcellus boom and didn't have the proper technology to treat the water.[8] Pennsylvania operators stopped sending water to municipal treatment plants in 2011.[9]

Produced water does not come just from shale wells but from the million-plus active oil and gas wells producing from all types of reservoirs.[10] In 2012, the industry handled roughly eight times more produced water than the water used in fracking. Of this produced water, nearly

45 percent of it is reinjected from whence it came in enhanced oil recovery techniques to simulate oil production. Officially, this is called water-flooding; the wise guys in the business call it washing rocks. Another 40 percent of produced water—nearly 350 billion gallons per year, or the equivalent consumption to that of about 10 million Americans—is injected into saltwater disposal wells.[11]

Drilling new disposal wells or converting old oil and gas wells that are no longer producing into disposal wells is an old practice, the default one in many areas, and the safest method in most cases. It has lately also become the most notorious, as injecting produced water into disposal wells has caused induced seismicity, as the industry likes to call it, or earthquakes, as human beings do. The produced water pumped at high pressure is activating some natural faults, especially if it is being injected into hard basement rock below from where oil and gas is produced. The earthquakes have occurred occasionally throughout North America but most famously in Oklahoma, where the number of seismic events over three on the Richter scale skyrocketed from one or two per year historically to 585 in 2014.[12] While a 3- to 4-level earthquake has the same dish-rattling impact of heavy truck traffic outside your house—also a fact of life for those living near shale development—Oklahoma also experienced fifteen earthquakes above 4 on the Richter scale in 2014. The largest earthquake in Oklahoma history, a 5.6, occurred near the town of Prague in 2011. While the tremor didn't injure anyone, it destroyed at least sixteen homes.[13]

Some in the industry like to remind the world that those earthquakes have nothing to do with fracking. That is little comfort if you're suddenly homeless in Prague. And there is no doubt that the shale revolution has increased the disposal of produced water. From 2010 to 2014, Oklahoma oil production shot up by 90 percent. Gas production rose 26 percent.[14] Water production rose the same percentage, at ten times the volume.

The industry is starting to accept that there are places that high-volume disposal wells just won't work. In a pattern that will become familiar in this chapter, the solutions to problems like disposal well seismicity are oftentimes remarkably straightforward. In Youngstown, Ohio, a series of earthquakes in 2011 ended after a disposal well was shut down.[15] Even in Oklahoma, where denigrating the oil business is as socially acceptable as rooting for the University of Texas Longhorns, regulators in 2015 finally caught up to the mounting evidence—and massive bad national publicity—by initiating a more restrictive system for produced water disposal around areas with a history of earthquakes.[16] Operators of deep disposal wells were forced to either prove that they were not injecting into basement rock, plug wells, or reduce disposal volumes. Companies in earthquake-prone "yellow light" areas were commanded to take pressure readings daily, monitor background seismicity, and go through a public process to get new permits.[17]

Today's greenest, safest, and most pricey way to manage fluids is a closed loop system in which all oilfield fluids are kept in steel tanks or moved by pipes, never exposed to the air. However, even in a closed loop system, mishaps are possible. Valves burst, hoses split, couplings can uncouple—reminding us that there is no guarantee that the loops will be forever closed. And even if the best designed systems totally eliminate the possibility of accidents, they can't eliminate criminal behavior. In Pennsylvania in 2011, a Wastewatergate was uncovered after the owner of a small waste disposal company was caught having ordered his employees to dump millions of gallons of contaminated water from gas drilling, restaurants, and sewage sources down the drain, into streams, and into mine shafts at night.[18]

As NOTORIOUSLY HAPPENED AT DIMOCK, poor casing and cementing of oil and gas wells can also on occasion. The industry has tools to detect problems with well integrity, how long and safely well casing and cement hold up. The most obvious symptom is a sudden drop in oil or gas production because the hydrocarbons are leaking somewhere out of the well. The oil company then has to diagnose the proximate cause—it might have to remove the casing altogether—and the underlying reason. Some casing has flaws in its manufacturing. Even with good casing, everything corrodes, including steel and cement, given enough time underground. Or the problem could have occurred in the installation and sealing of the casing. Sometimes well cement is inadequately set or lost within the reservoir, and gas can leak through fractures, gaps, or pore spaces within it. Completing wells is a complicated task, sometimes happening in turbulent weather, with technical surprises in how a rock responds to downhole tools. The industry cased and cemented 72,000 miles of wells in the on-shore United States in 2014, enough to drill through the earth over nine times.[19] A few mistakes are inevitable given that volume of activity. Each well involves an oil company contracting services from multiple oilfield service companies. Each service company hires workers in a competitive environment. No service company can boast that all of its workers are the best it can imagine.

Groundwater has some natural protection: the nearer the surface, the lesser is the pressure and temperature acting against the steel and cement. (Stick your jewelry in the refrigerator and in the oven and discover which method leads to faster decay.) Groundwater also has regulator-mandated protection, with surface and sometimes intermediate casing. But the extra layers of casing do not guarantee that groundwater will always be safe. A 2014 study under the auspices of the National Academy of Sciences investigated the footprint of trace chemicals in polluted water in eight clusters of incidents in the Barnett and Marcellus Shale boom, including Dimock. The study concluded that poor casing—or, in one case, a different failure in well construction before fracking—was responsible for contamination every time.[20]

Old wellbores can also cause water contamination. When operators decide a well is no longer useful, they will pull the steel casing out of the well to reuse it and install and cement plugs in the producing zones. If this is not done right, zombie molecules of gas could leak up into groundwater through the dead wellbore.

Finally, risks to water come not just from extracting oil and gas. Tanks that store oil at the wellhead can leak. When tornadoes come to places like Oklahoma—and tornadoes love Oklahoma—the tanks can get tossed around like beanbags. Connections between those tanks and trucks can be improperly sealed because a truck driver is thinking about his girlfriend. Trucks can flip over. Additional risks exist in local gathering and distribution systems, in the national oil and gas pipeline networks, and increasingly along rail lines carrying shale oil by—too often tipping and exploding—trains. Yes, those risks would have been there had the shale revolution not happened, but mo' oil, mo' problems, as a shale-boom Biggie Smalls would rap.

BUT WHAT IS THE PROBABILITY of, say, spills or cement failures? My oil industry friends reading the above may still be cringing. After all, you judge a baseball player by his entire career, not by his worst at-bat. Accidents can and do happen, sometimes with awful consequences. But I could have also written exceptionally boring paragraphs about hundreds of thousands of wells perfectly cemented, tens of thousands of frack sites where not a lick of chemicals ever fell to the earth, 27,000 active oil industry disposal wells and over a hundred thousand injection wells silently accepting produced water with less noise than the Toby Keith thumping out of some guy's truck.[21]

Frustratingly, comprehensive data on the frequency and magnitude of accidents is elusive. Each state has different reporting rules and requirements. Some track citizen complaints, which may or may not be ultimately attributable to oil and gas drilling once investigated. Some track spills from any cause. Few make aggregate data easy to find. And none do a good job of categorizing the data by cause: oil leaking out of a wellhead installed twenty-five years ago feels less relevant, in my assessment of the boom, than a porous cement job done last week. The EPA tried to calculate data in its landmark 2015 report but it ended up estimating the national number of shale-related spills at between 100 and 3,700 per year,[22] which sounds like telling a man on a second date that you suspect he'll end up being somewhere between a passing acquaintance and the love of your life.

There is some regional and anecdotal data. The dogged National Resources Defense Council has catalogued forty incidents, some as early as 2001, some not proved, but many involving multiple families, in which the NRDC claims oil and gas drilling caused water contamination.[23] The Pennsylvania Department of Environmental Protection posts redacted versions of "Water Determination Letters" summarizing its testing of homeowners' water to investigate whether drilling was responsible for some contamination. (These letters introduced me to a new term: the "aesthetics" of water to describe its taste and smell.) From 2008 through the first quarter of 2015, the DEP determined that 256 Pennsylvania water well contaminations were due to oil and gas drilling in a period in which over 21,000 oil and gas wells were drilled in the state.[24] The Colorado Oil and Gas Conservation Commission tracks oil spills above one barrel of oil. Since 2010, the commission records, 500 to 800 spills have occurred each year, mainly from tanks and pipelines.[25] In a deadpan spreadsheet, it also reports that the total spilled in 2014 was about 100,000 gallons of oil and 675,000 gallons of water, 0.003 percent of the oil and 0.005 percent of the water produced from the state's 50,000 wells.[26] In North Dakota, more than 18 million gallons of oil and chemicals—and 5.2 million gallons of nontoxic substances—spilled or misted into the air, mainly from pipelines, over eight years.[27] The state produced 61 billion gallons of oil in that period.[28]

Are some of these regulatory determinations unfair, as the industry claims, because, for instance, naturally occurring methane is the cause of gas in groundwater? And even if all the determinations are fair, are 256 contaminated wells an unavoidable sacrifice for the greater good in a state that produced 15 percent of the country's gas and supplied almost 1 percent of the primary energy of the world in 2014?[29] How do we measure the harm—as irritating? as catastrophic?—of the few families who now have to get water trucked in or treated at oil company expense, instead of from their own well? And does the tiny percentage of statewide oil spilled in Colorado even matter to you if you live on the Poudre River, into which 7,500 gallons of oil spilled because a collapsing riverbank knocked off a storage tank's valve?[30]

AT LEAST WHEN DISCUSSING WATER, the industry and environmentalists are fighting over the meaning and frequency of the unusual: are accidents so common that the whole boom is too risky on a local level, or are they so rare that some of us (an "us" that hopefully doesn't include "me") are just going to have to live with them? And is there a way in which we can have fewer accidents or avoid them altogether? Air and land issues—land not just in terms of polluting the earth but in the lives of people and animals on it—are less about avoidable accidents than the usual reality.

Air quality and community disruption issues have accompanied every oil and gas boom in history. Drilling and fracking rely on convoys of trucks, belching diesel exhaust. A modern well pad, according to oil company Encana, requires about 3,000 or so daily truck trips spread over nine months. These trips peak for a couple of weeks at fifty or sixty trucks passing by someone's house each day.[31] Some equipment parked at the well site during drilling and completion is run nearly constantly, adding to the exhaust. (A growing number of oilfield service companies use natural-gas-fueled equipment, which is less polluting if no less quiet.) The moving of frack sand at high speed in the completion process generates dust in the air. Even when there is no active drilling, methane and volatile organic compounds can leach off wellheads, compressor stages, gas processing facilities, and storage tanks. (Methane leakage is a headline issue when looking at the boom from a global perspective, as I discuss in Chapter 10.) Before associated gas—gas that is produced alongside oil in many wells—can be connected to a pipeline, it is flared.

Is this boom-affected air noticeable, annoying, dangerous? The industry reminds people that chefs don't die from being in a kitchen all day, with stovetops constantly burning gas—and converting methane to carbon dioxide and water. But flaring, organic compounds, equipment exhaust, and dust in unusual circumstances can start to add up. A family living sixty miles northwest of Dallas was unlucky enough in 2008 to find their house surrounded by twenty-two new gas wells, during the manic period of the Barnett Shale boom. In 2014, the family was awarded $2.9 million in a lawsuit against the oil company most responsible for the drilling because they convinced the jury that the drilling activity—and the wells themselves—had led to migraines, dizziness, nosebleeds, burning throats, and rashes.[32]

Local disruptions almost never mean the health calamities that happened to that family. And, as will be discussed, some local impacts that were more common at the start of the boom are considered unacceptable now. (New North Dakota regulations, for instance, seek to cut flaring in that state by half, to only 15 percent of the state's gas production by 2016.[33]) But even with a more thoughtful industry and stringent regulations, an oil and gas boom still generates petty aggravations. Imagine living in a rural area beset by the shale revolution. Imagine, even worse, being a Have Not with no mineral rights of your own. Your neighbor, who's getting rich for his trouble, may allow oil companies to perform twenty-four-hour drilling operations. Maybe he doesn't worry about being woken up by the yelling workers, the beeping of backing up trucks, and the bone rattling from steel knocking against steel because he can afford golden earplugs handcrafted by Belgian monks. But you have to listen to the fracking racket. And every time you want to run an errand, you have to deal with the trucks from "his" oil company, with their exhaust and kicked-up dust. What's the point of living in the countryside if you can't even keep your window down while driving? Some of those trucks making him rich are so slow-moving that if you're stuck behind one, all attempts at promptness—and you live to be prompt—will be thrown out the window (if you dared open the window). So every time you go anywhere you allocate twice as long as you used to. You might still be late if your pickup gets damaged by one of the new potholes everywhere, massive enough to swallow a Labrador, created by trucks that are a curse on roads built for low-density rural life.

The only thing worse than trucks traveling too slowly is trucks traveling too fast. An average of 145 oilfield and pipeline workers died from workplace accidents in 2012 and 2013. Nearly half of those accidents were from crashing vehicles.[34] If these oil guys want to kill themselves, that's their business. But whom do you think they're colliding into?

And that's just on the roads. Towns and communities are changing, too. A bunch of roughnecks—dudes who happily call themselves roughnecks—living alone in cheap motels and man camps is probably not going to lead to more book clubs. It's going to lead to more fistfights, more teenage pregnancies, more and better drugs. In 2000, Williston, North Dakota, one of the capitals of the North Dakota oil boom, boasted a crime rate half of the country's average. In 2012, it was 20 percent higher than the country's and 44 percent higher—oh, Babylon of the Bakken—than New York City's.[35] And that's just the rate of crime. With more citizens come more incidents. There were forty-nine assaults in Williston in 2012. There were eight in 2000.[36]

Environmentalists often talk about the impact of the boom on the tourist industry. This may be aspirational in many cases. Artesia, New Mexico, is not on many travelers' bucket lists unless they like refineries, cow sheds, pungent air, and flat dry land. But surely there is a retired couple in southeast Ohio who sank their life savings into a bed-and-breakfast only to find that the deliciousness of their scones couldn't drown out the thundering of a passing pressure pumping fleet or the aesthetics of water that evoke NASCAR more than *Walden*.

Oil and gas booms change a place. Some of the changes aren't even quantifiable. Wild animals have traditional roaming areas altered. Livestock are fickle, even if their water isn't polluted. Loud industrial activity can cause stress and neurological or reproductive problems.[37]

There is also human life. Seamus McGraw's memoir *The End of Country*, recounting what happened when gas drilling came to his hometown in northeastern Pennsylvania, extraordinarily conveys the trade-offs and tough truths. Many rural areas are not the Edens of their urban defenders' fantasies. "All I needed to do," McGraw writes, "was look around at the many formerly thriving farms on and around Ellsworth Hill, places that after nearly forty years of bad federal and state farm policies had failed, places where a sense of desperation and loss was as thick as the brambles that covered once carefully tended fields."[38] The land McGraw profiles "was rode hard and put away wet": any value from the rock, timber, or soil that could be extracted was extracted, long before the gas boom, because to make a living off land that infertile left no other choice. [39]

But who gets to decide the future? Rural Pennsylvania kids, not fond of loss as thick as brambles, have been moving to New York City and Philadelphia for generations. But who invited oil companies to town, speeding up the pace of life, denigrating the simple joys of hard farming, pumping money into the system, shredding neighborly relations when one family wins the lottery with oil or gas money and another family doesn't or when one family declares the risks of drilling worth it and another dreadfully disagrees?

Some businesses tied to the pre-boom economy, like a restaurant or motel, may hit smaller jackpots. But all businesses will find it harder to attract employees. In 2012, a Williston native told me of the McDonald's in his hometown offering $3,000 signing bonuses to kids to work the fryer. The restaurant, still unable to attract enough employees, closed most days at three. For businesses like farming, whose revenue does not benefit much from a shale boom, increased labor costs could prove fatal.

And, who knows, maybe the son of the West Virginia woman did not become gay because of water and sand pumped down a well near her house. But maybe fracking, as a synecdoche, brought to town a handsome East Texas roughneck, who locked eyes at a bar with her quiet son. . . .

Many of these annoyances and accidents are not new. The industry has long had strategies and tools—and inherent profit-seeking incentives—to mitigate the local environmental impact of oil and gas drilling. On the most minor level, the industry responds to accidents. Spills happen, but companies with specialized expertise exist to contain them have expanded with larger fleets and newer technologies. Specialists clean up spills with industrial vacuums; others remediate the soil with biocides. Some states mandate transporting spilled-on land to treatment facilities. It's like re-hab for dirt.

The industry also avidly wants to minimize the periods of maximum local consequences. Few people outside the oil business, I find, understand this. The public has visions of permanently installed fifteen-story drilling rigs huffing and puffing for years in someone's backyard to, I guess, pull oil and gas out of the ground. But the main disruption of a shale well comes at its birth, with drilling and completion operations that cost companies thousands of dollars per hour.

While there is some preparatory activity to drilling a well, the "spud to sales" time—from the time the drill bit first hits the rock to when the oil and gas hits the market—tends to be from twenty to forty days depending on the basin. If multiple wells are drilled from the same pad, activity will continue on the pad for as many months as there are wells. But after the wells are drilled and completed, the activity quiets, the fumes die down, the drilling rig is gone, the pump trucks drive off, the oil and gas factory mainly works passively beneath the land, and the risk of accidents dissipates. The area around the wellhead is reclaimed, resoiled, and replanted.

Pressure of the overburden for the most part pushes the oil, gas, and associated water to the surface, oftentimes with the help of compressors, pumps, or other artificial lift equipment. A gas wellhead just sits there, connected to a "Christmas tree" of pipes and valves and chokes not much larger than, metaphorically straightforward, a Christmas tree. There might be a compressor and tanks nearby. For onshore oil wells, most well sites are a few hundred square yards with storage tanks, separation equipment, and a horsehead pump jack—the icon of the oil business—slowly pumping the oil up from low-pressure reservoirs. (Some wells have even lower visibility with an electric submersible pump belowground.)

The industry doesn't ignore these wells. An oil company maintains dirt or gravel roads to allow access to the wellhead, visited by a "pumper" in a pickup, usually daily, to make sure nothing bad has happened. If oil is stored at a well site, a marketing company will come weekly to pick up the crude.

Depending on the concentration of wells in an area, the end of activity at one pad could bring quiet. In Pennsylvania, a former drill site can be absorbed back into the landscape, the gas equipment cloaked in a grove of trees. (The more permanent scars to the landscape are pipeline routes, covered in grass where trees once were.) Air quality should also improve. The family that won the lawsuit in Texas due to the noxious air acknowledged that their health problems cleared up after the drilling stopped and equipment to improve air quality was installed. State air quality studies have not shown any long-term health effects of compressor stations or gas wellheads, although as with everything in the local environmental debate, where there is a study, there is an anti-study.[40]

The end of operations at one well could, however, be like a rambunctious day care center after one infant has fallen asleep. Parts of West Texas and southeast New Mexico look like a zoo of steel, with tanks and equipment spread to the horizon, the pump jacks like strange nodding birds, the tanks fat hippos basking in the sun. (These industrialized deserts, not surprisingly, are sparsely populated.)

Every once in a while, there might be a burst of activity to repair a well, or perforate another oil-and-gas-bearing zone, with a small work-over rig. These workover operations take much less time than the initial drilling and require no new well site disturbances. The largest worry on the horizon for landowners is refracking. In some areas, operators are bringing back the pumping equipment, sand, and water to apply more effective techniques than were deployed in the original fracks. A refrack could involve several weeks of headaches, like a loud sloppy uncle you thought had moved to Manitoba announcing that he decided to occupy your living room couch for a month or two.

Gasland, fond of the statistic that there is drilling in thirty-four states, shows a map of the country dripping red, fracks invading—and ostensibly polluting—every corner of the country.[41] But an accurate map would illustrate that the shale revolution takes up surprisingly little space on a national level. Indeed, the footprint of American oil and gas drilling is concentrating in ever-smaller areas, even as production volumes grow. (Of course, the million producing wells already drilled also take up space, albeit quietly.) As discussed in Chapter 8, operators in 2015 focused their drilling even more in core areas of the most productive basins. Drilling ceased in areas outside the cores, from poor results or too low oil or gas prices. Rigs are also working on multi-well pads, with fewer farms and ranches disrupted. In the most active U.S. basins such as the Marcellus and Permian, oil and gas companies are seeking to lower their costs by drilling four to seven horizontal wells per four- to six-acre pad. Assuming a national average of four wells per six-acre pad and 25,000 wells drilled per year on a steady state basis—this would be down from 37,500 wells drilled in 2014—the industry would drill each year on about sixty square miles out of the 3 million square miles of the continental United States. If a 3,000-square-foot house were the country, the amount of drilling in a year would occur on a playing card.

The oil industry has long paid for everything, too. An oil company can't park a drilling rig on someone's land and let spills and accidents happen as they will. Part of the costs of drilling a well, and a job of the landman, is negotiating surface rights. Drilling leases often cover in minute detail what areas can be used for the pad, in what condition the land must be reclaimed, and what hours drilling and fracking are allowed. There can be other conditions. Sometimes the oil and gas company will buy water from a farmer's private well. Sometimes the industry will build a family a road they can later use. Also, like a ward boss in a city machine, landmen are talented at knowing how much cash to throw to the neighbors, to make them if not rich than at least compensated—and perhaps morally tied to the area's drilling activity. A neighbor might be paid $10,000 even if the oil company has no intention of doing anything but running a temporary pipe in front of her house.

As Seamus McGraw's *The End of Country* bittersweetly conveys, taking oil or gas money, even a lot of it, doesn't mean that you will dance with ecstatic joy about having a rig on your land. We all have two minds on many things. But if someone sitting next to you on a plane announced that he was going to play the bongos while gnawing on a raw onion the whole flight, you might tolerate the beatnik more if he gave you $300 when he sat down.

THE AMERICAN SHALE REVOLUTION CAUGHT everyone by surprise. None of it was supposed to happen, certainly not at that speed. The industry in the early days of the boom could seem heartless occasionally, like when Cabot fought the claims of the homeowners in Dimock.[42] But even in the early days, from what I saw, most folks in the oil business sympathized with the people who lived inside the boom. That sympathy, though, wrestled with everyone frantically trying to make sure that a specific land rush—and an upside-down industry—didn't leave his or her company behind. As I talk about in the book's next part, not every oil company made it through.

The initial land rushes also led to drilling in areas in which the rock, terrain, and water situations were unfamiliar to oilmen, at least to those who weren't 140 years old. And sometimes, before the boom, it seemed like everyone in the business *was* 140 years old. Given how long the onshore U.S. oil industry had been in decline, there was a shortage of engineers, geologists, and skilled blue-collar labor. It was a not uncommon story, as happened to my company in 2011, for an oil hauler to call up to say your oil couldn't be trucked that week from the well site because the hauler couldn't find anyone to drive the trucks. All the qualified drivers now had fracking jobs because they could earn a dollar an hour more. Labor shortages led to the need for "other" hiring standards: if you had a clean driving record and recent clean drug test, you were hired, sometimes regardless of other signs that, well, working may not have been your core competency. But as the boom matured, a new generation of engineers, geologists, rig hands, and other specialists joined an industry that was, after all, paying $112,000 on average per year.[43] And many of the men and women who joined the industry at the start of the boom now have a decade of experience. In many areas, the labor pool is also becoming less transient, more connected to local communities and land.

And so as the shale revolution reached a more mature phase, as the experience of the workforce increased, as the scrutiny from the media, environmentalists, and regulators sharpened, the industry got better at minimizing its local environmental impact. This is hard to prove as the data on how accident-free and nuisance-causing the industry is, at any time, is vague. But as one who lived through the boom, saw creative businesses emerge to reduce local impacts through, for instance, frack sand dust control equipment or noise abatement walls, and observed what our own companies were doing, I can report that the impact has been mitigated.

We didn't get better because everyone in the business suddenly became 15 percent more sympathetic to the locals. We got better for two more hardheaded reasons.

First, incentives to further mitigate local disruptions and minimize accidents became tangible. Pad drilling is the industry's favorite environmentally friendly showpiece. Operators didn't shift to it as a nifty way to display directional drilling technology. They did so because no one wants to pay for more surface rights, build more well pads, or deal with more sure-you-paid-me-but-I-didn't-think-it-was-going-to-be-this-bad complaints than they need to. (The euphemism in the oil business for these headaches is dealing with the local "culture.")

The safety innovations don't stop at pad drilling. More intermediate casing is being used, for instance, in Pennsylvania, to better protect groundwater with a third layer of cement and steel.[44] Some companies began using well site ground mats and groundwater monitors to better protect against water pollution.[45] Others have begun testing nearby water wells before and after drilling. In some areas, they have to, by law.[46] The industry is also now recycling more water, which minimizes the risks from other disposal methods. (Pennsylvania is the leader in this effort, with 90 percent of frack flowback recycled.)[47] In recycling, frack flowback or produced water is kept in tanks or lined pits, treated, and then reused for fracking. The effort for this was once thought to be too expensive, but with technology and more experience, it has become cheaper than using freshwater in many places. At the operating division of my firm, we developed a pioneering system in New Mexico based on building a double-lined produced water pit with an electronic leak detection system. The pit is expensive but well worth it: it saves us the dollar-per-barrel cost of buying new water and $0.85 per barrel for transporting produced water to a disposal well. It cost only $0.35 per barrel to treat the produced water for new fracks.

It's not just the land that's being looked out for. Like similar pits, ours has an "avian protection system," which includes testing the water for toxicity and, to make sure as few birds as possible pull up to it as the local bar, using low-tech stern-faced plastic owls and, when necessary, motion sensors connected to air horns.

Of course, landowners, local environmentalists, bird lovers, and oil professionals are not always strolling arm in arm, whistling on their way to the Happy Land of Win-Win. Oil companies make choices. They calculate the risks of certain accidents, of adopting a you-can't-please-everybody nonchalance when dealing with local culture. They measure that against the costs of making every single well a demonstration project for the company's annual report. No two companies, or two people within companies, will reach the same answer on what the right balance is.

But the industry is not irresponsible as a core characteristic. In 2013, Delphine Batho, France's environmental and energy minister, defended her country's ban on *le fracking* by saying, "We have to have our eyes wide open about what is going on in the U.S." After all, the United States "has invented environmental dumping."[48] This was just the latest French outburst, likely formed from intensive study of both *Gasland* and *There Will*

Be Blood, about an America covered in slime, destroyed by ubiquitous drilling rigs, filled with citizens gleefully flouting regulations if they are not otherwise occupied shooting each other, getting fat, and distracting French schoolchildren from avant-garde ballet with *Iron Man 3*.

But Batho didn't understand the deeply instilled culture of HS&E in the oilfield. Almost every board meeting of every company in the oil business starts with a review of HS&E incidents, even if it's just an oilfield worker getting a scrape on his hand. Until I got used to it—where is the hidden camera?—I would be disoriented when meetings at an oilfield service company's headquarters, in a generic suburban office park as dangerous as a marshmallow, would start with a safety briefing.

The industry is focused on HS&E for human decency, and for human greed. Oil companies, like all companies, want to make the most money they can. While one can increase margins by cutting corners—rushing cement jobs, buying suspicious Chinese casing—operators know that these are fool's strategies. The best way to make less costly widgets is by drilling and completing wells efficiently, using less land and materials, and not having to redo bad work.

A good way to make money is also not to stupidly lose money. And of the many things that the American oil industry doesn't want to do—drill dusters, see commodity prices fall, listen to French politicians—highest on the list may be not wanting to get sued. In the oil business, when accidents happen (in a spill) or shoddiness occurs (from poor well integrity), a lawyer appears about eight seconds after the spill hits the ground, as if he were a genie caused by the spill itself. Getting your company sued is a good way to get fired. From the local perspective, one of the benefits of the more institutional, bureaucratic phase of the boom, with more drilling done by larger companies, is that the size of an oil company is directly correlated to the size—and paranoia—of its legal department. A friend at Chevron told me that his company is well aware that it costs much more for Chevron to drill wells, with its engineering redundancies and safety processes, than it costs smaller companies. This makes sense: accidents are more expensive to Chevron because plaintiffs press their claims not just on the size of an accident but on the size of the defendants' pockets. Other major oil companies seem to recognize that fact. In an analysis of spills in

North Dakota, *The New York Times* reported that Norwegian oil giant Statoil produced 9,000 gallons of oil for every gallon it spilled, over two and a half times better than Harold Hamm's Continental.[49]

THE SECOND REASON that we in the industry got better at mitigating the local environmental impacts of the shale revolution is that we had to: the regulators got better, too. Some anti-shale activists incessantly raise the point that fracking was declared exempt from federal oversight in the Bush administration's 2005 energy bill. Dick Cheney not only headed the task force that devised that bill but, before he became the vice president, led Halliburton, the company as associated with fracking as Hershey is with chocolate. Oh, they cried, what conspiracies of oil and money and war and water lie in the dark heart of America. Of course, Cheney's 2005 energy bill was applauded by the industry. But fracking has *never* been regulated by Washington except on federal lands. The bill just continued the status quo. Fracking on nonfederal lands, like almost every part of the oil and gas drilling and completion process, is regulated by the states.

And U.S. state regulators, alongside the federal government in certain limited situations, have steadily advanced new rules to account for the increasing scale and complexity of the shale revolution. Regulations create pretty obvious incentives to comply. Even more costly than a fine in most cases are a pause in operations demanded by a regulator. A company we invested in had activities on one well pad halted for close to a year of forty separate information submittals and painstaking remediation. They were attempting to start drilling again after a regulator issued a cease and desist order because the company's well site construction contractor moved dirt onto a federally protected wetlands area. The violation: about twenty square feet.

The reaction to regulatory stories like that is what you'd expect from an industry in which political diversity is considered a healthy mix of Tea Party and Republican. Some of my friends in the business are certain that they are under siege from the Democrat president and his Bicoastal Alliance of Rich, Skinny Hypocrites. They complain about red tape and bureaucrats with nothing better to do with their time. Some see patterns in each regulation and vigorous enforcement: the country seems bent on committing economic and security suicide by adding on so many new costs that U.S. oil and gas production becomes permanently unprofitable. No one will be laughing when the industry can't make money, the shale revolution dies, we import more oil from Saudi Arabia and Russia, and Vladimir Putin takes over Warsaw.

I hear this stuff all the time. I laugh patiently. I needle my friends by telling them that when Putin declares me a vice commissar, I will assign them to a nice gulag. (Gruel with less sawdust for you, old friend.) But I don't take the bellyaching seriously. The U.S. oil and gas industry's problem in 2015 was not margins squeezed by regulators. It has, most likely, never been. The industry's problem was that the profits available from drilling in the best areas led to a glut of oil and gas.

The initial complaints against new regulations, I find, are a defense mechanism. When your wife tells you that leaving your shoes in the middle of the hallway is dangerous, you might cry, "When will I be free from civilization's oppressive rules on storing footwear?" (That, granted, might just be me.) But you pick up your shoes a few minutes later, realizing that the person most likely to trip is you. The people in the oil business, I've found, view each new oilfield regulation as yet another thing to worry about in already busy and complicated days. But once new rules are announced, people in the industry, a practical set used to solving problems, accept them, integrate them into their work practices, and get on with life. They complain more about the paperwork, and slow regulator response time, than about the regulations themselves. Because frankly, many regulations call for sensible oilfield practices that the best operators are already following. Bad and lazy actors can damage everyone's reputation. Following regulations helps mitigate liability.

In general, state regulators are refereeing the oil and gas industry's activity, trying to make sure it is contained, productive, and safe. Many of these regulators, in the early days of the boom, were caught short-staffed. In 2006, regulating deep gas drilling in Pennsylvania felt as relevant as regulating the telegraph office or—looking at it another way—taxis to the moon. But regulations have now largely caught up with the boom. All parts of drilling and completing an oil and gas well have long needed to be permitted. Regulators are decreasing the risk of accidents by updating the rules for the particularities—and volume—of shale drilling. In Pennsylvania, for instance, new rules have been steady: requiring disclosure of chemicals on FracFocus; dictating how closely one can drill to a water well; mandating that flowback cannot be sent to wastewater treatment plants unless it is pretreated; tightening air quality standards at compressors and wellheads; demanding pressure testing of all cement jobs; and more.[50] Municipal ordinances across the country have also gotten stricter, limiting the hours a company can work, the noise it can make, the visibility of its equipment.

Not every rule or regulation is perfect, not all enforcement is consistent, and not every action against an oil company is fair. At some point, regulations could burden otherwise worthwhile All-American oil and gas wells, preventing companies from profitably drilling them. (Besides New York state, some municipalities have banned fracking, including Denton, Texas, a college town in the heart of the Barnett. It was like Miami banning bikinis. The state of Texas later passed a law prohibiting Denton's prohibition.) From the other side, environmentalists point out that better regulations, and more rigorous enforcement, in one state could easily be applied in others. North Dakota fined oil companies only $1 million for spills from 2006 to 2014, compared to $33 million by Texas over the same time.[51] Details, trade-offs, local impacts matter. Each debate on each regulation deserves a full hearing. A thoughtful report issued in 2015 by Michael Porter of Harvard Business School and consultants at the Boston Consulting Group detailed, among other recommendations, important steps to target consistent and universal regulatory compliance across jurisdictions.[52]

But so far, American democracy with all its lobbying and noise and occasional grubbiness has worked. Regulations are getting smarter. The industry has adapted. The shale revolution is, among other things, the product of a reasonable and functioning nation.

YET HAS THE INDUSTRY improved enough? Weighing individual pain against societal freedom is one of the toughest ethical dilemmas in the world. In 2010, there were forty-six hospitalizations and three deaths from E. coli in beef in the United States. We haven't banned meatballs.[53] One problem with understanding—and discussing—the shale revolution is that we don't know the equivalent of the forty-nine E. coli victims. We know that there hasn't been an epidemic of accidents or truly damaging earthquakes given 3,000 or so wells drilled and fracked each month during the most active days of the boom, with only a handful of consequential accidents reports each year. We know that the industry is getting better at minimizing the impact of the boom on air, water, and land through a desire for profits (and avoided lawsuits), an ethic of responsibility, and an awareness that operators are being watched ever more closely by regulators, activists, and the press. But we don't know exactly how many water wells have been contaminated or how many spills have happened nationwide. We don't know the cause of all the water contamination incidents that have happened. We don't have a national database on lives disrupted or ruined.

I suspect that better data would force both sides to be more contemplative. Just because the industry is not doing much harm with fracking specifically, shale drilling is not an ice cream truck come to the playground. And for environmentalists, claiming everything is equally and overwhelmingly bad makes it hard to know where to focus their activism and concern.

Better data is needed, for sure, but there are limits to its practical use. For how much local pain outweighs the benefits of the boom cannot be measured on a desktop balance scale. For one, the scale itself is usually preset by our sympathies. Environmentalists sympathize with the people whose lives are shaken by shale drilling: the family getting their water trucked in, the retired couple kept awake by a rig. People in the oil industry sympathize with themselves, of course, but also with the suddenly oil-rich farmer able to keep land in his family or a twenty-year-old kid securing a high-paying oilfield job close to home. And outsiders have it easy, in their ability to have abstract sympathy. Local battles, between those who yearn for drilling and those who fear it can get tense, nasty, and heartbreaking with neighbors no longer speaking to neighbors.

Almost all (non-European) environmentalists know that the U.S.

countryside and water supply haven't been destroyed by drilling or frack-ing. Some, though, invoke a concept used more often in the climate change debate: the precautionary principle. That is, if your action can harm the environment and the public, the burden of proof is on you, before you act, to show that what you are about to do is tolerable. The default should be no change to the environment. This principle was the logical founda-tion of the New York state health department report cited by Andrew Cuomo when he instituted New York's ban on fracking.[54] It is a fair posi-tion: we don't yet have complete data on the local impacts of the shale revolution. It might be foolhardy—and all too American—to allow more drilling until we do.

The industry responds that we've been drilling here for 150 years and fracking for seventy. Indeed, compared to thirty years ago, we are drill-ing with only a third to a half of the rigs we once were.[55] And the oil industry's culture of safety and transparency, like every industry's in an era of Google searches and increasing environmental awareness, is more eco-nomically necessary and effective than ever. Saul Bellow once said, "Public virtue is a kind of ghost town into which anyone can move and declare himself sheriff."[56] The industry asks, who gave environmentalists a badge to proclaim us a bunch of bad actors, invoke the precautionary principle, and demand that we cease? We have decades of data and seven-teen years since George Mitchell's first Barnett success. Where is the wide-spread harm? Prove that, rather than list forty anecdotes on your Web site. This is a fair position, too.

Practical observers add one more fact. Will the hundreds of billions of dollars to be spent by the U.S. onshore oil and gas industry be stopped—the boom arrested, peak oil worries restarted, coal consumption roused—if there were twice as many accidents? Almost certainly not. Twenty times as many? That's harder to say. Whatever the validity of the arguments, we haven't banned fracking yet and are unlikely to in the areas driving the shale revolution. (New York is decidedly not one.) And when even a Democratic president supports more domestic oil and gas drilling, you can guess the direction of the political momentum. The precautionary prin-ciple is a thoughtful ethical guidepost, but we are in the post-cautionary period of the boom.

And we are in a period in which the local perspective is passionately and probably disproportionately argued about. *Gasland* plays an important role in the history of the oil and gas renaissance, more important than Josh Fox probably could have hoped for. It ignited a movement that, as misplaced as its concerns can sometimes be, has been a necessary check on the industry's self-image and actions. It also began a way of seeing that we, as Americans, were unaccustomed to when it came to oil and gas: judging a boom from the local point of view, by the people and communities most affected by it.

Life is unfair. Accidents happen. We can be glib about this, until something unfair happens to us. What occurred in Dimock, Pennsylvania, or Prague, Oklahoma, are key events of the boom, every bit as important as Norwegian oil companies coming to North Dakota. But what happened in Dimock and Prague will never tell us whether the boom is good or bad, nor will fifty more incidents like them. Some environmentalists understand this: the chief problems with the boom, they say, are global issues, not local ones. Some in the industry would happily take them on in this shifted debate. But the debate shouldn't shift. It should expand. The boom has different impacts and looks different when considering it also from the perspective of life (climate change), liberty (implications for America), and the pursuit of happiness (making money). There is no easy reconciliation into a single answer after studying it from those vantages either. But they together complete the story, even if the whole story may never get nominated for an Oscar.

Part III

THE FINANCIAL PERSPECTIVE

7. THE TWO TRILLION–DOLLAR REVOLUTION

IN OCTOBER 2014, I HAD LUNCH WITH ONE OF OUR FIRM'S INVESTORS in the airy dining room of the institution where she works, one of the world's largest charitable trusts. We settled into our conversation with talk of the view, people we had in common, how my colleagues were doing. But when my grilled octopus with pickled sea beans arrived, she slumped in her chair in exaggerated frustration as if to signal that small talk was over. We'd both been entrusted with generating better-than-average profits from investing in the energy sector. Like me, she was then facing a crescendo of anxiety and perplexity. The anxiety: after a decade in which American oil and gas investments generated more profits than almost any other investment type—including corporate bonds, government bonds, safe stocks, risky stocks, gold, real estate, health care, clean tech, venture capital—was she the gambler at the table, the chips stacked high, about to overstay her luck? The perplexity: would the energy investors who had made all that money for her trust ever be able to repeat what they had done?

I spend my work life communicating with institutional investors like her, people who entrust some portion of their capital to specialist energy investors like my firm. These people are allocating the capital that nearly everyone in the world relies on to some degree: college endowments used for scholarships and research; charitable foundations supporting medical breakthroughs, social services, and—in a few what-a-crazy-world examples—anti-fossil-fuel advocacy; pension funds enabling the retirement of teachers, firefighters, and other private and public sector workers; sovereign wealth funds investing a nation's savings. And, yes, before I let loose with a Celine Dionish song about how Capitalism Is All About You and Me, institutional investors also include rich families who use their gains to buy Junior a private airplane or, who knows nowadays, a private circus.

At lunch, I stared at my sea beans, whatever those are. And I wondered, to myself, if I was going to give the Golden Decade speech for the fiftieth time. It becomes dangerous in my job to deliver prepackaged bits. You can appear slick, become rote. Then again, the Golden Decade speech had the advantages of being both true and, well, all I had.

From 2002 to 2012, the oil business experienced a Golden Decade. In the first part of the decade, with the economy rising everywhere, global oil prices quadrupled and U.S. gas prices tripled. In 2008, just as that commodity-price-driven wealth creator for the industry ended with the global recession, the U.S. oil and gas renaissance expanded in the best and biggest of the basins (Marcellus, Permian, Eagle Ford, et al.). This renaissance created mountains of wealth for the oil industry completely unrelated to the causes in the first six and a half years, except as far as the rising prices from that first half of the decade had encouraged the experimentation of the second. Indeed, the second half of the Golden Decade killed off the first half, as swelling production volumes had, at the time I was talking, already crashed natural gas prices and capped the price of oil. What is remarkable is not that an industry had two separate drivers of growth. A tale of two tailwinds can be told of many industries. What is remarkable is the overlap. Feast years usually follow famine years, in microeconomic cycles. That is how business works. But over a decade, acknowledging some local and subsector weakness, the oil industry had barely three consecutive quarters in the dumps. It's as if the Internet boom of Twitter and LinkedIn happened six months after the boom of Yahoo and Amazon, with no bust in between of Webvan and Pets.com.

I finished my speech with a highly precise, highly made up number. The Golden Decade ended on January 1, 2013.

She laughed at the ironic final flourish. But she wanted more. If the

Golden Decade wasn't to be succeeded by hundreds of billions more in windfalls, couldn't it at least be followed by a period of stable, stagnant wealth? It could be like Paris. I wanted more, too. But the signs that afternoon were noisy. On the one hand, E&P stocks had underperformed the broader stock market in 2011, 2012, and 2013 (as they would in 2014).[1] Oil prices had dipped below $90 per barrel just that month. On the other hand, there had been autumn swoons in 2011 and 2012, too, and nothing had moved oil from its near four-year residency in the $100 per barrel neighborhood.

And then in the four months that followed, oil prices fell by half. Had we had lunch the next spring, our conversation wouldn't have been about predicting the shape of financial life after the Golden Decade. It would have been about survival strategies in the hereafter.

Which is the challenge of providing a financial perspective on the shale revolution. Like the industrial and local perspectives, the financial perspective is crucial to comprehending the boom's first-order impacts. Those economic impacts are not just score-keeping or gee-whiz anecdotes of billions skipping from one pocket to the next. The impacts complete many stories of the shale revolution: the local story, of neighbor being enriched and neighbor disturbed, cannot be told without them both; the national story of incomes and wealth created by the boom must be weighed alongside the cumulative local effects; and the industrial perspective is unfinished without looking at which people benefited from the industry's revived fortunes.

Understanding the financial perspective on the shale revolution is also practically a necessity for many people, like my lunchtime companion. The prerequisite to figuring out how to invest the future savings of the world is reckoning with the Golden Decade. It is trying to fathom whether wealth came (and went) in the shale revolution by innovation, desperation, heroism, inertia, vision, or luck.

The financial perspective of the shale revolution differs, however, from the industrial and local perspectives in having a less linear narrative. Indeed, if the endpoint of the boom was 2015, the boom seems more like a bust. But what happened in 2015 is not the opposite of the boom, some tulip market implosion that proves that it never mattered at all. In the shale revolution, the variable prices for oil and gas—and the variable money generated—are the financial and commodity markets working as they are supposed to work as they absorb unexpected new sources of oil and gas at rule-breaking costs.

And even amid the corporate pain of 2015, there were still areas, in drilling in parts of the Permian Basin, in the competition between the shales and other sources of oil and gas, in which it seemed nothing fundamental had changed at all. And that comes back to one of the challenges of the financial perspective of the shale revolution. We aren't looking through a microscope at a fixed pebble. Shifting and colliding microorganisms are coming in and out of view. Oil prices wobble or rise, as do companies. And every time one tries to fix the financial facts of the boom (and put them in a book), the facts buck, refusing to be frozen.

This is no more true than with the first financial fact of all: how much money, exactly, has been made in the shales?

I OFTEN WISH there were an official Oil Wealth Clock in Houston, tallying the billions generated in the shale revolution. I've never even seen an estimate. This may be because calculating the money created in the boom demands accounting for the idiosyncrasies of corporate histories and individual transactions that marked—or transferred—billions. One's estimates also have to be set in time, a hard thing to do after a decade in which oil prices have doubled twice and halved twice, and the next move is still uncertain at the start of each trading day.

However, we can make some educated if imprecise assumptions of the boom's impact on companies and individuals. The boom benefited some Americans as revenue and some as wealth. That distinction is important. You will be richer if you get a raise. You will also be richer if the sloppy uncle who stayed with you, uninvited, left you his shockingly large estate. The distinction between revenue and wealth also tells us *who* got richer from the boom: the labor (and service companies) who helped extract America's shale oil and gas; or the owners of the companies that possessed it.

The "raise" is an easier number to calculate. From 2000 to 2007, U.S. oil production steadily declined at 2 percent per year and gas production at 1 percent. From 2007 to 2014, oil production grew at an 8 percent annual rate and at nearly double that pace in 2012, 2013, and 2014. Gas production grew more slowly, at 4 percent per year, only because of limited demand. These old and new trends mean that in eight years, the United States produced about 6 billion barrels of oil and 28 trillion cubic feet of gas more than it would have had we continued on our old trajectory.[2] Coincidentally, this eight-year cumulative total is about the same as the total oil and gas the United States consumed in 2014. It's as if all of America went to Starbucks, handed in a frequent drinker punch card, and instead of getting a ninth venti latte for free got—molto venti—all the oil and gas we needed for the year.

But the industry didn't give away this oil and gas. It sold it. If one assumes that producers, in aggregate, got 15 percent below the publicly traded commodity price—this accounts, broadly speaking, for regional price differentials and transportation costs—then the total incremental revenue for oil and gas producers in 2007–2014 was nearly $600 billion. Even at 2015's lower oil and gas prices, the U.S. oil industry's raise from U.S. production increases was about $150 billion, the extra money it would not have achieved on the old decline rate. (That being said, on the old decline rate, if the shale revolution had never happened, oil and gas prices would be much higher today.) The supplemental revenue could double to $250 to $300 billion per year by 2020, particularly given that our status quo output would have reflected six more years of steadily falling production.[3]

Wealth—the car, house, and obscure coin collection left to you by your weird uncle—must be measured differently. It's best to start with proved reserves, the amount of oil and gas in the ground we can produce economically at today's prices and available techniques. Estimating proved reserves in a single oil or gas field is a subjective exercise, with lots of eye rolling from one reservoir engineer (usually a buyer of assets) about the outlandish assumptions from across the table (usually from another engineer trying to sell her something). That being said, BP estimates global reserves every year. For a quarter century until 2004, U.S. gas reserves fell in total by a gentle 3 percent and oil reserves by 19 percent, with barrels produced and consumed offset to some degree by new discoveries and "field extensions"—companies finding ways to extract more hydrocarbons from fields already producing. (Over that time, global oil and gas reserves doubled.)[4] For decades, the proved reserves of the United States were always about six to eight years' worth of domestic gas demand and four to five years' worth of oil.[5]

And then the shale revolution came. By year-end 2014, the United States' 48 billion barrels of proved oil reserves were 57 percent higher than five years earlier. Its 345 trillion cubic feet of proved natural gas reserves were 69 percent higher than at the start of shalemania in 2005.[6] And that's just proved reserves. Research firm ITG estimated in 2015 that the total "resource" extractable in the continental United States alone, across reserve categories and at reasonable long-term prices, was 1,440 trillion cubic feet of gas (fifty-four years of domestic consumption) and 123 billion barrels of oil (eighteen years of consumption).[7] Seven years earlier, it estimated that gas resources were one-third that level; oil resources were one-sixth.[8]

Companies buy and sell reserves in the ground for a fraction of what they sell produced oil or gas for: it still costs money to extract and ship oil and gas and, given how reservoirs behave, it may take decades for a bought field to produce all of its recoverable reserves. If you estimate, in a reasonable long-term assumption, that oil in the ground is worth $20 per barrel of proved reserves and gas $1 per thousand cubic feet, the total value of U.S. proved reserve wealth alone was $1.3 trillion at the end of 2014. That is $550 billion more than it would have been had the boom not happened, $700 billion if you include the new reserves already consumed. My guess is that if America decided to sell all of our oil and gas reserves to the Chinese—we could throw in for free a few office buildings in Manhattan, a Vegas casino or two, reality television—we could get about double the $700 billion if we also sold our probable and possible reserves. (This is the official oil industry reserve category that ITG groups in with its "resource" estimate.) If you assume that the incremental resource now extractable in the continental United States, almost all of which is associated with the shales, is worth a quarter as much on a per unit basis as proved reserves—or $5.00 per barrel and $0.25 per thousand cubic feet—then the total oil and gas reserves that became viable because of the boom would be worth about $1.35 trillion. As the shale revolution continues, as more wells are drilled, the value of the contingent shale resource is likely to grow.

In the United States, private individuals and companies own the oil and gas in the ground even if they are leasing drilling rights from the federal or state governments. The $1.35 trillion in "new" reserve wealth thus went to the equity owners of E&P companies: the men and women who started, run, and work at those companies; shareholders of public stocks; investors in private companies; and the most admirable category of all, middleman professional investors, like at my firm, who invest on the behalf of others.

The boom also created secondary wealth. E&P companies spend almost all of their revenue, including the raise from the shale revolution, on salaries, rent, interest, taxes, coveralls, copy machines, hunting boondoggles, lease bonuses, royalties to landowners, and—the bulk of it—services and equipment from oilfield service firms. As I talk about in Chapter 12, industry groups are fond of touting the most multiplicative "multiplier effect" of the hundreds of billions of dollars generated in the shale revolution. The groups take credit not only for the extra oil and gas revenue but also every candy bar bought by every roughneck and every new television bought by every Oompa Loompa at the chocolate factory.

Whatever the final multiplier, the $1.35 trillion in incremental wealth in oil and gas reserves does not include other ways in which America is richer. The portion of the oilfield service industry focused on U.S. onshore wells, by my math, was worth $60 to $70 billion more in 2015 than in 2004—an admittedly squiggly number to catch given the bankruptcies in the U.S. oilfield service sector in 2015. The equity value of the pipelines, gathering systems, and export terminals may take the boom's total to $1.8 to $2 trillion. That's two trillion dollars of wealth that came to America from shale reservoirs still largely considered a single North Texas trick a dozen years ago.[9]

THE TWO TRILLION DOLLARS doesn't include the wealth gained by the farmers, ranchers, government entities, and others who leased land to oil and gas companies. When a landman knocked on a farmer's door, he sometimes brought an offer that would allow the farmer to wake up, in a few months, with millions more in his pocket than he could have expected in multiple lifetimes. In many cases, the offer was just thousands, but as Seamus McGraw masterfully conveys, those thousands of dollars could buy health, peace of mind, optimism, and in many cases the ability to continue to own a farm and make a living off the land in a nation increasingly fond of making a living off financial services. That knock-on-the-door wealth is a credit to the boom, one of its most heartwarming aspects. It also helps explain the success of the U.S. shale revolution compared to the still infant shale extraction efforts in other countries, almost none of which have private mineral ownership. In America, for all the NIMBYs objecting to fracking in their neighborhood, there were also YIMBYs—Yes, In My Backyard—arguing for it on behalf of their personal wealth.

But the boom was not a fair parent, distributing equal slices of the pie to every YIMBY. The shale revolution's oil and gas hydrocarbons are relatively ubiquitous in source rock. So, broadly speaking, ranches next door should have the same amount of oil and gas underground, unlike in conventional trap reservoirs. Yet if geology is consistent, financial history is not. Some people own large tracts of land. Some own smaller parcels because their father sold pieces off to keep the farm going. Rights to oil and gas "minerals" under the land can be "severed" from the surface rights to live and farm on it. The person who sold you some land—or your grandfather, hard up during the Depression—may have sold those mineral rights for a few hundred dollars decades ago.

In some areas of the country, like in West Virginia, mineral rights tend to be unsevered across depths. The owner owns every pebble and molecule from the surface all the way to the center of the earth—and who knows, to Pyongyang if we could drill that far. In many other places, mineral rights have been severed by vertical distance: you may have the rights to everything to, say, 5,000 feet deep, but some owner before you sold the rights to the oil and gas below that. In the land rushes, some landowners got a knock on the door and popped the champagne (or a Yuengling) in celebration, only for a landman to do more research in the jumble of paper files in a county courthouse and discover that the deep rights were sold fifty years ago. In some cases, no one kept track of the rights. A farmer in North Dakota might die with six children, and no one bothered to go to the courthouse to probate his estate because the family figured things out fairly on its own. It didn't matter: keeping track of deep onshore oil and gas rights in the United States used to be as fruitful as keeping a VCR factory in sparkling condition. But as the boom took off, oil companies made it their business to discover who owned America's oil and gas rights. The knock sometimes came to the door of a lucky granddaughter in St. Louis who couldn't imagine what the oil business had to do with her.

The unequal distribution of land payments also came from the leasing process. There are few activities as nakedly capitalistic as the American landman hungrily seeking to lease as much rural land for as little money and as few headaches as possible. (Strangely, considering their name, landmen are among the least male-dominated oil industry professions. A landman told me that, still, only once in thirty years has he ever met a person who called herself a landwoman.) Before a land rush begins, leasing land may be easy. A landman can present herself as a lonely eccentric, humoring her employer's moon shot. After the industry starts drilling wells in an area with sufficient volumes to inspire the dreams of mass profits, a land rush starts. The countryside crawls with oil company landmen and, more often, independent brokers. They arrive in all shapes and ethical settings, sleazy liars and candid churchgoers and competitive jocks just looking to keep score.

No landman will be employed for long if she pays the highest price to every landowner. In the early stages of a boom, landmen have the information advantage: how prospective certain land is for oil and gas; what she is offering the neighbors; how oil business math works (especially in areas that hadn't seen leasing in decades); how math works (when dealing with some). The landman's basic pitch is that while her bosses will be furious at her—the imagined bosses are always furious—for being so generous with her terms, the landman wants to do right by good people. And she is being truthful when she says that her company is taking on all the capital risk.

As a land rush matures, landowners start getting more savvy. Lawyers appear. People have Google. And so as a land rush heats up, companies pay higher rates and bonuses, because of competitive frenzy, because of landowner demands, or because well results have improved enough for an oil company to pay more. The tumultuous history of when and how land was leased yields a chaos of lease terms around four main variables: the lease bonus, or upfront, nonrefundable cash payment; the royalty rate, or how much money the landowner gets off the top from the oil company's revenue from wells on his land; the term, or how much time the company has to drill before the lease expires; and the compensation and rules of surface use, for example, on where and when the oil company can drill.

Lease bonuses, those quick payments that allow people to wake up rich, are the most gossiped about number in boom-struck communities. When should we lease? Early on in a boom? At the end of the boom? At some voodoo-sensed hour of maximum price? Some stubborn cusses who laughed at offers for $100 per acre later leased acreage, in the shaleoniaire-making Haynesville bonanza, for $30,000 or more.[10] Those folks gloated that they were taught right: never be impatient. Yet when the roulette wheel comes to town, there are no lessons. A company I know was prepared to lease land from an entire subdivision outside Fort Worth to paragons of patience, for a stunning $25,000 per acre at the peak of the Barnett boom. Alas, the meeting to sign the leases was scheduled a few weeks after Lehman Brothers—and the global economy—collapsed in August 2008. The company executives canceled the deal, saved millions, but have never forgotten the faces of the crushed homeowners who had already, in their minds, spent the money on new cars, new kitchens, college tuitions. Neighbors who had "impatiently" leased earlier, for far less than $25,000, scoffed that they were taught right: never be greedy.

And some people benefited from a strange sort-of luck: you leased your land, you deposited the check, but the oil company changed its mind. Regularly, people became millionaires and never suffered the inconvenience of drilling because neighboring wells were disappointing or oil or gas prices plummeted. The industry condemned the leased acreage as goat pasture—not worth drilling unless you enjoyed losing even more money.

Not having a frack job roaring on your farm is nice. Yet those "lucky" landowners also never received the stream of royalty payments that should, over the long run, render the initial lease bonus less crucial. If you and your brother each owned a half section—320 acres, a half a square mile— in West Texas, you might have lucked into acreage prospective for an oil play. Your brother, probably because your mother always loved him more, never quite grew up. When the first landman he meets offers him $1,000 per acre, he jumps at the $320,000 to buy a rare Wonder Woman figurine. Two years later, as operators better understand the play, you lease your land for $10,000 per acre, or $3.2 million. You could buy a sixty-foot boat and name it *Wonder Woman*. However, assuming you each got a 15 percent royalty, and the oil company drilled a typical well and sold the produced oil for $60 per barrel, you'd each earn $5.4 million or so in royalties over the life of the well. Over 40 percent of that money would come in the first five years. He would thus have plenty of money for the whole Justice League, you for buying your mother's affection. Now, if you negotiated a 25 percent royalty and he got 15 percent, you'd make $4.6 million more than him in royalties. You could buy a second boat. You could call it *Wonderer Woman*.

It is hard to calculate how many primary landowners shared in the boom, but my guess is that it has been about 2 million people, standing in for the interests of 2 million families. They may have split around $50 billion in lease bonuses. Very rough estimates feed those guesses. We know that active shale development in 2015 covered about 25 million acres.[11] The total areas leased to date may have been double that, given how much land and how many plays have been abandoned without success. A single acreage block in which multiple wells can be drilled, called a drilling spacing unit, can require a phonebook of leases with different owners that are different heirs to different depths of different areas through which multiple horizontal lateral wells may go. Being a landman is sometimes like playing Tetris with legal rights. Regions vary in lease complexity: the New Mexico portion of the Permian has many simple leases even though they are owned by 320 million people, in the form of the U.S. federal government; the tangle of mineral rights in East Texas, one of the oldest oil-producing areas in America, is the landman's nightmare. Finally, companies are loath to disclose how much they spent on leases, to avoid anchoring prices for others in the area, to not tell their competitors where they think the good drilling is, and to not anger people paid less than their neighbors.

But we have two ways to reach a broad estimate of total leased acreage. One way comes courtesy of the company that was an exception in disclosing how much it spent: Aubrey McClendon's Chesapeake loved, after the fact, to brag of its scale, and *Forbes* reported in 2011 that the company over the previous five years had signed 600,000 separate leases for 9 million acres of drilling rights and paid out $9 billion in lease bonuses.[12] Later reports would up that total to $12 billion and 14 million acres. It's not impossible that Chesapeake, which swaggered into the butcher shop game to buy every chicken and chop, accounted for one quarter to one-third of all acreage leased in the boom. That assumption would imply 4 million leaseholders nationwide. But in North Dakota, according to a landman who worked there, landmen could assemble an average drilling spacing unit with only five to eight leases per square mile. That would imply, nationwide, about 600,000 leases. My estimate of 2 million leaseholders benefiting from the shale revolution is at a midpoint between Chesapeakean complexity and North Dakotan sparseness.

Those leaseholders are a subset of the total number of royalty owners, which include people receiving checks from the million or so non-shale wells still producing, ones drilled long before the boom. The National Association of Royalty Owners estimates, broadly, that there are 12 million current royalty owners.[13]

Lease payments have subsided, unrelated to oil and gas price booms and busts. For most land in the shale revolution has already been leased. There hasn't been a major new play discovered since the Utica Shale in 2010 and a midsized one since the Oklahoma SCOOP play in 2013. Oil companies are now primarily focused on drilling on the best leases they already have. In 2014, for example, Pioneer Natural Resources spent $3.4 billion on exploration and development costs—drilling and completing wells. It spent one-fortieth of that on unproved land.[14]

The river of royalties, however, has not been dammed. Landowners get monthly checks from producing wells, regardless of who the operator is. If we assume a 15 percent national average royalty, leaseholders of U.S.

onshore wells (including the federal government as a landowner) would have earned about $60 billion in royalties in 2015, half of that comprising "extra" royalties that would not have been paid had it not been for the shale revolution.

Oil executives burst into Santa Claus grins when discussing the landowners of the shale revolution and the billions "we" brought them. The payments are, indeed, an essential part of the moral calculus affirming the benevolence of the boom. However, oilman Santas drive Porsches, and their North Pole is Aspen. The biggest beneficiaries of the boom, the ones who collected most of two trillion dollars from the shale revolution, weren't landowners or even Wall Street hotshots. They were the future billionaires and multimillionaires who ran and worked at the companies exploiting the best shale plays: midsized companies that became giant companies (like Continental, Southwestern, Pioneer, and Range), and private companies that, in no more than a breath, became large companies or acquisition targets (such as Antero, Rice, Enduring, Athlon, CrownQuest, Chief, GeoSouthern, and East).

A decade ago, I had barely heard of any of them.

8. THE INTERNET OF OIL

BARRING DIVINE INTERVENTION, I NEVER WOULD HAVE BEEN ABLE TO predict the names of the companies that would win in the U.S. shale revolution. However, had I been smart enough to read a book published about twelve months before Mitchell Energy detonated the boom with the S. H. Griffin #4, I might have predicted the *type* of winners that emerged from nowheresville.

In 1997, Harvard Business School professor Clayton Christensen published *The Innovator's Dilemma*, a book that, while not uncontroversial, has become integral to how the business world, especially the technology world, understands itself. The book reveals patterns by which sophisticated industry leaders adjust their strategy. The leaders habitually abandon selling simpler, lower margin products or services for more differentiated ones. In the process, they cede the lower end of the market to smaller and initially less capable companies.

The dilemma is that for smart companies, moving upscale is the right thing to do, but time and again, the scrappier firms selling the less sophisticated products thrive by satisfying the large market abandoned by the smart companies. And within a few years, with the democratization of technology, the products made by once second-tier firms end up being just as effective as the former market leaders' products. Disruptive innovations, as Christensen famously called them, are not about leaps in human possibility, like nuclear power. They are about the first Toyotas or smaller steel mills: competitors that at first find ways to supply good enough stuff.

The shale revolution seems to fit that pattern. Heroic underdogs like George Mitchell and Harold Hamm reversed the gravity of the oil and gas business by drilling and fracking in second-rate basins in places like North Dakota and Pennsylvania while ExxonMobil bet its future on projects of mind-blowing technical complexity and cost. I am dumbfounded that disruptive innovation hasn't yet become the framework for understanding the boom. People in the oil business go to Harvard Business School, too. Maybe this conceptual absence is because the "new" product of the shale revolution is exactly the same as the old product: commodity, interchangeable oil and gas. It's how that oil and gas is made—and how much they cost to extract—that has changed.

The tech industry also seems to have colonized disruptive innovation as its private idea. A 2014 *Atlantic* essay, for example, challenged the ubiquitous claim of constant disruptive innovation in the technology sector and in the United States. I swallowed the article in three gulps, curious if someone would at last welcome the shale revolution into the world of disruptive innovation.[1] But the article didn't even hint at the shales. It often seems that the technology sector, driving Teslas to each other's pitch meetings in Menlo Park, provincially think of innovation in the oil patch (if they think that it's possible at all) as akin to someone replacing leather with performance fabrics on horse saddles: perfectly reasonable but irrelevant to the march of time.

Finally, the lack of understanding of the oil industry's deep disruption comes back to the Resource Triangle. Investors have long thought of buying oil and gas reserves as a "real asset" strategy like ports, farms, skyscrapers, pipelines—things that have some intrinsic value. The price of real assets can be cyclical, for sure: 2008 proved that. But unlike a consulting firm or a folk-rock band, something of value should remain in a real asset regardless of how its value fluctuates in a cycle. Real assets that have some supply constraints, like buildings in Manhattan, should also over time go up in value: if someone offers you Rockefeller Center for 50 percent of the price it was last year, you should probably buy Rockefeller Center. When the Resource Triangle and the unbreakable arrow connected to it still ruled how we conceived of the oil and gas industry—it had, after all, been true forever—we were certain that reserves would become increasingly expensive to develop. If someone offered you an oilfield for 50 percent of the price it was last year, you should buy the oilfield.

Then came the shale revolution, the Internet of oil, to change how oil and gas—and money—could be made.

My early career involved assisting in the analysis of companies like Shell and Exxon, the leaders of the global oil business. As Christensen argues sympathetically when writing about their equivalents in other industries, market leaders like these are not typically disrupted from what we might expect: blinding arrogance or strategic stupidity. Leading companies usually sell high-quality products and services in which they have a clear competitive advantage.

In the oil and gas business a decade ago, the talented engineers and geologists at Big Oil were doing what was necessary to supply the energy-thirsty world with oil and gas. They dedicated themselves to plays that everyone agreed were the *only* sizable sources of oil and gas left. What they do still amazes: create from scratch an entire liquefied natural gas exporting industry in Qatar, which now supplies 5 percent of the world's gas; drill wells from rigs in rough waters two miles above the sea floor; deal with Russians.[2] This is our high-tech.

Before the shales, the market leaders had largely ceded the low end of the market, U.S. onshore fields, not because they loved the ocean, or vodka, but because the continental United States was filled with small, depleted, and near impermeable reservoirs that were too small to be meaningful to the largest companies in the world. Owning an oil well that produces 1,000 barrels of oil per day could change your life. It wouldn't pay for ExxonMobil's paperclips.

As we'd expect in Christensen's model, the disruptive innovators in the oil business started with the ideal scale for the new opportunities. They were private entrepreneurs, often backed by private equity firms like where I work, who would never have to work again, nor their children, if they made ExxonMobil's paperclip money. The innovators were also smaller public companies, headquartered in silly places (silly in the oil business defined as "not Houston"), that were still small because they had never done anything impressive enough to become big. As the concept of disruptive innovation would predict, the future disruptors' strategies rested, self-aware, on lower margin, second-rate products. The pioneering U.S. shale producers fully assumed that using horizontal drilling and tons of stimulation to extract oil and gas from bad rock meant that they would produce high-cost hydrocarbons. But as oil and gas prices rose—and never underestimate the importance of higher prices as kindling for the boom—the companies figured that even bad rock was worth their time.

Harold Hamm, the boom's Lincoln, is everyone's favorite case study because he's the richest case study. With a $12.2 billion fortune, according to the *Forbes* 2015 list of Rich People Who Remain Not You, Hamm is the only executive of the American oil boom to have accumulated Russian-oligarch-sized wealth.[3] (Disruption good, kleptocracy better.) Hamm is even extraordinary at divorce and managed in 2014 to pay his ex-wife $2 billion *less* than people were predicting. She still got $975 million, paid in a handwritten personal check available for all to see—if not, unfortunately, for all to cash—on the Web.[4]

Hamm's own friend and lawyer admitted that the shack-raised Hamm "talked like a hick," causing people to think of him as a "dumb country bumpkin."[5] (Even today, Hamm pronounces it "multa-stage" fracking.)[6] For many years past when it was considered good business sense, he owned both a land drilling contractor and an E&P company. Until recently, he headquartered his company in Enid, the Wheat Capital of Oklahoma. It's as if Twitter came out of Fresno.

For decades, even as Hamm got steadily richer, his career was undistinguishable from a hundred other oilmen. He had success, for sure, but he also had seventeen straight dusters in 1983. An acquisition in Wyoming was an $80 million bust.[7] When I rejoined the oil business in 2004, I could have known about Harold Hamm, just like a Phillies fan can know the name of the second-string shortstop of the Padres. But I didn't. When I finally heard about him, probably in 2010, the consensus was that he was a hillbilly lucky enough to have been stupid enough to try to explore for big finds in North Dakota.

Yet the more I study Hamm's career, the more I admire it. At some point, Hamm made the decision, as he told Gregory Zuckerman, that "I wanted to put myself in a position to find the ancient wealth"—money more than success, money bigger than a single human's existence.[8] (Hamm doesn't plan on taking all that ancient wealth past his human existence; in 2011, he signed onto the Giving Pledge to give away at least half of his net worth in his lifetime.)[9] I've met a few other million-dollars-is-fun-but-a-billion-dollars-is-where-it-gets-interesting types and have always found it hard to read the origin of that wiring through their self-possessed gaze. But however it began, Hamm rested his hunt for ancient wealth on two key insights: that most people analyzing how much oil could be extracted from a field failed to understand how technology would eventually allow an operator to extract more; and that people (unpatriotically) underestimated the amount of recoverable oil in America in general and North Dakota in particular.[10]

With these insights guiding him, Hamm pursued a high-risk strategy to secure large amounts of oil in place even if the conventional wisdom was that that particular oil was permanently imprisoned in unextractable reservoirs. Not heeding worries about diversifying his holdings, he encouraged his employees to lease more and more acreage in North Dakota.[11] As with George Mitchell, a series of bad wells did not shake his faith in advancing technology or the hydrocarbons in the ground. Hamm was remarkably open-minded, too, studying his competitors, listening to his employees no matter how young, adopting without cynicism whatever worked.[12] (I suspect the roots of this humility are an autodidact's appreciation for information; Hamm learned the oil business out of high school from studying guys in the field and from occasional audited college courses.)

Hamm also did what every investor and executive knows to do but few have the nerve to pull off. He ran into the burning building as others were running out. After oil prices crashed in 2008, Hamm spent money to lease more acreage in the Bakken[13] that his company, Continental, in some ways didn't have. At the time, most of the rest of us in the business, including me, assumed that there were even odds that the remote, expensive, too complicated Bakken Shale would never be heard from again.

As much as Hamm's contrarian impulses impress, Mark Papa, the Jefferson of the boom's Mount Rushmore, even better exemplifies the disruptive innovators of the shale revolution. The company he led, EOG Resources, transformed from an average conventional gas producer with an above-average embarrassing history—its original parent was Enron—into one of the world's largest and most technically admired oil and gas companies, all through the development of crummy rock. Many companies adapted technology. EOG was the driver of multi-stage fracking in shale oil reservoirs, one of the three key advances of the boom.[14] All oil companies have computers. EOG realized that the speed of information, in a disrupting world, called for investing in the best IT systems and people in the industry. Many companies take credit for opening up a shale basin, sometimes with thin claims. EOG indisputably inaugurated the Eagle Ford Shale play in South Texas when it leased up the play's best acreage in 2008 on the untested theory that it could apply, on the opposite side of the country, its own advances in the Bakken. The Eagle Ford is now one of the big six basins of the shale revolution. From a globally irrelevant amount of oil and gas supplied in 2007, the region produced 2 percent of the world's oil and gas at the end of 2014.[15]

Papa, like Hamm, was not the flashiest executive—perhaps because he had seen what happened to the loudmouthed Enron. Papa had an ego, for sure, but we in the industry thought of EOG as the anti-Chesapeake. Chesapeake would seemingly put out a press release if Aubrey ate a good lunch; EOG, it felt, wouldn't put out a press release if it had discovered oil itself. But Papa, without flash, with an outwardly conservative temperament, had conviction. In 2007, he announced that EOG, once thought of as a classic onshore U.S. gas producer, would shift almost all of its drilling to oil and natural gas liquids. I figured that it was like Michael Jordan deciding that the world would be better off if he played baseball: we were going to see EOG, too, come back to its gifts. But Papa understood early that the shale wells being drilled by EOG were exceptional but not unique. And so, in a rare occurrence in a business prone to assuming other operators are more lucky than good, EOG extrapolated how everyone's successful wells would lead to too much supply.

Reading about Papa and others who won big often hits me harder in the stomach than in the brain. I have expended an embarrassing amount of mental energy asking how to reverse the flow of time. Some space cap-suley machine? A witch's brew with paprika and goat hooves? Shame-fully, I have most often resorted to the same technique I used when I was seven. I shut my eyes tight in bed and wish really, really hard for time to reverse. There were so many multibillion-dollar opportunities that I could have seized if I had had a playbook from the future. For instance, Harold Hamm, facing financial pressure during the global financial crisis, con-templated in 2008 selling half of Continental's position in the Bakken even as it acquired more acreage. An investment bank solicited offers from dozens of companies. No one was interested. When I finally get my time machine, I will buy that half interest for $500 million. (I suppose I will also need $500 million.) Hamm, I suspect, would have taken the offer, which would have been more, for a half interest, than the total reported value of Continental's proved Bakken reserves at the end of 2008.[16] By the end of 2014, even after oil prices plunged again, I could have sold that interest for probably fifteen times my original investment—and written about the five perspectives you gain from owning both a French château *and* an Italian palazzo.

I suspect that Hamm and Papa didn't regard themselves in the early days of the shale revolution as disruptive innovators. Even more precise horizontal drilling and multi-stage fracking were thought of as clever engineering solutions that companies were applying to second-tier rocks in the hopes of making just profitable enough widgets. It only turned out later, in the classic slow-dawning Christensen pattern, that these new U.S. techniques completely redefined the cost and availability of the widgets. Digital photography was originally just convenient and cheap. Only later did it produce higher resolution photographs than film.

Surprisingly, *The Innovator's Dilemma* is less applicable to the oilfield service industry that advanced much of the technology of the shale revo-lution. While some entrepreneurs developed, say, better drill bits or more effective proppants, the oilfield services necessary for the boom were as well provided by giant incumbents like Schlumberger as by smaller businesses. Indeed, unlike ExxonMobil or Shell, in which size and skills were an impediment to experimenting with "low-tech" U.S. onshore oil and gas fields, the scale and strategic advantages of the giant oilfield service companies—in logistics, in integrating different services, in advancing and adapting new technologies—were ideal for serving developers of the shales.

THE SHALE REVOLUTION SHARES another characteristic with the changes wrought by the Internet. The Internet has infiltrated every aspect of daily life, but "who" disrupted our lives was never just Mark Zuckerberg or Jeff Bezos.

The corporate history of the U.S. shale renaissance was not some Night of the Living Rich in which every developer of every crappy reservoir woke up at the same time, got wealthy, and bought a private plane with mud-stained cash. Hamm, Papa, and George Mitchell succeeded for specific reasons: being early in a shale basin and being relentless in trying techniques until one worked. But there were diverse ways to win in the boom—and just as many to lose.

Through some combination of buying, selling, and developing shale gas and oil reservoirs, E&P executives tried to get rich—or, in the anodyne Wall Street term, create value. ("I'm not European-castle-owning rich. I just created value.") There was no pretested recipe for buying, developing, and selling that worked to win part of the $1.35 trillion in new reserve wealth. There were successful land flippers, equivalent to vacant lot hunters who benefit when a hipster opens an artisanal barbershop in a formerly marginal neighborhood. These companies leased land from farmers for peanuts and then sold those leases without drilling a well when a land rush began. Other companies pursued a "dot map" approach, in which they leased land, drilled a few science experiment wells, and then sold their assets to another company with the anecdotal well results "derisking" the acreage. Companies like Devon or Anadarko were like full-on real estate developers: they aggressively drilled wells and leased new acreage and swallowed neighboring companies like Mitchell Energy whole. In effect, they reinvested their profits to add buildings to their mixed-use developments and improve the value of their land with better tenants paying higher rents. These companies, if they were private, went public and cashed in after an IPO. If they were already public, executives and employees could see their wealth rise with their companies' stock price, as less rich Harold Hamms.

At each stage, the risks were real. Much like for landowners, a company would face the choices of caution versus confidence, patience versus pace, with countless examples of lucky bastards who had gotten rich holding on and poor bastards who had lost by prematurely selling out— and vice versa. Some companies paid millions for acreage that would turn out worthless. Other companies saw ravenous rivals agreeing to terms that one could classify only as ATFD—Are They [Bleeping] Drunk?—and then watched as acreage in suburban Fort Worth that was leased for $26,500 per acre, with a 25 percent royalty rate, on a three-year term ended up actually making the drunk rival millions when the Barnett Shale wells worked.

Take Ohio, for example, which eventually roused the imagination of frontier-oriented E&P companies. Why Ohio? Well, why not Ohio: shale plays underlie—and feed—shallower reservoirs, and oil and gas production had dribbled out from shallow Ohio reservoirs for decades. Hell, the state was the largest producer of American crude in 1896.[17] So a few companies shook cobwebs off old Ohio well logs and geological maps. Eventually, they focused on the deep Utica Shale there. Pioneers began drilling vertical test wells, then a few horizontal multi-stage fracked wells. By 2010, the industry was abuzz with the possibility that the entire eastern half of Ohio was going to be an Abu Dhabi on the Erie. There were parts of the Utica that would give up oil, parts that would give up gas, and parts that would give up "wet gas"—gas mixed with natural gas liquids like butane.

After more wells were drilled, some operators crowed about greater successes and others begged for patience. ("We've drilled only a few science experiments.") Eventually, after enough wells, the industry had a better sense of the reservoir quality, the unit costs, and profitability of each part of the Utica. It turned out that the "oil window" of the Utica was open only to marginal returns. The dry gas portion in the southeastern corner of the state, however, boasted insanely productive wells.

Over just two years in Ohio, companies could judge their decisions in retrospect, whether they were right to sell, stupid not to, or unlucky in delays. The winners would look with half-justified pity at the companies that lost money, because their me-too strategies were unable to replicate the financial results of those quicker to read the market or the technical results of more talented operators. Sometimes losing meant not selling quickly enough. One company famously reported to its investors that it had a deal to sell all of its Utica Shale position for $6 billion. This meant $6 billion in profits, because the company had gotten the Utica acreage for free when it bought some shallow conventional wells above it years earlier. But the negotiations took so long that the billions-offering buyer changed its mind, likely spooked by some well reports. The jilted seller still holds most of its Utica acreage.

Sometimes losing meant selling too quickly. A few companies, I'm sure, smugly congratulated themselves after jettisoning acreage in the dry gas window of the Utica. It was a loser's area. America needed more dry gas like it needed more cable TV stations. The sellers later kicked themselves as they read about the buyers drilling huge wells there and becoming new stars of the oil patch.

And sometimes losing meant buying too quickly. In 2013, had you told an oilman that you could get him acreage in the Cline Shale in West Texas, his heart would have started racing as if you were offering him a month of whiskey and fishing, with his boss's approval. Now, if you offer him some Cline, he'll pat you on the back and say that he'll have to de-Cline. He would rather spend a month at the dentist. A company I know tried to sell Cline acreage to 174 different operators in 2014. Not one bothered to test the company's desperation with a price.

Like a modern dance performance, the early days of a boom in any area were randomness and strange posturing. (These performances would be faster and less random with each successive boom.) As each play matured, two patterns emerged. First, in most places, the core of the plays—where the oil and gas bearing rock is the thickest, where it is least interrupted by natural faults, where its rock characteristics are most responsive to fracking—turned out to be even better than people thought. The fringes of a play, on the other hand, were worse. The Mississippi Lime play, once thought to cover a dozen counties in southern Kansas and a half dozen in Oklahoma (and none—don't ask—in Mississippi) shriveled in a couple of years to parts of four or five counties in Oklahoma. Current estimates are that the cores, subjectively defined, usually represent the best 20 to 30 percent of any play.

Second, in every area of the boom, some operators consistently made better wells than others. Even the village idiots of the oil business can improve on shale well productivity by adopting neighbors' techniques to deliver more stimulation—more fracks and more proppant—to more parts of the reservoir. But oil and gas production is no different than other endeavors. Some people are just better, more intelligent, more patient, more data driven: they drill better wells because they spend time in the field and understand every step of the process tactilely, not as a plan on paper; they drill better wells because they study intensively what's working and what's not, thinking clearly about geology, engineering, and physics; they apply cold logic to the quality of acreage based on the underlying rock, not their longing to become the next Harold Hamm. More nimble organizations have also been able to adjust well designs quickly, extracting lessons from a well just drilled or one currently drilling, rather than downloading every well plan from some bureaucratized template. And those more nimble companies, with engineers as buddies (or brothers) of landmen a few offices away instead of in a rivalrous department on a separate floor, have been quick to capture the opportunities to lease new land as implied by their own wells. Mark Papa, not surprisingly, divided EOG into smaller, self-contained, play-focused companies—a collection of mini-EOGs.

IN THE SHALE REVOLUTION, the pattern of disruptive innovation—in which the second-tier caterpillars morphed into butterflies—applies not just to individual companies but to the oil and gas itself. In many areas of economic life, being in a second-rate line may not matter. Even if you're not selling bespoke blouses made with rare Japanese threads, you can still make money selling offensive T-shirts at the seashore. But in a commodity market, if there is enough supply from new gas wells that can be profitable at, say, $3 per thousand cubic feet, the market will settle—to simplify matters—with everyone getting $3 per thousand cubic feet. This is bad news for even boom-era shales that can profitably make widgets at only $4.50 gas.

For us in the oil industry, it still seems science fiction sometimes that in West Virginia, for decades a land of whispering wells drilled into shallow reservoirs, you can now extract 8 billion cubic feet of gas from a single honking well in the Marcellus. It's like your ne'er-do-well son announcing he got into medical school. It is equally incomprehensible that those unbelievable wells in West Virginia may not be profitable because there are so many more 12 billion cubic feet wells in Pennsylvania, driving down the price. It's like your once ne'er-do-well son *not* getting into medical school after achieving straight As at Yale.

Critics of the shale revolution point to companies that lost money after oil or gas prices fell as evidence that the boom is nothing but a bubble blown up by the combined hot air of Wall Street sharps and Texas wildcatters. (Those critics love to mention the corporate origins of EOG.) Yet this left-wing gotcha has a twin in right-wing cynicism: my oil industry friends declare that the demise of solar panel manufacturers like Solyndra was the just punishment for liberal "crony capitalism." But regardless of the subsidies for the solar industry, the collapse of the price of solar panels did not mean that the original impulse to invest was corrupt. Nor does losing money in the oil and gas business mean that the impulse to invest in the shale revolution was an underhanded financial scheme. The lost money means that both impulses were too popular, bringing in too many competitors, leading to oversupply. Markets are often as innocent and as inevitable as that.

Just as the supply chain management (and the sales tax exemption) of Amazon forced lower margins on other retailers, the U.S. shales brought about lower prices and margins for all kinds of oil and gas fields around the world. Goldman Sachs estimated that the cash return on capital employed for natural-gas-focused E&P companies declined from a range of 20 to 24 percent at the start of the boom in 2004–2006, to about 10 percent in 2014.[18]

The "new" price for oil and gas has disrupted few oil companies as much as the biggest of them. Disruption works differently in the oil industry than in many others because of the commodity nature of the end product: if you don't like your assets, and you have enough money, you can buy new ones—and maybe sell your old ones—and remain an oil company through it all. There hasn't been a mass extinction of former leaders in the oil business. Indeed, given how stably gigantic ExxonMobil and its predecessor entities have been for a century, it often feels that the company will be selling oil and gas after human life ends, on the planet of the apes. (Critics of Clayton Christensen say that big companies like IBM and U.S. Steel have also adapted better than his theories seem to allow.)[19] But the American shale revolution profoundly disrupted ExxonMobil and its international oil company peers in two major ways. The glut of supply brought about by the boom has made some of their high-tech, international megaprojects too costly to continue. Some fields that once seemed globally necessary now just feel odd. If the oil company owners of those projects never revive them, the billions invested to date will be lost. And even if they do revive them—and they may—the billions will likely provide glum returns.

As I discussed in Chapter 4, the boom also compelled international oil companies to declare that if they can't beat 'em, join 'em. Or, more accurately, buy 'em. ExxonMobil and other major oil companies have acquired assets of U.S. disruptive innovators and sometimes whole companies. Each buying decision was rooted, I'm sure, in a desire to make money on that transaction. But the purchases were also strategically necessary for the big companies to shift to lower-cost reservoirs in a world marked by ample oil and gas.

To date, for the most part, the return of international oil companies to onshore U.S. basins has been awkward, like Heavy Metal Night at a country club. ExxonMobil's profits from its $35 billion purchase of large independent XTO in 2010 were flattened when, in the two years after the deal closed, near-month gas prices fell by 39 percent.[20] The Australian commodities giant, BHP Billiton, has begat a phrase in the U.S. oil patch: "pulling a BHP." Within six months in 2011, at a height of mania for the Haynesville and Fayetteville gas shales, it paid nearly $5 billion for

Fayetteville Shale assets from Chesapeake and $15 billion to buy E&P company Petrohawk.[21] Within a year, BHP had written down the value of its gas assets by $3 billion.[22] In late 2014, slouching, it put its Fayetteville assets up for sale.

As uncomfortable as these acquisitions have been, I suspect there will be another wave of the international majors shifting to the U.S. shales. To keep production at least stable, the shifting will need to replace their existing megaprojects, which at some point begin to naturally decline, with fields that can make money at prevalent prices. The large companies have convinced themselves—and some will succeed—that they can transform organizations in which hundreds of people worked together to design one production facility in the deepwater Gulf of Mexico into companies in which fewer people are tasked with flexibly drilling many more wells.

Others in the industry are skeptical of whether a dinosaur can ever become a mammal.

Disruptive innovation also, I believe, best explains the oil price collapse of 2014. There are other theories, for sure. When prices fell, I was lectured that if I could get my oilman head out of a barrel, I would understand that Saudi Arabia was purposely lowering prices for geopolitical ends: to cudgel Iran and Russia then fighting against Saudi interests in Syria. (These cocktail party Kissingers seemed to pick up the secrets of Saudi foreign policy from their brother-in-law whose college roommate's childhood neighbor worked in the State Department.)

Yet disruptive innovation as an explanation spares you the effort, if denying you the entertainment, of conspiracy theories. From 2011 to 2013, oil demand had grown just fast enough, although still objectively slow, to absorb the massive additional supply from U.S. shale oil. In 2014, when U.S. oil production grew another 16 percent, the global market had changed. Demand growth in China had slowed. Brazilian and Libyan oil production had rebounded. What confronted Saudi Arabia was not just a proxy war in Syria but a declining call on its oil—the amount it could produce and not oversupply the market. It would have faced the same maddening either/or (oversupply the market and lower prices, or cut production and encourage more competitive supply) even if every Iranian in the world pledged loyalty to the Saudi king. Saudi Arabia chose what it thought of as the least bad option.

Saudi Arabia will do fine, as long as oil is consumed. With oil in reservoirs even less expensive to extract than from U.S. shales, Saudi is not going to be disrupted. But its options are now defined by a new world in which oil *can* get cheaper, a world made possible by the shales. When speaking to investors in late 2014, I borrowed a distinction from Martin Luther King Jr.'s "Letter from a Birmingham Jail," one he used more nobly to describe the role of the church in transforming society: the "thermometer" was the price of oil; the "thermostat" was the shale revolution.

Almost all existing oil and gas wells will be kept producing in the world whose temperature is set, in large part, by the shales. The wells have been drilled; the money spent; there is no reason to shut off the taps. But, in 2015, oil companies exposed to *new*, high-cost projects became worried. (Even more panicked were companies that built $600 million offshore rigs to drill those projects.) U.S. oil companies were not invulnerable. Many operators in second-rate shales that responded less productively to fracking anticipated, fear-struck, their own corporate remains.

And so, overall, the industry in 2015 shifted capital and people to preserve *growing* production in the best parts of the most disruptive shales. They shifted away from international and fringe shale projects. The companies that could make that shift most gracefully and profitably were the ones, of course, with the most high-quality shale acreage as a percentage of their assets. This was not Shell or BP.

This situation riles up the majors. Decade after decade, they tell you, they were doing the work of the world in providing everyone with oil and gas while grubby U.S. E&P companies were selfishly playing around with chicken-spit assets in Oklahoma or West Virginia because they couldn't do anything else. And how were the majors thanked? At the end of 2014, the combined market capitalization of Shell and ExxonMobil was 28 percent—$211 billion—less than at the end of 2007. The biggest and smartest and scariest oil companies have, in effect, lost money after the greatest oil and gas boom in thirty years. And this is not just Wall Street math. Shell's production in 2014 was 3 percent less than it was a decade before.[23]

And, holy petroleum, look who benefited: bottom-feeding public investors who bought into nothing companies like Pioneer Natural Resources (up almost five times since the end of 2003) or Range Resources (up almost 8.5 times). The emperor of Enid, Oklahoma. Slick-haired New Yorkers at private equity firms. Those people are splitting two trillion dollars because of what? Disruptive innovation? Fracking?

9. *GUAR AND LEASE*, OR ANOTHER SIDE OF DISRUPTION

TOLSTOY WOULD SMIRK.

When I get caught up with using *The Innovator's Dilemma* as the uncanny explanation of the shale revolution and the stories of Harold Hamm and Mark Papa, I remind myself what Tolstoy would think. This is not, for me, terribly unusual. I remind myself in many contexts what Tolstoy would think (when writing, when making conclusions on cause and effect, when eating breakfast). He is one of my writer heroes, a framed picture of him, long-bearded and sternly glaring, often above me as I write.

The epilogue of *War and Peace* is, notoriously, one of the strangest—and worst—endings of any of humanity's masterpieces. In it, Tolstoy explicitly lays out his theory of history. He does so more subtly (by a bit) in the 1,500 pages of warring and peaceing before that. Throughout, he shows his contempt for explanations that rely on heroic decisions or even simple causality. So many actions that at first seem to be exercises in free will can come to be seen, with distance and time, as acts of necessity. Historians, to Tolstoy, stretch to come up with "ingenious arguments for the foresight and genius of the commanders."[1] The irony is that the most ostensibly powerful people—generals and kings—have the least room for free action. As Tolstoy wrote about a fictionalized Napoleon at the Battle of Borodino:

Napoleon fulfilled his function as the representative of power just as well and even better than in other battles. He did nothing to harm the course of the battle; he bowed to the more well-reasoned opinions; he caused no confusion, did not contradict himself, did not get frightened, and did not run away from the battlefield, but with his great tact and experience of war calmly and worthily fulfilled his role of seeming to command.[2]

There are many oilfield Napoleons seeming to command in the history of the shale revolution. Had Tolstoy written *War and Peace* about the boom—*Guar and Lease?*—he would have been as unimpressed by Papa and Hamm as he was of Napoleon or Russian generals, those "most enslaved and involuntary agents."[3]

An alternate financial history of the shale revolution is a less heroic one. In that history, everyone did exactly what they had to do.

CLAYTON CHRISTENSEN SYMPATHIZED with the role that necessity played in the corporate decisions of both disruptive innovators and those disrupted. He might partially agree with Tolstoy. And so might George Mitchell and Harold Hamm. As much as both men liked to be thought of as visionaries (and they were), they have been candid that limited options and desperation directed some of their decisions. Hamm started exploring in North Dakota because he didn't have the money to compete in better places.[4] In 2007, he bet his company on the Bakken because, at sixty-one, it was his last chance.[5]

Gregory Zuckerman reports George Mitchell's recollection that he had had no choice in the 1990s but to focus on the Barnett: "it was really the company's only shot at avoiding complete collapse."[6] For all his famed perseverance, Mitchell thought about selling all his energy assets and dedicating the company exclusively to real estate in 1996, two years before the Barnett breakthrough, after a jury awarded plaintiffs against Mitchell Energy $204 million for water contamination incidents, unrelated to fracking. (A Texas appeals court later voided the award.)[7] The company was in triage, and the industry was bumbling along at low prices, which were about to get worse. Had someone bid a fair price on Mitchell Energy's declining gas assets, George Mitchell would have likely sold out, erasing himself from the mainstream history of the shale revolution.

The smaller operators who "chose" to innovate in that revolution did so for all sorts of good reasons but also this: what else were they going to do? Oil companies have depleting resources. If they don't find new fields, they will eventually have nothing left. In the 1990s and 2000s, a few U.S. E&P companies tried to follow the big boys into international and deepwater plays, but most stayed where they had experience, in onshore gas plays in the United States. The new LNG import terminal projects being announced were a sign of the energy industry's clear lack of faith in volume growth from those U.S. gas producers, like your mother bringing home takeout after your father tells her that he's cooking tonight.

The U.S. E&P sector sometimes reminds me of the Pima Indians, who over millennia developed a culture—an evolutionary adaption, a collective body—ideal for living in near starvation conditions in desert Arizona. When modern America moved onto their lands, when food became more available, their genetic adaption to store calories did not quit. In a century, some of the thinnest people in the world became some of the fattest.[8] There are many reasons why an oil and gas renaissance has happened only in the United States, Canada, and to a lesser extent Argentina. But the character of the men and women in the U.S. oil industry must be chief among them: a fearlessness in the face of risk, a scrappy creativity in keeping businesses running, a grit to try again after failures, and a sense of fun in getting all the meat off the bone in a market declared spent.

In some ways, the U.S. oil industry's character produced impressive results. It kept the U.S. onshore E&P sector afloat in the two decades between the oil price fall of 1986 and the start of the shale revolution. Yet that character also has its compulsions. As hedge fund manager David Einhorn joked, "If you give a driller a dollar, he's going to drill a hole."[9] The hole may not always be profitable. There were reasons that some independents were looking outside the United States or in deepwater. Onshore natural gas drilling returns in the United States were mediocre or worse. But the industry never stopped hyping and pursuing new plays, even ones that were obviously going to be busts, because they could in-

vest with Other People's Money as long as people dreamed. U.S. operators, then as now, engaged constantly in hectic buying and selling of
assets, activity that caused stocks to move and money to change pockets
but often in the end not much value created for the industry as a whole.
(Much value, to the contrary, was destroyed.) One day, we may all live in
a hyper-efficient global economy in a borderless world. But even before
the boom, half of the drilling rigs in the world were operating in the
United States not because that's where the best oil and gas exploration
opportunities were. It's because Alamo-remembering, never-surrendering
Texans and Oklahomans could project enough confidence to attract
capital.

Aubrey McClendon is the swaggering, never retreating Teddy Roo-
sevelt on the Mount Rushmore of the boom. It was a mutual friend
who, in an e-mail to Aubrey, called him the Steve Jobs of the shales. And
Chesapeake was most responsible for turning shale drilling into a disrupting national phenomenon. But what *made* Aubrey's reputation? It was
a land acquisition strategy implemented in highly limited conditions: when
Chesapeake was a private company with eight employees; when it was
nearly bankrupt after seventeen years in business[10]; when it was worth
$31 billion ten years later[11]; when it was buying gas properties because gas
prices were going up; when it was buying better gas properties because
gas prices were going down; when it was declaring itself an exclusive
devotee of gas, the fuel of the future; when it was buying oil properties
because margins were better; when it had the money to spend; when it
didn't have the money to spend; when Aubrey was worth $2 billion;
when Aubrey lost $2 billion; when assets were up for sale; when assets
weren't for sale; before the boom and during the boom; under new moons
and under full moons; for better, for worse, for richer, for poorer, in sick-
ness and in health, to love and to cherish, till death do Aubrey and the oil
and gas property market part.

Chesapeake's strategy was always the same, fueled by optimism: being
a fast follower to technical and regional pioneers; being unafraid to pay
high prices to sometimes heedlessly acquire land and properties; and being unashamed to raise capital from anywhere it could, however it could,
to fund its sprees. (Chesapeake's strategy also seemed to consist of being

exceptionally tough on oilfield service companies and royalty owners, but that's a different story.)[12]

Defenders of Aubrey point out that before widespread drilling allowed the industry to delineate new plays, leasing *all* the land, or trying your damned best to, was a savvy way to ensure that you also got the best acreage. This was the case almost everywhere from 2003 to 2008 and in select places, like Ohio or West Texas, after 2008. Aubrey defenders also point out that many equally aggressive E&P companies failed because they were too late, too tentative, or too narrow in where they sought land. Or they had the right idea but didn't have the capital to follow through. And Aubrey, like Hamm and Mitchell, was never distracted by deepwater or international projects in areas he knew nothing about. (In 2015, he seems to have crossed that border of his appetite, with a highly speculative project in Australia.)

Did Chesapeake lift off in the mid-2000s because Aubrey's decisions brought success? Or did Chesapeake succeed because, for a five-year period and no longer, the fates were finally aligned to massively reward strategies and people like him? Probably some of both. Yet watching Aubrey feels sometimes like seeing the country's best restaurant critic blissfully eating from a box of day-old donuts. People respect the critic for the sensitivity of his palate. But maybe the man just likes to eat.

And there is a question of how much Chesapeake succeeded at all. The enterprise value of the company, for all the speculation on whether it would survive its latest crisis in 2013, was nearly four and a half times higher at the end of 2014 than at the start of 2004, when the boom was just beginning.[13] However, given how much of the growth was fueled by debt, new shares, and complicated structures, and given how much of the acquired land was divested after various crises, a shareholder of Chesapeake would have seen those shares appreciate only 52 percent in that time, or an unboomy 4 percent per year.

WE LOOK FOR CAUSES because we want to judge. We look for effects because we want to find patterns for the future. The story of the boom, financially speaking, is sometimes conventionally explicable when thinking about Continental or EOG or even Chesapeake. These companies were contrarians, early adopters, technology leaders. They won at disruptive innovation. But the story of the boom is also about inertia, irony, unintended consequences, and outrageous chance.

In the boom, people got lucky passively: their grandmother's rhinestone brooch turned out to be made of diamonds. Some companies held shale rights for decades, from a stubborn ability to somehow scratch out a living—or a corporate strategy—from conventional reservoirs above the shales. Cabot Oil & Gas, one of the pioneers of the Marcellus in northeast Pennsylvania, had been working shallow Appalachian gas for decades. In 2003, the market capitalization of Cabot had still not broken a billion dollars after thirteen years as a public company. As its performance in Dimock attests, it did not emerge at the start of the boom as the most technically sophisticated operator in America. At the end of 2014, because of the Marcellus, the company's shares were worth $12.3 billion.

Other companies got "lucky rich" through effort, no matter how initially misdirected. They searched at rummage sales for an oil painting to go above the couch—something emotional like a sad clown playing checkers—and discovered later that there was a Rembrandt in the frame behind *Bozo Gets Queened*. Those companies pursued sensible business ideas, by pre-boom standards, that would have turned disastrous after the boom had shale acreage not slept under their conventional targets.

The luck story everyone in the industry most likes to tell is Terry Pegula's. Few in the industry had ever heard of Pegula before 2009 even though he had assembled shallow gas wells over 650,000 acres, mainly in Pennsylvania. No one I've talked to knows exactly how Pegula, a down-to-earth, blue-collar guy, acquired all those leases. He seems to be of the if-it's-free-it's-for-me school of acquisition. According to a friend in the industry, Pegula was given some of his assets as long as he agreed to plug and abandon old wells. The former owner thought it was saving money by allowing Pegula to bury its corpses. In 2000, Pegula acquired other Pennsylvania assets from Devon Energy, the buyer of George Mitchell's company the next year, in a transaction so small that Devon wasn't obligated to disclose it.[14]

Pegula didn't discover the Marcellus Shale. He took on his assets in

Ohio and Pennsylvania in a strategy, it seems, to produce coalbed methane. Pegula also wasn't on the forefront of shale drilling and completion techniques. In 2009, the private equity firm KKR bought one-third of Pegula's company, East Resources, by investing $330 million to fund East's drilling. We rubbed our eyes in disbelief: East Who? The company had drilled all of one horizontal well. Eleven months later, Shell bought most of East for $4.7 billion. KKR and its investors made $1.2 billion in less than a year.[15] Pegula did better: as of 2015, he was worth $3.8 billion, from the Shell transaction and a subsequent sale of his Utica acreage to Aubrey for $1.8 billion.[16] Pegula is now so wealthy that he has joined the Official Club of Too Much Money and Too Much Time on His Hands, also known as NFL team owners, by buying the Buffalo Bills for $1.4 billion.[17] He owns the Buffalo Sabres, too.

Throughout the boom, one of the games I often played with my industry friends was What Was Their Original Business Plan? When we heard the news of a company selling out for a wild sum or going public in a monster IPO, we looked in our files—half sneering, all jealous, amazed, depressed, demanding justice—and saw that the Bakken powerhouse was originally targeting properties in the Middle East or that the multibillion-dollar Wolfcamp Shale producer had pitched us a few years earlier on a strategy to buy shallow, nonshale fields.

On a few occasions, I've informally advised the friend of a friend, the daughter of one of the more improbable beneficiaries of the shale revolution. Her father is a New York stockbroker-cum-oilman who moved out to a raggedy oil province in the late 1970s, the previous time the oil business attracted dreamers there. For decades, he operated a fourth-tier oil company. I call it fourth tier, but if there is a fifth tier, it would be him. When one of his employees, in 2009, described to me his assets and operations, I saw no coherence in the business or value in his barely producing stripper wells. I suspected that the entire company was a drilling partnership, a now largely discredited business model that relied on hyping investments to naive investors with pitches of price spikes and tax benefits.

Then the boom came to his area, and the stripper wells turned out to be above a major shale play two miles deep. His family "farmed out" the right to drill in the shale for about $50 million. According to his bemused (and now rich) daughter, the father didn't thank heavens for his luck. He said I told you so. He had been absolutely right to hold on when others in his backwater had given up. It was hard to argue with $50 million.

The fact that a company changed its business plan, or started targeting a deeper zone, does not mean that its success depended wholly on luck. Everyone in the U.S. oil and gas business, from Chevron to a Louisiana roughneck, responded to the shale revolution. It altered every assumption of which oil and gas reservoirs should be pursued. Cannier companies adjusted more quickly. But when it came to the decision to buy and—more often—to sell, everyone was reminded of Ecclesiastes: time and chance happeneth to us all. Some in the industry seem to understand this, others less so. Creationists and evolutionary biologists argue about the anthropic principle, the thesis that the universe's evolution to the point where intelligent beings—us—can contemplate it means that the direction of the universe's existence is defined by humans' contemplation of it. I have observed the oilmanthropic principle, a belief that the history of the shale boom—heck, maybe the natural history of the planet back to the plankton 500 million years ago—developed so that a specific oil and gas executive could unlock specific rocks and fulfill his destiny of being rich.

Some of my friends in the industry took high umbrage at President Obama's admonition that "you didn't build that" in explaining how society plays a role in helping businesses succeed.[18] "We built it" became shorthand among oilmen—and others—to dismiss the suggestion that business success was anything but the direct effect of wisdom, foresight, and grit. In the shale revolution, "we built it" surely applies to Mark Papa. But for wildcatters drilling exploration wells in shallow acreage in South Texas who suddenly became rich when Mark Papa's EOG discovered the Eagle Ford, a better chant would probably have been We Lucked Into It.

IN THE YEAR before oil prices plunged in late 2014, Aubrey McClendon went at it again, buying over $14 billion worth of properties and aggressively raising capital.[19] He has never been dumb: he understood that the market was different than it was in earlier land rushes. He just believed that the same strategy would work again. Whether the flighty billions return to his bank account is still the most popular show in town. There are other dramas of boom babies and boom billionaires (and some ex-billionaires) trying to do it again, because they have something to prove, because life is meaningless if you don't own a pro football team, because of the love of the hunt, because if you give a driller a dollar . . . Yet none are as entertaining as *Aubrey's Return*. The oil price dropped as Aubrey was still assembling his billions in acquisitions. After the drop, seemingly every lunch and dinner in Houston was overtaken at some point, by speculation on whether Aubrey was finally going to go bust. Adding to the speculation, Chesapeake sued Aubrey in February 2015, claiming that he stole its corporate secrets, the locations of shale acreage sweet spots that Aubrey's new venture bought.

We all talked obsessively about Aubrey not only because he is the industry's biggest star but because his current incarnation adds, to the financial drama, a Shakespearean plot straight out of *Henry IV*. Aubrey's primary backer, with a mind-bending amount of capital and typically overcomplicated Aubrey structure, is a private equity firm run by John Raymond, the son of Lee Raymond, the famously brusque retired king of ExxonMobil. Who knows what the father thinks of his Prince Hal throwing in his lot with that slender Falstaff, a glutton who, in the Exxon headquarters of the 1990s, was probably thought of as a blowhard, if thought of at all. Then again, the Exxon of the 1990s ignored the Barnett Shale a few miles away from its headquarters.

WHAT WE TALK ABOUT when we talk about Aubrey is a fascination with the most charismatic and vainglorious among us. But we also talk about our biggest fear, by putting a human face on it: whether our best days were short and behind us. Indeed, at lunch when I gave my Golden Decade speech for the fiftieth time, the investor and I talked about Aubrey. Her trust had direct exposure to him through several investments.

She wanted to know what I thought. Could he do it again? Could any of us? Should she expect the energy sector to provide "normal" slow, eight-year, double-your-money type returns over the next decade—the typical goal of an endowment or foundation—or could she expect a tripling of money or more as some of the best energy investors had achieved in the past? Frankly, a Silver Decade would be fine with her. Her institution is not looking to get rich off oil money. Already rich, it seeks only to prudently grow its capital. An oil and gas bubble bursting calamitously would make it harder to achieve that goal.

One of the shortest routes to embarrassment in any fluid industry is to make bold market predictions. Putting those predictions in a book is the ideal way to tattoo future humiliation on your face (well, like tattooing anything on your face). As I argue at the end of this book, I think that the shale revolution, as measured by volume, will continue for years. The world has few better alternatives—some would argue no better alternative—to supply itself with oil and gas than the U.S. shales. But the pace of the boom will be determined at any given time by oil and gas prices. Some investors will wager billions of dollars on the direction of those prices.

I am not one of them. I cannot predict oil and gas prices any more than I can predict the majority party in Congress in 2026 or if the Rolling Stones will still be on tour that year. This inadequacy will be crushing to a relative who expects me to know all about all because I'm "in commodities." (I fear one day he's going to ask me about sugar beets.) I can, however, outline the contours of how the shale revolution *could* evolve, financially. If the Golden Decade created wealth from two consecutive causes, the industry could extend it from a reprise of one of those two: another surge in oil and gas prices or the opening of even more new shale basins to profitable development. Many predict resurgent oil and gas prices in the future. A few forecasters, with an almost animalistic sense of market behaviors, remind everyone that all businesses are cyclical and that no matter how many witty books are written declaring this a new world, cyclicality always wins. We may, for instance, be underestimating renewed demand growth. We have become accustomed to economic news alternating between uninspiring and full-on frightening. It is not beyond imagination that global economic growth will revive at some point to allow for the planet's 7 billion people, as has been happening for two centuries, to steadily consume more energy to increase their living standards.

Others predict that the supply of oil and gas to meet demand will be acutely inadequate at some point in the next few years. Remember: the global production of oil and gas from existing wells declines in aggregate at about 3 to 5 percent per year. Someone has to drill new wells. In 2015 and 2016, large international nonshale projects are coming online. A company that already invested $10 billion in a deepwater West African oilfield will invest the last billion dollars, regardless of current prices, just as you would finish knitting a sweater even if a year of effort has resulted in something ideal for a person who has the neck the width of a French fry and both arms on the same side of his chest.

However, the industry's sharp reduction in spending on new megaprojects will mean less of those in the future. And at some point, the world may need the oil and gas from the fields that never got sanctioned. Saudi Arabia would have to step in. Prices could skyrocket.

Commodity prices could also rise again if the U.S. energy renaissance turns out to be short lived or overhyped, as skeptics argue. The world's expectations of stable—maybe even declining—oil and gas prices rely on ample and growing American supply. Increasingly lonely and weary, shale skeptics wait for their vindication: the shales are expensive; no one can make any money; the reserve estimates are inflated; the decline rates are too high; it was all a cockamamie scheme funded by debt. When the bubble of the shales finally bursts, they predict, the market will need to reset at prices that make conventional projects profitable. Shell will have the last laugh.

These skeptics are bullish on investing in energy. So, strangely, are their opposites, the biggest shale enthusiasts, who think that there is going to be later fabulous acts of the boom, not because of prices but because of land. The land rushes, they claim, are not as dead as the obituaries would have them. After all, previous land rushes caught the industry by surprise. Companies run by Harold Hamm, Aubrey McClendon, and others are developing new plays in Oklahoma, ones they haven't named after towns or first farms like the Marcellus or Bakken but after low-level punning acronym names that sound like menu items at the Dairy Queen: the SCOOP, the STACK, the CNOW. And the most optimistic folks in the industry wait eagerly for a fracking boom in the Monterey Shale not far from Santa Barbara, perhaps if every single citizen in California were re-placed by someone not from California.

YET NONE OF THE ABOVE is the inevitable, or even the likeliest, future. At lunch, at the trust, the investor finally pressed me: "What follows the Golden Decade?"

I couldn't hide anymore. I answered, "Normal life."

I believe that financial success from the shale revolution will be much harder to come by, even as shale production expands. It will not be im-possible, for sure. Some companies will secure profitable drilling locations in core shale plays that other operators passed over, because earlier wells were completed poorly or because some crotchety farmer refused to lease prime acreage to oil companies but his children—"you'll love the nurses at the home, Pops"—like the sound of being rich. There will continue to be entrepreneurial oilfield service companies that invent businesses and products that make drilling, fracking, and other parts of the process more efficient.

However, a booming, leaping, radically disrupting industry is a better creator of wealth than a normal industry facing normal competitive mar-kets with normal oversupply threats and normal opportunities to generate investor returns. The late autumn orchard has fewer apples to be picked. In the shale business, there is not enough land still held by crotchety farmers to provide opportunities to the hundreds of E&P companies looking for it. And no new major American shale play may be unlocked. For sure, I was not prepared for the emergence of the SCOOP, a profitable but smaller play in Oklahoma, and not just because it shares its name with a type of Frito. Shale plays lie beneath where we've already discovered oil and gas. We may find some new plays in Oklahoma. We are unlikely to find them in Oregon. And, yes, oil and gas prices could rise in the future. The world may need the "disrupted" barrels in the Canadian oil sands or Cline Shale or deepwater Angola five years from now or twenty years from now. But demand for oil and gas may have by then faced its own inflec-tion point. The current onshore shales—shales of increasing efficiency and decreasing unit costs—could join production from existing wells and the usual low-cost Middle East sources to provide the reasonably priced hydrocarbons the world wants.

LOOKING AT THE SHALE REVOLUTION from a financial perspective is important for another reason besides helping us decipher Christensenian or Tolstoyan causes in an effort to make sensible investments: the wealth created in that financial history is also part of the boom's tally of costs, gains, curses, and gifts. Economists argue over the long-term, nationwide impact of the boom, as I talk about in Chapter 12. But it has had clear individual benefits, especially if you're American, besides allowing you to pay less to fly, drive, and heat your home.

You may not have been fortunate enough to get a $975 million divorce settlement—you should have been more thoughtful in whom you unhappily married—but you got some portion of the boom's two trillion dollars in new wealth if the mutual fund in your 401(k) account was invested in the right oil and gas stocks. If the pension fund of your city's police officers was invested with well-positioned energy investors in the Golden Decade, those pension funds, all things being equal, are in better shape than those that weren't—and are less likely to call municipal budgets away from schools or parks. Your alma mater has almost certainly been able to build a new lab or offer more scholarships (or maybe, with current values, construct another indoor rock climbing wall or frozen yogurt buffet) given how much wealth was generated for endowments and charitable foundations in the boom. Indeed, if the boom's benefits can ever be precisely tallied, a surprisingly large amount will be found to have gone to American college endowments, who were early investors in "real assets" following the Yale Model pioneered by chief investment officer David Swensen. As a few endowment investors have told me, energy was the best asset class for their endowments for a decade.

Yet in dorm rooms far from the endowment offices and climbing walls and new labs, vocal bands of students are urging their colleges to divest from the oil and gas business altogether. They argue that the financial wealth from the boom—from fossil fuel investing in general—is bloodstained.

The financial perspective on the shale revolution may be important, they claim (although few might claim that), but a global perspective—on how the boom affects climate change—is necessary to understand issues that will determine the fate of the world. On that, for certain, the kids have a point.

Part IV

THE GLOBAL PERSPECTIVE

10. WHEN RACHEL CARSON MEETS AL GORE

I'VE HEARD AND READ BOTH ENOUGH TO BE ABLE TO PARAPHRASE THE points and the passion.

Oil industry friends tell me that land and ocean temperatures haven't changed all that much in fifteen years despite the environmentalists' "models."[1] They tell me that the grand total of global warming in the last 130 years has been—no one disputes this—0.85 degree Celsius.[2] Despite life as we know it not ending, no scientific debate has been this moralized since Galileo. Why do environmentalists refuse to talk about the data rationally? What other purpose could they have in using the term "denial" other than to silence debate by comparing skeptics to Holocaust deniers? In what normal scientific world did their predictions, built on computer models highly sensitive to infinitesimal changes in inputs, become such an impregnable consensus that either you "believe" in global warming or you don't?

Do you want to talk about denial, some friends in the industry ask. People are living safer and healthier lives than any time in the history of the world, with a large part of that increased standard of living due to the moral good of capitalism and the greater availability of energy. Environmentalists deny this. They see death in everyone's happiness and ghosts in every profit. Of course, global warming became an issue only after the Soviet Union fell.

Environmentalists have the luxury to scold because they are freeloading in the rich world that fossil fuels have created. Do they ever pause to thank the oil and gas industry for providing 56 percent of the world's energy? The coal industry for providing 30 percent?[3] Do they care that the energy industry allows a Chinese peasant, whose parents starved under Mao, to truck his food to market? Do they care that cleaner modern hospitals and greater wealth have reduced the world's infant mortality rate by half in twenty years?[4]

If the oil industry allows environmentalists' sentimental, self-righteous calls for less energy and less consumption to win, billions of people will be worse off. But not the environmentalists—of course not them, in their Pacific Heights mansions, aboard their private jets, thinking they're fooling people because they drive an electric BMW. The reason environmentalists have to call the oil industry evil is the only other option they have is to call evil everyone who flies, drives, uses plastics, receives products from anywhere but their own private potato patch. The moment they face the fact that oil and gas companies sell oil and gas because people want to use oil and gas, that there is no separate morality of buying and selling, their entire edifice of propaganda crashes. That's the moment that terrifies them because that's when people will stop donating to their organizations. And self-preservation through hate-raised dollars is the whole point of their campaigns anyway . . .

These lectures pain me for their twisted arguments, their bitter theses, their avoidance of the main issue—and their element of truth, the pebble in the shoe.

Then I listen to environmentalists. They tell me that the oil industry defines itself by its blindness and greed. How, they wonder, can engineers and geologists, who pride themselves on bringing empirical solutions to technical challenges, decide that climate change is the one topic in which a sign of brains is to disagree with almost every scientist who is studying the issue? Of course, there's no consensus on every input into every climate model, but the idea that stuffing the atmosphere with carbon, water vapor, and other particles traps in the sun's heat is not some "theory." It is the basic fact that prevents that heat from bouncing back into space. Without it, the earth's average temperature would be 2 degrees Fahrenheit.[5] Without it, none of us would be alive.[6] And climate change is not some theory from 1989. The first modern scientific paper on the influence on carbon dioxide on the atmosphere was presented in 1895.[7] The phenomenon was first theorized in 1824.[8]

A sentient person, environmentalists tell me, cannot dismiss the fact that the earth's temperature *is* hotter every year unless he is willfully denying it. What other words would you use? Well, the "genially unconvinced" see hurricanes, droughts, death, melting ice caps, dying coral, acidifying oceans and conclude—here's rational for you—that it's all a bunch of disconnected facts? That's *not* denial?

Oilmen wonder why no one thanks them for providing the world with energy. It's because no one can get in a word edgewise as they're too busy thanking themselves. Of course, these Mother Teresas extract fossil fuels solely for the good of humanity. It must have been for the good of humanity that they have also left a 150-year trail of spills, political manipulation, and warmongering. The world was able to live with that, actually. It affected only the people unlucky enough to live near their drilling rigs and pipelines (well, except for the warmongering). But they are not just killing Nigerians or poisoning Amazon tribes now. They are extracting the carbon that is killing the planet. The problem is not just that many of them seem too lazy, corrupt, or pig-headed to understand the basic facts of climate change. The problem is that the oil industry—ExxonMobil, the Koch brothers, and the rest—have been active propagandists to prevent others from understanding climate change.[9] They have sponsored front groups to spread misinformation. They lobby politicians to stop the legislation necessary to save the world.

That misinformation, the malevolent political influence are what turned the oil business from idiotic, greedy, truth-denying asses into enemies of the earth . . .

AND THEN THE SHALE REVOLUTION walked into this debate.

The new facts of previously unimaginable U.S. oil and gas production didn't alter the anger, exasperation, and cynicism on both sides. Nothing probably could. Yet the newfound abundance has altered the math of climate change. This part of the book and the next one, on the national perspective, broaden the view of the boom from its direct industrial, local environmental, and financial histories to see how it is altering the global environment, economy, and power of nations. From a global perspective, the U.S. gas boom has given birth to the possibility of unprecedented common cause between environmentalists and the oil business. Natural gas can and is displacing coal, which emits twice as much carbon dioxide for the same amount of fuel. Acceleration of this displacement may be one of the most practical weapons to reduce carbon dioxide emissions that the world has.

The leaping production of U.S. shale oil and gas has also lowered the price of oil and gas of all types. This is extending the era—and stimulating the use—of fossil fuels, with potentially disastrous consequences. Can environmentalists and oil industry advocates stand together for gas consumption while accepting the divide on the larger issue of fossil fuel use? Some are contemptuous of the effort. Others are trying—I am trying—to hold two contradictory ideas simultaneously in our minds.

DETAILING MY CONCLUSIONS AND BIASES on climate change could swallow the book, which is after all about the shale revolution. But candor about my premises is necessary before I discuss the issues.

First, I believe the scientific consensus that climate change is happening now because of fossil fuels. The evidence for yet more changes is overwhelming. Climate change is a serious threat to human life. While I am more hopeful than most environmentalists that we can address these issues with technology, efficiency gains, and a cleaner energy mix, I believe that continuing to consume energy as we do will have terrifying effects over the coming decades.

Second, I am not a one-man oil industry freak show. From my experience, most but not all people in the oil business divide into two camps on climate change. One camp, whose voice I tried to capture above, is deeply convinced that climate change is liberal hype. Climate change is not happening or, in the much more frequent argument, has consequences much less harmful than claimed. The other camp, like many outside the oil industry, don't think a lot about climate change at all. No one has counted the relative proportion in each camp, although the donations to politicians with fervently anti-regulatory agendas probably come from the most passionate climate change skeptics, not from every oil industry professional as a tithe.

There are, however, other points of view in the business. A few oil companies, from giants like Statoil to private businesses like Imaginea, a Canadian oil company run by a friend, put environmental responsibility at the center of their business models and try both to limit the direct impact of oil and gas drilling on the local environment and to minimize unnecessary carbon emissions (such as through reduced gas flaring). Almost all Big Oil companies also now officially "accept" man-made climate change, whether for PR purposes or from corporate changes of heart. This doesn't mean that all of their employees share every opinion of every corporate environmental statement. Some do, for sure. But many employees are probably just as indifferent or just as passionately skeptical as others in the business. The corporate stances do, however, mean that major oil companies are no longer the institutional funders of disreputable propaganda as they once were.

Steve Coll's *Private Empire* charts the fascinating evolution at Exxon-Mobil on the issue. In 1997, in a representative example, Lee Raymond delivered a speech to the World Petroleum Congress in which he argued that "the case for so called global warming is far from air tight," questioning whether burning fossil fuels is the cause of global warming and whether global warming is happening at all.[10] Fourteen years later, Raymond's successor as CEO, Rex Tillerson, had a Nixon-in-China moment when he acknowledged the risks of man-made climate change and expressed support for carbon taxes. It's still not clear to me whether that support was strategic or sincere.

Finally, I believe that providing energy to the people of the world is an equally just cause to fighting climate change. In energy use debates, it is entertaining to mock air-conditioning empty wings of American mansions to keep the houseplants comfortable and driving a 5,500-pound Escalade to drop off a 55-pound child at school. It's easier to gloss over the more difficult challenge: how can we get energy to those who need it more? The world has over 7 billion people, 2.2 billion of whom live on less than $2 per day.[11] Over 1.3 billion people don't have access to electricity, and 2.6 billion don't have access to clean cooking facilities.[12] Filipinos consume one-tenth of the energy per capita of the environmentally conscious Dutch. Bangladeshis consume one half of the energy of Filipinos.[13]

More people deserve more energy. And fossil fuels are tremendously powerful, portable, efficient sources of it. A semi-trailer using a single gallon of diesel can carry 45,000 pounds of cargo and 35,000 pounds of itself six miles in six or seven minutes. If you were a Tom Sawyer who could recruit friends to help carry the 22.5 tons of cargo in a world without oil or trucks, you'd have to convince 900 of them how fun it would be to lug 50 pounds each on a two-hour walk.

The fight against climate change and the fight to improve the living standards of the world's poor are the two biggest challenges of our time. On my more self-loving days, I remind myself that I'm part of the solution to one of those. But I can't ignore that if climate change is as bad as the worst-case scenarios, I will have, yes, collaborated with an apocalypse caused by fossil fuels. This makes me uneasy many nights. Some nights, I don't think I can take that collaboration any more. I wake up seized, in my whole body, by the need to do something—anything—else.

But, for many reasons, I haven't yet quit.

How do I live with myself? The same way I put on socks made in a sweatshop in Vietnam or eat an unhappy, unloved chicken slaughtered by an unhappy, underpaid illegal immigrant in Iowa. Most of the time, I don't think about it.

OF ALL THE ODD THINGS Aubrey McClendon did with his money, the oddest surely had to be his $56 million pledge to the Sierra Club.

As recounted in Russell Gold's *The Boom*, one of the essential histories of the shale revolution, Aubrey formed an alliance in 2007 with Carl Pope, then in his fifteenth year as the head of America's most famous environmental organization. While the alliance was public—Pope and Aubrey made appearances together nationwide—Pope didn't tell the Sierra Club's board of Aubrey's enormous donation to its "Beyond Coal" campaign.[14] It boggles the mind how Pope managed to keep that pledge secret for three years given that, starting in 2008, Aubrey's donations represented 12 percent of all of the donations made to the club.[15] When the board found out that the club's secret admirer was the King of the Frackers, it told Aubrey he could keep his final $30 million. That may have been good news for Aubrey, much less rich in 2011 than he was in 2007. Carl Pope got off less easily. By late 2011, the club's board informed him that he would need, according to Gold, to "cut all ties with the organization that had been his home for eighteen years."[16]

Pope has no regrets. He told Gold, "I think Aubrey McClendon will undoubtedly turn out to be one of the major contributors to giving the world a shot at protecting the climate."[17]

I have no idea what Aubrey thinks about climate change. For his donation came not for the reason one usually supports the Sierra Club (i.e., one agrees with the mission of the Sierra Club), but because he was trying to increase demand for U.S. natural gas.[18] Chesapeake, by then, was America's largest gas producer. If Aubrey could have increased gas demand by promoting flaming bursts of methane on the Fourth of July, he probably would have launched a front group to lobby against unpatriotic fireworks and their "Asian technology."

In 2014 in the United States, one-third of the gas consumed was used by power plants to generate electricity. A slightly higher amount was burned to heat homes and offices. A slightly lower amount was used for industrial use, such as fuel to manufacture glass or as a direct feedstock to make plastics and fertilizers. Transportation here consumes an insignificant amount of gas, mainly in gas-powered buses and other fleet vehicles but also in a few cars owned by half-crazy–half-brilliant guys who also, for convenience, wear the same blue outfit every day.

For gas producers hoping for higher demand for their products, U.S. industrial, residential, and vehicle use is growing at a frustratingly slow pace, when it is growing at all. People are predicting an acceleration of gas demand with cheaper gas. (Environmentalists can snicker that residential and commercial gas demand won't go up much if global warming continues, as America consumes almost 50 percent more gas in winter months than in the summer.)[19] But a surge in U.S. gas demand hasn't happened yet; a lot of sources of gas demand grow only as fast as the economy allows.

The three demand sources that make gas producers' mouth water with possibilities of higher sales and potential higher prices are more use by the chemical industry, more liquefied natural gas exports, and higher consumption by power plants. There are two particular reasons for enthusiasm for the last source. Gas-fired power plants tend to be used, for technical reasons, at peak times when an area needs more electricity. In 2012, U.S. gas-fueled generators, operating part-time, produced only 29 percent of the power they could have at theoretical full capacity.[20]

Also, as Aubrey recognized, advocating for gas to increase market share against the country's most common fuel used in electricity generation is like arguing for Tax Free 2016. We in the oil and gas business are thankful daily that we generally have a better public reputation than the hill-dwelling, mountain-destroying, miner-killing, union-busting, dust-spewing, river-poisoning, Mitch McConnell–loving executives of the American coal business. Natural gas's killer app is electricity generation. To generate the same amount of energy as bituminous coal, natural gas emits only 57 percent of the carbon dioxide.[21] Fifteen years ago, an electric utility might have congratulated gas for being so clean but would have done little about it. What utility would want to pay more for—and be dependent on—imported gas from Qatar when it could use a cheaper, more stable, more secure fuel from West Virginia or Wyoming?

Then came Mitchell Energy's breakthrough. Within ten years, the United States had developed an oversupply of gas. Utilities responded. In 2005, coal fueled 50 percent of electricity generation, and gas accounted for 19 percent; ten years later, coal fueled 39 percent and gas 27 percent.[22] This was not a function of an individual power plant switching between two different sources of fuel, like getting beer from the Bud Light tap instead of the one for Miller Lite. Older coal-fired power plants were shut down, or used less, and utilities in aggregate constructed new gas-fired plants or generated more electricity from existing ones. Increased gas use has reduced coal use in a flat market: for all the American obsession with electronic gadgetry, with the dead nowadays probably being outfitted with Fitbits to measure their vitals in the afterlife, the United States consumes roughly the same amount of electricity as it did a decade ago.

The shutdown of coal-fired plants was not always an immediate capitulation to the superiority of gas. The Sierra Club's "Beyond Coal" campaign, originally supported by Aubrey and now funded in large part by Michael Bloomberg, coordinated local coalitions, often including corporate energy consumers, to block construction of coal-fired power plants and convince utilities to retire older plants or not retrofit them. The campaign marshaled a mix of arguments, from local air quality concerns to climate change to the fact that investing in coal plants to meet clean air regulations would lead to higher energy prices.[23]

Through the combination of gas gaining market share on price and the opposition to coal on local and global environmental concerns, the United States used 17 percent less coal in 2014 than in 2004.[24] In April 2012, perhaps in an unwitting nod to Earth Day, we consumed less coal than in any month since May 1981, when there were 84 million fewer Americans.[25]

I'VE FOUND THAT THESE FACTS, one of the most startling good news stories of the shale revolution, are not widely understood. Bike-or-Vespa Eurosnobs still consider the United States to be the big outlaw of climate change. And indeed, the United States of pickup trucks and politicians who see climate treaties as plots for World Socialism emitted 15 percent of the world's carbon dioxide in 2013, according to the Global Carbon Atlas—three and a half times its share of the global population.[26]

However, in 2012, a year of plunging natural gas prices, a year of an 11 percent fall in U.S. coal consumption (the second steepest fall in recorded history),[27] the United States reduced its carbon dioxide emissions by over 12 percent from 2007 levels. There was a 25 percent fall in coal-related emissions in those years. While U.S. emissions rebounded by 3 percent in 2013, the five-year reduction in U.S. carbon dioxide emissions by 2012 was 725 million metric tons. This is equivalent to a year's *total* emissions from Germany, the sixth largest CO_2 emitter in the world. [28] To the atmosphere, it's as if Germans powered all their pretzel bakeries and Audi station wagon factories with nothing but wind and good intentions.

Equally mind-bending, sixty-two other countries experienced emission drops from 2007 to 2012. The United States' reduction was 18 percent higher than the drop from all of those other countries combined. In other words, in those five years the consequences of the shale revolution and the United States' reduced use of coal effectively matched the carbon emissions reduction from every other effort by every other country successful at reducing emissions at all.[29] This data is even more impressive considering that the U.S. economy, for all the draggy pace of its recovery, was 2 percent larger in 2012 than it was in 2007.[30] Italy, which had the second largest drop in carbon emissions, achieved its reduction grimly, with an economy 7 percent smaller than five years earlier.[31]

Even before the reduction in U.S. carbon dioxide emissions became clear, a celebration of the global climate possibilities of shale gas forged strange alliances. Aubrey McClendon and Carl Pope made their secret pact. In a famous 2009 *Financial Times* op-ed, Robert F. Kennedy Jr., one of the country's leading environmentalists, declared, "Converting rapidly from coal-generated energy to gas is President Barack Obama's most obvious first step towards saving our planet and jump-starting our economy."[32] Kennedy's essay was the first in which I saw the term "bridge fuel" to describe how gas could ease us from a "deadly coal addiction" to a future of renewable energy.

From a political point of view far from a Kennedy's, octogenarian corporate-raider-hedge-fund-manager-oilman T. Boone Pickens also championed wind energy and natural gas as the twin fuels of the future. (Boone, the Aubrey of the Eighties, couldn't help calling his brilliant idea the Pickens Plan.) Pickens, a Republican who had once donated $2 million to the anti–John Kerry Swift Boat group,[33] lauded gas as a particularly ideal companion to renewable energy sources because of how gas-fired power plants work. [34] Solar needs the sun. Wind, as advertised, needs wind. But we need predictable and scalable sources that can produce power during dead air at midnight. Coal-fired and nuclear plants are horrible for this. They need to be run constantly to work effectively (with the most complications at nuclear plants, as stopping them involves stopping nuclear reactions). New gas-fired power plants, which are also cheaper to build than coal or nuclear plants, have quick-start turbines, using technology derived from jet engines. These "aero" turbines can launch, like an engine, multiple times per day to provide electricity at high-use times and to compensate for—and complement—the intermittency of solar and wind. Some gas-fired peaker plants run for only 400 hours or so per year.[35]

Over the last few years, the facts on natural gas became so encouraging, almost unbelievably so, with a checkmark by every virtue of abundant, relatively clean, cheap, geopolitically safe, solar- and wind-friendly, that many in the oil and gas business caught the bug. Aubrey launched a pro-gas advocacy group called the American Clean Skies Foundation,[36] a name as hard to oppose as the American Puppies for World Peace and Ice Cream Foundation. Some of my friends in the oil business embraced gas as a clean fuel without completely abandoning their belief that climate change concerns were lefty hype. Sure, coal has other problems besides causing climate change, such as the pollution from large particulate matter, but it was amusing to watch my friends' advocacy of natural gas fit into an I'm-100-percent-not-guilty-of-what-you-accuse-me-of-but-I'm-doing-less-of-what-I'm-100-percent-not-guilty-of-anyway argument.

The NFL follows the same mental-moral twists to respond to its concussion-focused critics.

I also use the line at home, about pretty much everything.

An early lesson I learned in the oil business was to never expect the ambivalent public to thank you for the products you provide, no matter how necessary they are to people's lives. But as shale gas production started to displace coal, I felt for the first time in my career firmly on the side of the angels. I was so excited about being a liberal oilman—a gasman—without remorse that my imagination got carried away. I wondered when RFK Jr. was going to invite me to some star-studded Gala for Gas, at which my tablemate Angelina Jolie would be awestruck by yours truly for saving the world.

Yes, Angelina, it is hard work, but I do it for the children.

Then came *Gasland* and the *New York Times*'s "Drilling Down" series, and my fantasies of some enduring green-and-black, environmentalist-and-industry alliance collapsed. The evils of fracking took center stage. Carl Pope was defrocked. Boone faded from the spotlight. By 2013, Kennedy was calling once planet-saving natural gas a "disaster" and a "catastrophe." He added that even if gas is better for the climate than coal, its other problems, especially the local impacts of gas drilling, made it "untenable."[37]

Kennedy represented the majority view among environmentalists, from what I observed. Shale gas confronted them with an inherent tension between what I think of as Al Gore Environmentalism (against climate change) and 1970s-style Rachel Carson Environmentalism (against local pollution). This conflict, at least, was decided firmly in favor of Rachel Carson. Perhaps environmental movements, like any movements, need the oxygen of public response. By 2010, anti-fracking local protests were generating life-and-death rhetoric with a straightforward message and achievable plan. Texas oilmen were coming to poison our water. All we needed to do was convince the governor to keep out their rigs.

This was a different exigency than what was howled by many climate change activists: that the world's population must make almost unimaginable changes in how it orders its economy and in its existing modes and use of transportation, power, and heat. The Boulder City Council couldn't pass an ordinance to achieve that.

IN 2011, THREE CORNELL PROFESSORS brought to national prominence an issue that, they argued, put an end to my industry's—and my—claims of virtue. Sure, the reduction in carbon dioxide emissions that came from switching from coal to gas in power plants was real. But the professors, Robert Howarth, Renee Santoro, and Anthony Ingraffea, claimed that gas advocates ignored another greenhouse gas, methane. The professors brought together uncontroversial facts—that methane is the primary component of natural gas, that some methane leaks before gas reaches end users, and that methane has potent atmospheric warming characteristics—with calculations to conclude that so much methane leaks in gas drilling, completion, processing, transportation, and storage that natural gas was not only *not* an improvement over coal, it might in fact be worse.

It took me a while to process how central leaking would become in the environmental movement, primarily due to my skepticism of any anti-drilling arguments emerging from my alma mater. Ithaca is a famously liberal city. (When I lived there, the mayor was a member of the Democratic Socialists of America.)[38] As a border town close to Pennsylvania shale gas drilling, Ithaca had become a—if not the—capital of anti-fracking. The methane leakage argument had its roots in anti-fracking activism. Robert Howarth told *Philanthropy* magazine that "he had been approached by the Park Foundation in 2010 to consider writing an academic article that would make a case that shale gas was a dangerous, polluting fuel."[39]

I was also skeptical because of the timing of the leakage issue. In 2011, conclusive examples of *Gasland's* mass water pollution fears had still not been found. That year, a presidential commission, with thoughtful suggestions on how air, water, land, and communities could better be protected in the shale gas revolution it still supported, disappointed environmentalists by concluding, like the EPA would four years later, that it could find "few, if any, documented examples" of frack fluids contaminating the groundwater.[40] And then shale opponents came up with a completely different reason to oppose drilling, one technically much harder to disprove. Leaking became the new fracking.

The energy industry, of course, didn't issue a capitulating press release: "Oh, Man, We Forgot About Methane and Gas Isn't Actually That Good." It fought back with other data.

The arguments on both sides are tough to penetrate; there are multiple areas of honest disagreement and interpretative contention that require knowledge of molecular chemistry that does not come if, theoretically speaking, you spent the last three of your own four years in Ithaca crowing about how easily you filled your science requirements with Astronomy 101 and 102.

According to the EPA, methane accounts for one-tenth of all U.S. greenhouse gas emissions, with natural gas and petroleum systems responsible for a third or so of that methane.[41] (Agriculture emits about the same amount, with "agriculture" the euphemistic way of describing primarily pig burps, cow farts, and shit piles. How they measure those, I do not want to know.) Coal use accounts for about 26 percent of all U.S. greenhouse gas emissions, primarily in the form of carbon dioxide.[42] And so if methane traps significantly more heat as a greenhouse gas than carbon dioxide, then even a small amount of incremental methane in the atmosphere could offset the benefits of burning less coal.

The first controversy is over how much methane actually leaks. Numbers from each new study ping-pong across the possible. The default understanding was from the Environmental Protection Agency, which had concluded that methane leakage from all U.S. "natural gas and petroleum systems" was only 1.5 percent.[43] The Cornell professors made national news with the claim that 3.6 to 7.9 percent of methane produced over the lifetime of a well leaked during extraction and transportation, from drilling to delivery.[44] At those levels, they concluded, the impact of natural gas's greenhouse gas emissions was 20 percent worse and "perhaps more than twice as great" as coal's over a twenty-year horizon. They also argued that shale gas wells were indeed something new, more prone to "fugitive" methane than conventional gas wells for two reasons: gas can leak between frack stages; and, more important, previously unaccounted for gas comes back to the surface along with the frack fluid flowback. When the liquid is disposed of in ponds and pits, the gas is released into the atmosphere. (It'd be like the carbon dioxide slowly bubbling out of a Pepsi when you pour it into a glass.) Other studies would come out supporting Howarth, Ingraffea, and Santoro's ranges—or with more frightening estimates. A 2014 study based on airborne surveys calculated natural gas leak rates of 3 to 17 percent in southwestern Pennsylvania.[45]

For many years, the studies were based on extrapolation or distant measurements. In 2013, University of Texas scientists under the sponsorship of the mainstream Environmental Defense Fund released the first comprehensive empirical study of methane leakage from gas drilling. After visiting 190 production sites across the country, the scientists estimated that 0.42 percent of methane leaks on average from the drilling and completion process.[46] This was slightly lower than the EPA's 2011 estimate of

0.47 percent from these activities, and the study's authors concluded that the EPA's 1.5 percent leakage estimate across the entire natural gas system seemed a generally reasonable estimate—and capable of being reduced further.[47] Unsurprisingly, Anthony Ingraffea scoffed at the "fatally flawed" UT study.[48] I'm sure he privately assumed that asking permission from Pioneer or Southwestern to study how much gas they leaked was like asking Bernie Madoff for your account statement.

Even if the sides could agree on the exact level of leakage, they offer highly variable estimates of how bad methane is relative to carbon dioxide and the maximum leakage below which gas would still be better for the climate than coal. Scientists form their estimates around assumptions that, one assumes, have facts: the weight of methane versus carbon dioxide molecules; how much relative heat the molecules trap; the duration of methane's residency in the atmosphere. Methane dissipates in about a dozen years; carbon dioxide, the atmosphere's worst houseguest, sticks around for thousands.[49] Some comparisons also seem to account for methane emissions from coal mining (about one-third of that from natural gas systems); others seem not to. With all these inputs, we have crazily dispersed outputs. The World Resources Institute claimed that even 1 percent leakage offsets gas's benefits.[50] Andrew Revkin of *The New York Times*, adjudicating the claims, cited the conclusion of Richard Muller, a Berkeley physicist and leading climate change scientist, that it would be "acceptable (although not good) to have *10 percent* leak."[51]

Finally, the sides argue over whether methane leakage is a growing or shrinking problem. Anti-shale activists argue that the boom in gas drilling will be a boom in gas leakage, aggravating global warming. The industry counters that data from the EPA (not a source it's in the habit of citing) shows that methane released in the United States has been steadily *declining* since at least 1990—10 percent alone from 2003 to 2013, 23 percent more than the decline rate of carbon dioxide emissions.[52] Methane emissions from natural gas and petroleum systems fell by over 4 percent during that period, a time when U.S. gas production rose by 32 percent.[53]

The oil and gas industry also points out that methane leakage will continue to decline. Partly in response to political pressure from environ-mentalists, the Obama administration implemented a comprehensive strategy to reduce methane emissions from all sources.[54] (Republicans pushed back on regulations of one of those sources, and cow methane emissions were excluded from certain data-gathering requirements, a victory for freedom and flatulence everywhere.)[55] On natural gas methane emissions, a rule issued by the Obama EPA in 2012 went into effect at the start of 2015. Operators must now stop releasing methane into the atmosphere during the drilling process by either using "green completions," in which off-the-shelf equipment separates gas from the frack flowback, or controlled flaring to convert methane into carbon dioxide and water.[56] (Gas flaring represented only 0.2 percent of total U.S. carbon dioxide emissions in 2013.)[57]

For all the industry bellyaching about what a friend calls Obama's War on Oil, I have come across astonishingly few industry complaints about these new regulations. Green completions may be a case in which self-interest and globe-interest merge. For the government demanding that pipelines, storage tanks, or frack flowback processes leak less, for the public good, is like the FDA forcing Dunkin' Donuts to better lock up its Chocolate Frosteds so donut thieves don't get fat. Capturing and selling methane is, after all, the whole point of drilling a gas well. In 2014, Devon Energy boasted that it had exclusively used green completions since 2004—well before any regulations. From capturing gas in 4,000 wells, Devon sold 25 billion cubic feet of gas that it would have otherwise lost.[58] That gas, by my calculations, was worth around $140 million over that time excluding the unquantifiable benefit to Devon's corporate image. That $140 million wasn't all profit, as a company needed to rent equipment to capture the methane. But that equipment is readily available, costing about $1,000 per day per well.[59]

The industry will be able to meet new methane reduction standards. In almost all cases, according to science writer Charles Mann, complying with new regulations is less onerous than forecast and comes with more unexpected benefits. (The most famous energy sector example is the cap-and-trade system to fight acid rain, passed into law in 1990 with bipartisan support.)[60] The Environmental Defense Fund, which is leading the globally important work to reduce natural gas methane leakage to below 1 percent system-wide, estimates that 40 percent of the projects to capture methane at the well site will generate a positive return on capital.[61] I suspect that that estimate will prove conservative.

Perhaps predictably, I strongly agree with the arguments that the most comprehensive empirical methane leakage data concludes that it's a much smaller current problem than the Cornell scientists contend. I also believe that corporate self-interest and new regulations will make it a smaller problem still. As I talked about in Chapter 6, the negative environmental impacts of shale development, with solutions and best practices available to all, are being better addressed by the year. The tango of the industry and its critics works.

And yet, as of this writing, only one-third of the EDF's sponsored studies on methane leakage have been published.[62] Other studies may prove a higher level of leakage at other points in the gas supply chain. If the science becomes definitive that the increased use of natural gas is not reducing greenhouse gas emissions, the final balance of my judgment on the shale revolution would become unsettled. One of the boom's most beneficial consequences would have been a mirage, and one of the world's easiest and most practical strategies for reducing greenhouse gas emissions—one already working—would be lethally flawed.

THERE IS ANOTHER POTENTIAL MIRAGE: was the displacement of coal by shale gas only temporary? The near record 11 percent drop in U.S. coal consumption in 2012, which reduced total U.S. emissions that year by 4 percent, turned out to be fleeting. Coal consumption rose 4 percent in 2013 before declining again by only 1 percent in 2014.[63] (Gas consumption rose 2.5 percent per year over that time.) While there were a few reasons for that increased coal use, including the where's-your-global-warming-now-hippie Polar Vortex winter of 2013–2014, it became clear that electric utilities didn't use more gas in 2012 because it was virtuous. They used it because it was cheap. As the price of gas rose by 30 percent in 2013, electrical utilities' switching from gas to coal stopped.

To reaccelerate the decline in coal consumption, we will first need gas prices to remain low, relatively speaking, against coal. This seems achievable: a decade into the gas boom, technology and applied experience are still lowering unit costs. Even more supply will be stimulated by the construction of large pipeline systems to export gas from Pennsylvania, Ohio, and West Virginia, home of the most productive shale gas basins. In the first half of 2015, gas prices were only 14 percent higher than they were during the first half of 2012 when switching from coal gathered pace.[64] Coal prices, on the other hand, seemed to have reached a practical floor, as their current level seems to be giving coal companies the two-poled choice of fighting bankruptcy or being bankrupt. In early 2015, U.S. coal use started falling again.[65]

Encouraging a further decline in coal consumption may also require further regulation or coordinated social pressure and activism, the logic of Aubrey's alliance with the Sierra Club. As I talk about in the next chapter, tougher regulations against utilities burning coal have already been proposed. I'm not alone in the oil and gas industry in quietly, or openly, wishing for these regulations to be fully implemented. While oilmen believe that government meddling in the energy business is as productive as hiring a deaf man to tune your piano, when it comes to regulating coal, well, if you must . . .

BUT METHANE LEAKAGE or short-term market share skirmishes between coal and gas should not distract us from the larger issue, or the larger accomplishment: the United States has led the world in carbon dioxide emissions reduction because of shale gas. This has been an unexpected, outrageously important gift to the world, with an opportunity to become even more important because shale gas is the ideal companion to intermittent wind and solar power sources.

Without reducing coal-fired power emissions, there seems to be little hope of containing total carbon dioxide emissions and avert some of the worst scenarios of climate change. We must fervently, quickly capture the most climate benefits possible from shale gas, by increasing its use, by decreasing methane leaks. For there is another global impact of the boom. Even some of the denyingest climate change deniers call attention to the pollution-reducing benefits of the shale revolution's natural gas. But the revolution isn't likely to reduce the world's consumption of oil—or the emissions from it. The opposite, in fact, is true.

11. ON TO ALL OF THE ABOVE

IN FEBRUARY 2014, A FAMOUS NEW YORK INTELLECTUAL WROTE TO ME, "From your letter, I gather that the techniques used for fracking are now being applied to oil exploration and exploitation. I think few readers [of a magazine we were discussing] are aware of this, since fracking is usually associated with natural gas." I read his short paragraph twice, in disbelief. That month, 78 percent of all rigs working in the United States were drilling oil wells, rather than gas wells. (Ten years earlier, it had been 15 percent.)[1] Almost all of those wells were fracked. That month, because of fracking, North Dakota was already producing twice as much oil as Alaska—and more than the entire U.K.[2]

My disbelief was not that he didn't know those facts. He wasn't supposed to be an expert on oil production data. My disbelief wasn't even that gas still had a grip on the popular conception of fracking. I understood the history: the boom had happened in gas first; for many opponents of shale drilling, *Gasland*, its concerns clear in its title, set the tone; gas drilling, to New Yorkers, was what was happening nearby.

No, my disbelief at "few readers are aware of this" was that the man writing me, someone skeptical of the shale revolution, would ignore his best arguments for that skepticism: that not only is fracking no longer "associated" with just natural gas but it is much more often used to extract oil; and that, with one nuance, there are no environmental benefits of the increased supply of shale oil. By making oil more abundant and cheaper, the shale revolution will likely lead to more oil use. And that is making the world's other strategies to fight climate change more difficult and urgent.

THE LEFT-WING YURT DIVISION of the peak oil crowd, whose public prominence itself peaked in 2008, predicted that the implosion of our contemporary lifestyle would come equally by climate change and by the world running out of affordable oil. To my ears, they seemed more attached to describing the apocalypses from climate change, as they weren't the kind of people too attached to the luxuries of modern life, like hot showers. But the peakers didn't have to choose. The planet would right-hook humankind by not producing enough oil, or it would left-hook it with cascading disasters from warming. Either way we were going to get punched in the face.

Six years later, when the true abundance of oil became clear with the price plunge of 2014, the bout was different. At some point, we may run out of oil producible at reasonable prices, but the shale revolution has pushed back that date. Indeed, I suspect that an era of meaningful oil scarcity, from an industrial perspective, will come well past when the worst effects of global warming will have taken their most severe toll. (A collapse of civilization would reduce the consumption of oil then, if anyone then still cared.)

Cheap and plentiful natural gas has obvious environmental benefits, presuming methane isn't worse than I now think. And in theory, oil could join gas in the better-than-coal club. Burning gasoline emits 24 percent less carbon than burning coal to produce the same amount of energy.[3] However, unlike coal and oil, the fate of coal and gas are twinned because they are used for the same purpose: generating electricity. Only 4 percent of the world's electricity comes from consuming oil and petroleum products, over a quarter of that in the Middle East.[4] In the United States, fuel oil consumption has fallen from 15 percent of total oil consumption in the 1970s to about 1.2 percent now—among the lowest percentages of oil consumed for electricity in the world.[5] Oil and coal consumption here have decoupled, with one for transportation and one for power, with two minor exceptions: small diesel generators; and, in a mixed picture for environmentalists, electric cars that, if they consume the average American watt, recharge with 39 percent of their electricity derived from coal.

In general, global oil use, which produces 31 percent of global carbon emissions, largely rises or falls independent of competition from other fuels. And the shale revolution will likely stimulate that use. People may not drive less because they're warming the planet by dropping Maddy off at kindergarten in an SUV. They will drive less, though, if gasoline is $7 per gallon. The opposite is also true: the drop in oil prices at the end of 2014, according to analysts at investment bank Barclays, could increase global oil consumption by around 0.4 percent.[6] Not all increased oil consumption is due to lower oil prices, but preliminary data from the first half of 2015 seem to confirm that estimate with oil consumption 1.7 percent higher than a year earlier, compared to a 0.7 percent growth rate in the first half of 2014.[7] Price-stimulated oil demand isn't even higher because consumers in only a few countries, the United States and India in particular, feel the direct impact of lower oil prices with petroleum products not enveloped in high taxes or high subsidies. (U.S. oil consumption increased 2.1 percent in the first half of 2015, compared to 0.5 percent the year before.) A 1 percent increase in oil consumption—and emissions—from lower prices isn't much, but it would translate into the world adding total emissions from another Kuwait or another Czech Republic.[8]

The 2014 drop in oil prices is also delaying a shift to more fuel efficient transportation. In 2014, the sales of traditional hybrids like Priuses declined by 9 percent from 2013 levels. Sales growth of plug-in hybrids and electric vehicles also decelerated, disappointing expectations.[9] And in early 2015, according to *The New York Times*, 22 percent of hybrid car owners switched at their next vehicle to buying a conventional SUV, "nearly double the rate of three years ago."[10]

I can see one day the loudest shouts against fracking being a campaign to, in effect, save the Prius by stopping the Permian. I am surprised that we aren't there yet.

THE TWO MOST PROMINENT environmental campaigns against oil, one opposing the Keystone XL oil pipeline and another encouraging the institutional divestment from fossil fuels, are not about fracking. But like everything in the oil business, the shale revolution has transformed the facts around these campaigns, especially the first.

The obsession with Keystone XL, a pipeline that would bring 830,000 barrels per day of oil from Western Canada to the U.S. Gulf Coast, is a classic example of what I call the WHIRR: the Washington-Houston Inverse Relevance Rule. Oil industry issues that enflame the rhetoric of Congress, the political press, and environmental movements, like drilling in the Arctic National Wildlife Refuge in Alaska, fracking in New York state, or even the Macondo oil spill, almost always have as much direct bearing on the daily lives of the vast majority of people in the U.S. oil industry as the popcorn in theaters in Memphis has on who is going to win the Academy Awards.

Environmentalists have seized on the opposition to Keystone as a central stand—for some, the central stand—in the global fight against climate change because the largest source of oil in Western Canada is the Athabasca oil sands. The most famous line of the world's most famous climate change scientist, NASA's James Hansen, is that burning all of the oil sands would be "game over for the climate."[11] Oil sands deposits are indeed massive, even if oil sands production accounted for only 2 percent of world's total oil supply in 2014.[12] Oil sands projects extract bitumen, a tarlike substance that doesn't flow naturally through wellbores, in one of two ways: open pit mining or injecting steam to liquefy the bitumen underground. That intense extraction process and the later refining of the oil sands into usable products like gasoline generates more carbon emissions than other sources of oil. Oil sands mining's large footprint (with the same ugliness of all types of mining) rankles opponents further.

Most people in the U.S. oil industry think that Keystone XL should be built. Some point out that Keystone is not the only export option for Canadian producers, nor is its blocking sufficient in and of itself enough to stop the oil sands. If the oil sands can be produced economically, the bitumen will be transported somehow, by rail or pipeline, to the east, south, or west. Other Keystone defenders cite a fact made prominent by energy consultancy IHS: that the "wheels to wheels" greenhouse gas emissions from consuming oil-sands-derived gasoline are, on average, only 11 percent more than using gasoline derived from other types of oil.[13] On average 70 to 80 percent of carbon emissions associated with driving come from, well, driving: a vehicle's tailpipe emissions from burning refined diesel or gasoline. That gasoline is the same whatever source of oil entered the refinery to make it. If Keystone replaced 4 percent of U.S. oil with an 11 percent more emitting source, U.S. carbon emissions would increase by only 0.5 percent from the oil sector and 0.2 percent overall.[14]

A few supporters of Keystone in the U.S. oil business have these arguments near at hand. But I've observed that U.S. industry support for Keystone is like a basketball player being in favor of fair refereeing at a hockey match: a matter of casual attitude rather than passionate self-interest. While Shell, ExxonMobil, and Devon Energy (of the green completions) have oil sands projects, most oil sands development is undertaken by specialized Canadian companies of marginal interest to the U.S. industry.

In 2013, I attended a meeting in Las Vegas of two dozen executives of small North American E&P companies. Most of the companies talked about what you'd expect: horizontal drilling in Pennsylvania, slickwater in West Texas. Then the talented CEO of a large private Canadian oil sands company detailed his challenges: the cost of building roads in the middle of nowhere, the need for facilities to inject steam in the reservoir, the complexity of drilling two horizontal wellbores, the billions of dollars that would eventually be required. The rest of the audience stared, drop-jawed, as if the CEO were describing the great new toothbrush he had just made from carving whalebone and hand-picking bristles from a horse.

Why didn't he just go to CVS?

Ten years ago, it was obvious to everyone in the oil business that the world needed large oil sands projects for decades to come. Today, those projects—the archetype of oil sources being disrupted by the shales—are being canceled and delayed. This began even before the 2014 oil price drop and sped up after it. In 2015, the official Canadian oil producers' association reduced its forecast for oil sands production in 2030 by 857,000 barrels per day—almost exactly the same volume as Keystone—compared to its 2014 forecast.[15] One market analyst cited the "whisper mill" that the Fort Hills oil sands project may be "the last of the multi-billion dollar megaprojects the industry ever builds."[16]

And what will replace that heavy oil from oil sands projects now being canceled? Fantastically light—in some rail cars, dangerously light—crude oil from North Dakota that emits less carbon when it is refined and demands a much smaller local footprint to extract. Of course, one could say that barrels from Iraq, in a fungible global market, are displacing those oil sands barrels just as much. But in a competition for dollars, for pipe space, for American refiners' attention, what seems to be stopping the oil sands is not the acolytes of environmentalist authors like Bill McKibben and Naomi Klein but the followers of Mark Papa and Harold Hamm.

THE ZEAL FOR STOPPING or promoting Keystone seemed to advance by inertia in 2014 and 2015. As the WHIRR turns, Keystone was often front-page news—some days, it still is—and U.S. senators and representatives, always fond of expressing their deepest seriousness with the shallowest symbols, congratulated themselves on passing or blocking bills for or against Keystone. I'm sure a few senators were equally fond of backing marginal causes pushed by nonmarginal donors.

But leading climate change activists like Bill McKibben, while not giving up on the fight against Keystone, have also recognized that stopping it won't stop global warming.[17] He has shifted his efforts to a broader campaign to lobby institutions to divest their pension funds and endowments from the oil and gas business, "the richest industry the world has ever known."[18]

McKibben's campaign, launched in a *Rolling Stone* article and led by the 350.org movement it inspired, rests on straightforward and worrisome math: to keep the planet from warming 2 degrees Celsius in total—it has, remember, risen 0.85 degree so far—humanity can put only 565 gigatons more carbon dioxide in the atmosphere.[19] This is roughly equivalent to what humans already have emitted since the Industrial Revolution.[20] Oil, gas, and coal companies—private corporations and state-owned ones—control reserves that would emit 2,795 gigatons if burned. Thus they must be stopped.

The 350.org movement argues that the best way to prevent the burning of those reserves is to make it morally unacceptable to extract oil, gas, and coal from the ground. "We need to take away their social license," McKibben writes, "turn them into pariahs, and make it clear they're to the planet's safety what the tobacco industry is to our individual health."[21] The movement seeks to repeat the accomplishments of the divestment campaign against apartheid-era South Africa, in which campus outrage begat Main Street moral repulsion. Some institutions, like Hampshire College and the Wallace Global Fund, have already divested from fossil fuels.[22]

I, among other things, like to live in human society, and being threatened with pariah-ism tends to focus my mind on the logical failures of those who threaten my sociability. Many of my defenses go beyond the story of the American energy renaissance, but two are relevant. First, the rhetoric of the 350.org movement sees the fossil fuel industry as a monolith, with no competition between companies, strategies, or fuels. Indeed, one would get the impression that we gather annually at the Richest Industry the World Has Ever Known Convention to beat house pets, enslave children, and encourage each other to emit even more CO_2. (For the record, energy represented 8 percent of the value of the S&P 500 index of America's largest companies as of June 30, 2015, behind health care, consumer staples, consumer discretionary products, and especially financial services (17 percent) and information technology (20 percent).[23] I suppose, though, that compared to the richest industry ever known that the "sixth largest sector of the economy" doesn't have the same ring.) But the energy business doesn't have uniform economic interests: oil sands producers and Bakken oil producers, natural gas companies and coal companies all compete to sell different stuff with varying carbon footprints. Ignoring the variance of their emissions will lead to lost opportunities, such as displacing coal.

McKibben's rhetoric is also strangely focused on Big Oil and the supposed evil of companies like ExxonMobil and Shell with the biggest reserves and perhaps the biggest lobbying budgets to fight regulation that will reduce fossil fuel consumption. However, because of the boom, Small Oil has taken the mantle of innovation and growth.

The larger tactical, and I think ethical, problem with the divestment campaign is the focus on supply rather than consumption. Drew Gilpin Faust, president of Harvard, put it best when the university declined to divest from fossil fuels: "I also find a troubling inconsistency in the notion that, as an investor, we should boycott a whole class of companies at the same time that, as individuals and as a community, we are extensively relying on those companies' products and services for so much of what we do every day."[24] It sometimes seems as if environmentalists believe that the oil industry's business is to make carbon dioxide. Our business is to make fuel. Carbon dioxide is the by-product, the vast majority of which is emitted when people consume our products—in "your" wheels, not "ours." Yes, I believe that there is a moral difference between making money by producing oil and spending money by consuming it. I do not dispute that climate change is more on my conscience than on others'. But that moral difference is subtle, subjective, and probably not of the gap between a pariah and someone with a social license (whoever issues those) to use plastic or drive to work. Most environmental activists are deeply committed to their cause and live, as they must, in a world dependent on fossil fuels. But an anti-oil activist flying to a well-lit divestment rally sometimes feels to us like a party boy, cocaine crumbs still on his nose, ranting that someone has to stop those Colombians.

McKibben's comparison of the divestment movement to anti-tobacco campaigns is revealing of the challenges his movement faces. Evilness of tobacco companies didn't stop my smoking after a one-month, mainly fake-inhaling experiment in an effort to be Italian and/or Kurt Cobain. I stopped smoking because it causes cancer and because it's not socially acceptable among my crowd to smoke. The anti-tobacco campaign was effective at reducing demand. The oil divestment movement is an attack on supply, like Prohibition or the War on Drugs. Supplier-targeted movements have been famously ineffective.

I suspect that the same may happen with the divestment campaign. Of course, the oil industry will continue to fight in the political arena any attempt to reduce the demand for its products. But the best protection of the demand for oil and gas is not John Boehner or James Inhofe: it is the demand. According to economic historian Gregory Clark, "Living standards in 1800, even in England, were likely no higher than for our ancestors of the African savannah."[25] But starting with the Industrial Revolution fueled by coal and continuing for two centuries of supplementing coal with oil and gas, humanity has built the world we know. And many people like the modern world: suburban homes are nice (and can be heated on the cheap); flying to places on vacation is nice (minus the actual experience of flying); eating oranges in January in Chicago is nice. Small earth environmentalists may not agree with any of these values or joys, but oil and gas companies are producing the basic energy without which contemporary life in the developed world is unimaginable. And more and more people on earth want that sort of life.

IN SOME WAYS, studying the U.S. oil and gas renaissance is crucial for understanding emission reduction strategies and climate change. The world, after the boom, will not stop using fossil fuels because it has to. It will now have to stop using fossil fuels because it wants to. But in other ways, the shale revolution is not defining the central questions or answers of climate change. Getting oil from the Eagle Ford instead of Ecuador does not alter the emissions coming out of a car in Encino. And producing more natural gas from Ohio instead of importing it from Algeria will not determine how you balance the right of a farmer in sub-Saharan Africa for electricity with the right of a Bangladeshi villager to not be threatened by a rising ocean.

Strategies to reduce fossil fuel demand fill libraries and debate halls. They are sensible and far-fetched, expensive and cheap, disruptive and easy: carbon taxes, gasoline taxes, cap-and-trade systems, more nuclear power, more subsidies for solar and wind, new technologies that increase energy efficiency, better adoption of the technologies we have. Why aren't these campaigns more visible than the banners calling for divestment? Probably for the same reason Rachel Carson Environmentalism trumped Al Gore Environmentalism when it came to fracking. Carson-style environmentalism can generate passions in defending visible and beloved neighborhoods from someone else's actions. The reduction of fossil fuel demand has no Other, no villains responsible for recklessly destroying the world. The executioner is us.

An environmental movement focused on reducing fossil fuel demand has a benefit, though: it's more likely to have an impact. People in the oil business don't stay up at night worried that Swarthmore is going to divest shares of BP. We stay up at night worried about everyone driving cheaper Teslas. This has been a long worry. Oil industry folks endlessly quote the line from Sheikh Yamani, the Saudi oil minister of the 1970s: "The Stone Age did not end for lack of stone, and the Oil Age will end long before the world runs out of oil."[26] We can easily see how our business ends. It is gradually happening in the developed world. Fossil fuel demand there is cyclical and weather-tossed; politics alter it; accidents like Fukushima cause unexpected reversals. But the decades of strategies to slow energy demand have been working. U.S. energy use in 2014, for instance, was at almost the same level as it was in 2000 and 2 percent below where it was in 2004.[27] Future strategies to limit fossil fuel demand in Europe, Japan, and the United States are already parked downhill.

And there is no evidence that the cheaper oil and gas prices arising from the shale revolution are halting the momentum of the world relying on more renewable energy sources. This has surprised people in the oil industry and the environmental movement. Many in the oil business believe that solar and wind are liberal charity cases, which can be competitive with fossil fuels only with state intervention or with fossil fuel prices much higher than they are now. Many environmentalists seem to agree. They have a preteen crush on high fossil fuel prices when they result from carbon taxes, as that revenue can be used to support renewable energy. However, they will take high oil prices however they can, as they've long been worried about the unsubsidized profitability of solar panels and wind turbines in a low energy price world.

They needn't have worried so much. From 2010 on, solar and wind, competing primarily against coal and gas to provide cheap electricity, have become more cost competitive in many geographies even as fossil fuel prices dramatically fell. Capitalism works, innovation occurs, globalization leads to less expensive stuff. (Environmentalists point out, rightly, that government support works, too, in the guiding hand in China, Europe, and the United States.) Solar panels, thanks to the oversupply that arose from feral Chinese capacity growth, are 70 percent cheaper than five years ago.[28] The cost of wind power has declined 90 percent in two decades and by a third from 2009 to 2013.[29]

THE DRIVERS OF global emissions reduction—U.S. shale gas, lower renewable costs, stagnant energy demand in the developed world—face their defining obstacle in the growing fossil fuel demand from India and especially China. In 1993, the United States emitted 23 percent of the world's carbon dioxide and China 13 percent. Two decades later, U.S. emissions have grown only 4 percent—and now account for 15 percent of the world's. China's emissions have grown three and a half times. Now almost double America's emissions, they represent a startling 29 percent of the world's total. India, the number three emitter in the world, has doubled its carbon emissions in twenty years.[30]

On the one hand, those emissions are a direct result of one of the most astounding leaps in the history of human happiness: the massive and swift rise of the Chinese and Indian middle class (as well as in Brazil, Russia, and other countries). Over 1.7 billion more people had access to electricity in 2010 than in 1990.[31] On the other hand, the emissions should scare the stuffing out of us. For much of that middle-class rise has been powered by coal, which represents 66 percent of China's primary energy consumption versus 18 percent in the United States and European Union.[32] Between 2005 and 2010, China's total power generation capacity doubled, with a new coal-fired power plant built every week or two.[33] Chinese carbon dioxide emissions from coal alone are now 37 percent higher than *all* of the emissions from the United States.[34]

Reducing demand for coal from China, India, and other emerging countries is the grand battle in the fight against climate change. There are no easy answers. For one, Europeans and Americans are not innocent of Chinese coal. We've outsourced manufacturing to the most coal-consuming economy on earth and have increased the emissions inherent in the toys, pants, computers—and solar panels—we own.

It's also hard to see China's or India's primary energy demand falling. Or anyone wanting it to. If energy demand in China falls, over the long term one of the two engines of an ocean-crossing jet that is the global economy will have dropped off the wing.

I BELIEVE THAT THE DIFFICULT (but necessary) global effort to reduce oil and coal demand should be joined by a supply fight to reduce emissions: not a fight *against* supply but a fight *with* supply. James Hansen has argued that for any global attempt to stabilize the climate to succeed, "the principal requirement is that coal emissions must be phased out by 2030 and unconventional fossil fuels, such as tar sands, must be left in the ground."[35] Nothing over the last decade, probably ever, has done more to limit coal emissions and keep tar sands—the Canadian oil sands, mainly—in the ground than the American shale revolution.

Now, I recognize that this fact is convenient for me, an often lonesome liberal oilman. I also understand that more fossil fuels aren't the ultimate answer if you're looking to reduce the demand for fossil fuels. I'm also well aware of environmentalists' practical difficulties in acknowledging that oil and gas companies can sometimes be an ally in constructing a bridge to a clean energy future. Carl Pope got hurled off the bridge.

Yet if we don't let the perfect be the enemy of the good, the purehearted the enemy of the accidentally effective, could the U.S. shale revolution alone eliminate coal emissions and leave the oil sands in the ground? The growth of the oil sands is dependent on the price producers get for bitumen. Making it more expensive for producers to get it to market, as is the aim of Keystone's opponents, may work. A simpler way to ensure lower potential prices for bitumen is to have lower prices for every type of oil. That is what happened in 2014. One can, for sure, forecast scenarios in which oil sands projects revive in five or ten years because of higher oil prices. But the single best thing that could happen to the oil sands today, twenty times better than Keystone's approval, the object of all the prayers of Fort McMurray, Alberta, would be a U.S. ban on frack-ing. Oil prices would skyrocket. The oil sands would be necessary again.

Reducing global coal consumption is a harder challenge. The oil sands provide 0.7 percent of the world's primary energy. Coal provides 30 percent.[36] But coal use is relatively contained: China consumes just over half of the world's coal, the United States 12 percent, and just five other countries 21 percent more.[37] Efforts to shrink coal consumption in the United States have already begun. The EPA's Mercury and Air Tox-ics Standards (MATS) rules, for instance, were issued in 2012, although the Supreme Court delayed their implementation in 2015. These rules, aimed not at climate change but at coal-associated mercury, arsenic, and other metals air pollution,[38] have already reduced emissions as utilities shut down coal-fired power plants and made other clean air investments well before the Supreme Court ruling.[39] The U.S. Government Ac-countability Office forecasts that with MATS and other regulations, 13 percent of all U.S. coal-fired power plants, as measured by generating capacity, will shut down between 2012 and 2025.[40]

Reducing coal consumption in the United States seems straightforward for other reasons. As much as environmentalists like to talk about King Coal and Big Coal—why doesn't anyone ever talk about Big Hardware or King Yogurt?—I'm often unsure if coal's opponents know how small the coal industry is. The market capitalization of the *entire* publicly traded U.S. coal industry on June 30, 2015, was just over $5 billion, roughly the size of Diamondback, the twentieth largest independent E&P company in the United States.[41]

I sometimes wonder why high-profile billionaire environmentalists now spending their money on lobbying to shut down coal-fired power plants (or Keystone) don't simply buy all the coal companies in America, restructure their debt, pension out their employees, and as Kevorkians of coal usher the industry to a gentle death.

Winding down the U.S. coal business will be heartbreaking, if it happens. Some of the poorest and hardest luck communities in America have already been devastated by the slowdown in coal production. (One mitigating factor: some coal communities are also Marcellus or Utica Shale communities.) But you could fit all 80,000 people who worked in the coal mining and support industries at the end of 2014 into a college football stadium. You would need a smaller stadium each successive month.[42] Yes, the practicalities of further regulating the coal industry became more difficult when coal's biggest friend, Kentucky's Mitch McConnell, became the Senate majority leader in 2015. But a nearly bankrupt industry employing about as many voters as there are in Kenosha County, Wisconsin will not have disproportionate power forever.

We couldn't shut down the coal business today, of course, without turning off 39 percent of our phones and lamps and episodes of *Game of Thrones*. But we can steadily reduce coal use in the United States because shale gas is a cheap, available alternative. The logistics and capital demands of increasing gas production, transporting it across the country, and situating gas-fired electrical generation capacity in the right places are daunting. New pipelines and power plants will have to be built. But this effort is underway with, for instance, a 6 percent projected increase in gas-fired power plant generating capacity through 2023, representing nearly half of all new capacity from renewable and non-renewable sources.[43] Even without those new power plants, two similar percentages remind us how possible increased gas consumption is. In 2014, America used on average only 29 percent of its theoretically available gas-fired power-generating capacity. And American gas producers at the end of 2014 were drilling with only 23 percent of the rigs they were at the start of 2009.[44]

China, as always, is a more difficult case. But here, too, the world has one advantage: coal is more visible and more disliked there than it is here. To Chinese leaders, the bigger problem than coal's climate change impact is its large particulate matter, which causes health hazards, global embarrassment, and (most unsettling to the country's leaders) protests from citizen anger over foul air. In November 2014, the Chinese cabinet announced that it would cap coal consumption in 2020 at 4.2 billion tons, a still terrifying number 17 percent higher than 2013 levels. But it is a limit.[45] And China may not even reach it: in 2014, Chinese coal consumption slightly declined.[46]

Accelerating the reduction of coal consumption in China will require an all-out global effort to provide China with the same attractive alternatives as the United States already has: solar, wind, nuclear, and plentiful natural gas. While China has almost twice the technically recoverable shale gas as the United States, it has had limited technical success to date in extracting it, as I touch on in the next chapter.[47] A radical change in productive capacity (and water availability) for Chinese shale gas efforts would have to occur to make a global climate or local air quality difference compared to what can be more quickly done if China simply imports gas from Australia, Qatar, Papua New Guinea, Russia—or Pennsylvania and South Texas. Encouraging China to invest even more money and research in its current global leadership in "clean coal" carbon capture and storage technologies, techniques that have been long on press releases but short on captured carbon, should also be unrelenting.[48]

ANYONE WITH KNOWLEDGE of American climate change policy will quickly point out that my suggestions, all delivered with a dash of intellectual daring, can be summarized another way: the official policy of the government of the United States during the Obama presidency. President Obama's "all-of-the-above" strategy on energy is similar to many of his other accomplishments: overflowing with policies that are as effective at improving the world as seemingly ineffective at pleasing anyone.

But as the McKibbens demanded that Obama kill Keystone and the McConnells protested that he was killing Kentucky, the administration carried out policies to reduce fossil-fuel-related emissions: requiring car fuel efficiency standards to increase from 35.5 miles per gallon in 2016 to 54.5 miles per gallon in 2025;[49] proposing rules beyond MATS to cut power sector carbon emissions by 30 percent in 2030 over 2005;[50] introducing requirements to reduce methane leakage further; and reaching the first ever agreement with China to stop the growth in carbon emissions by 2030.[51] This agreement with China cleared the path for the Lima Accord in late 2014, with most countries in the world agreeing to further voluntary emissions cuts (of, granted, undetermined magnitude), following the example of the world's two largest economies.[52] President Obama implemented many of these triumphs of Al Gore Environmentalism not through any new laws, but through EPA administrative actions authorized by the triumph of Rachel Carson Environmentalism, the Clean Air Act of 1970.[53]

Obama also included domestically produced oil and natural gas in his all-of-the-above strategy.[54] He quietly but firmly declined to regulate fracking nationally (except, of course, on federal lands) or to inhibit the expansion of the U.S. shale revolution.

Will Obama's policies make a difference? One can make the math work. Decelerating Chinese carbon emissions and falling emissions from America and Europe could lead the world to emit less than 565 gigatons of carbon and potentially keep the planet from warming another 1.2 degrees Celsius.[55] The abundant natural gas from the shale revolution that is already lowering U.S. emissions would play a central, although not exclusive, role in that effort. One can also, heart in throat, make the math *not* work. As long as oil, gas, and coal are cheaper and more available than other sources of energy, as long as people continue, as they have for centuries, consuming more stuff in more places at more speed, the world will burn the available oil, gas, and coal. And the United States' unlocking of the shales has made global fossil fuels much less expensive.

There is no clear tally of the global environmental impact of the U.S. oil and gas renaissance. It is directly good and indirectly bad, like giving a cupcake to a child throwing a tantrum in church. But how directly good and indirectly bad is not something well understood. Too many people cite the data on carbon emissions, methane leakage, water contamination, or energy use that unequivocally confirms what they already knew. I am not naive that shale gas will instantly change the sometimes bitter words between environmentalists and the oil business. But there are areas in which their interests are profitably, beneficially, strangely coincidentally aligned. The green and the black can rant among their friends all night in the bars of Midland, Texas, or Portland, Maine. That's fine with me, as long as the good work of the day gets done.

Part V

THE NATIONAL PERSPECTIVE

12. RENAISSANCE AFTER RENAISSANCE?

SAUDI AMERICA WAS EVERYWHERE. IT HAD BECOME THE SHORTHAND WAY to describe the transformation of the United States from a spoiled consumer able to supply only one-third of its own oil appetite to a technology-driven world leader making some of the best oil and gas wells in the world. When 15 percent annual oil production growth in 2012, 2013, and 2014 joined the already steady expansion of shale gas output,[1] pundits moved from musing about effects of the American shale revolution to forecasting them. Saudi America, now the largest oil and gas producer in the world, would be even mightier than plain old America, with an eliminated trade deficit, increased employment, and cheaper energy giving our factories an unbeatable edge. Saudi America would also be, in a phrase that began being used, "freer in the world," with energy self-reliance allowing us to stand up to energy bullies everywhere and to disentangle ourselves from a half century of chaos in the Middle East that has resulted in Americans more hated and more Americans dead.

Oil and gas became what Homer Simpson said about alcohol: the cause of, and the solution to, all of life's problems.[2] With the American energy renaissance, we would show the Chinese that we could make better things at lower cost. We would create high-paying American blue-collar jobs and fight income inequality. We would tip America's balance of trade to patriotic levels not seen since the 1940s. And we would scoff at Putin's bluffs, turn kleptocracies into democracies, sanction the Iranians into submission, and tell the Iraqis that their national project was theirs again. All was inevitable. In 2012, Citigroup published what would become a famous report in the industry. It declared that "North America is becoming the new Middle East. The only thing that can stop this is politics . . . in North America itself."[3]

Two years later, Saudi Arabia, perhaps sick of the puns, had something to say about all this Saudi America hoo-ha. Tight-lipped but smiling, it declined to cut production to balance a market oversupplied with oil. In a few months, it would begin *increasing* production. Everyone in the business had known that there was too much oil. But a price crash still stuns. At my firm, our exploration and production investments recalculated downward the profits to be had from drilling each well; our oilfield service companies, with layoffs and salary cuts, prepared to be battered.

As I write this, over the past year alone, the price of oil has fallen by 59 percent, rebounded by 40 percent, and fallen again. The oil business will find its level at some price. (We in the industry remind ourselves that the best cure for low oil prices is low oil prices.) But once this correction passes, the future will be just as cyclical and messy. Markets rarely return to equilibrium, but shoot past it, fear overtaking greed, and the other way around. And so when looking at the shale revolution from a national perspective, it is critical to control for causes and effects. We need to see which benefits come to America from higher domestic volumes, which from lower oil and gas prices, which from natural gas, which from oil. Occasionally, some benefits are serendipitously coordinated. But, in markets, price is at war with volume. Forecasts of low oil or gas prices seeding new factories all over the United States crash into forecasts of American energy self-reliance.

POTENTIALLY TRANSFORMATIVE EFFECTS of the American shale revolution come, in part, because of how globally unique the revolution is. If every country had shale reservoirs of equal productivity, new U.S. sources of supply would be not a competitive advantage but a yawn. No one will be impressed if America finds a way to make cheaper, more abundant pillows. But while shale drilling has upset global oil and gas prices, it has not meaningfully altered, with a few exceptions, the domestic oil industry in any other country.

This is surprising. The United States' shale deposits are impressive but not out of scale with the rest of the world's. In 2013, the United States' share of the world's technically recoverable shale gas reserves was 9 percent, just under half its share of global gas production. U.S. shale gas reserves were fourth in the world behind China's (which are 68 percent higher), Algeria's, and Argentina's. U.S. shale oil reserves are higher on the global list, second to Russia, but only double Argentina's and Libya's.[4]

Yet you don't become the best bakery in town only by having access to flour. Shale reservoirs were the precondition of America's energy renaissance, not its cause. The causes should be familiar by now: never-say-die entrepreneurs, responsive and risk-embracing capital markets, most of the world's onshore drilling rigs, innovative oilfield service companies, large domestic markets, reasonable government regulation, low oil and gas taxes, millions of YIMBYs, and a laissez-faire political culture. Not everyone has liked shale development, but there has never been a day when it felt at risk of being derailed by politics in the most prolific areas.

A map of non-U.S. shale activity could be sold as a Global Guide to Disappointments. There have been two qualified successes at the end of 2014. Canada has some impressive rock and, if anything, more responsive capital markets and aggressive entrepreneurs. (Any romantic who thinks that Canadian capitalism is some easy listening version of the United States' has never been to Calgary.) However, the Canadian shales, as good as some are, have not offered the volume of profitable drilling opportunities to meaningfully alter the country's total output: Canadian natural gas production from 2004 to 2014 fell by 13 percent; oil production over that time, excluding the oil sands, was flat.[5] The largest challenge facing Canada is that oil and gas prices are now being set by U.S. plays, often bigger, better geologically, and closer to large consumer markets (and without needing new pipelines that environmentalists claim will be game over for human life). In a long-term battle to supply gas to Toronto, Alberta's Montney play is about six times further than the Pennsylvania Marcellus.[6]

Argentina's Vaca Muerta shale—the forbidding "dead cow"—has some of the richest oil bearing shale rock in the world, with the geological potential to be as big as North Dakota's Bakken.[7] It unquestionably has the best name. We in the oil business point out that the Vaca Muerta would be perfect if we could just slide all the rock below Argentina out of Argentina. For while Argentina is experiencing some technical success in unlocking the Vaca Muerta, it has demonstrated equal success in re-minding the oil industry of Argentina's talent for the passionately dramatic and the persistently self-defeating with its oil-related strikes, feuds, nation-alizations, high costs, and price and money controls.

China, where they seem able to construct a Manhattan in a month, suffers no lack of risk-taking entrepreneurs, capital, or government offi-cials supportive of moneymaking (and money-taking). It also has, as noted above, the world's most shale gas rock—and the most urgent need to de-velop it, given its levels of coal consumption. However, China's success in extracting gas from shales in the Sichuan Basin, the best area there yet identified, has been limited by the depth of that rock—almost twice that of U.S. basins—and the clayey nature of the shale, which responds worse to fracking than more brittle rock. Allotting the water necessary for a widespread fracking campaign in China may also prove domestically pain-ful, too: nearly 61 percent of Chinese shales lie in dry regions, and China already has a fifth of the world's population relying on only 7 percent of its freshwater.[8] In 2014 Chinese shale gas fields produced only 1.5 percent of the gas of those in Pennsylvania, at per unit extraction cost two to three times higher.[9] They feel more like U.S. *oil* shales: a way to increase local production, a domestic source probably better than imports, but not a Marcellus-like redefinition of how cheaply a commodity can be extracted. The fields will be developed, but it seems unlikely today that there will be a Chinese oil and gas boom equivalent to the American energy renais-sance.

And that's it for success. The other bakeries in town have suffered from one element missing—workers, supplies, ovens, etc.—or maybe all of them. If you want to crack up a room of Texas oilmen, say "Polish shale," a greatly hyped gas source in 2010 that has fizzled with repeated dust-ers. Poland's shale rock combines high clay content and poor porosity. Australia's Cooper Basin, in 2015, seems on its way to being the next laugh line. The development of Russian and North African shales has been hampered by limited suitable oilfield equipment, water issues, and capital hesitant to double the normal riskiness of the oil business with the "special" risks of evading sanctions or Islamic militias.

Then there are the usual NIMBY issues, aggravated in countries with no YIMBYs because individuals don't own the oil and gas under their land—or 2,000-acre ranches. In the densely populated U.K., the government gets the royalties but the locals get the headaches. And so despite the national Conservative government's strong support for shale development, permits for what were supposed to be Britain's first fracked shale gas wells were rejected by the Lancashire County Council in June 2015, four years after test wells were drilled, because of "unacceptable noise impacts" and "an adverse urbanising effect on the open and rural character of the landscape and visual amenity of local residents."[10] My English friends pointed out the ironies of banning, for being loud and ugly, something five miles from Blackpool, a seaside town whose most famous noise is the retching of bachelor parties and most famous visual amenities are a roller coaster right on the beach and the Blackpool Tower, which looks like the fat bastard son of the Eiffel Tower and, well, a drilling rig.

France has banned fracking because it's France, a nation prone to think the worst that can be thought of American inventions and the least that can be thought of property rights in a still capitalist economy. Without a landowner or significant oil company constituency for shales, with gas's smaller role in the national energy mix (14 percent versus 42 percent for nuclear, for instance),[11] there was no countervailing force to French environmentalists' exclusive focus on shale drilling's local impacts. ("The costs are a thousand times worse than the benefits," said the spokesman for a French environmental umbrella organization, in 2014.[12]) The country outlawed fracking in 2011 four months after *Gasland* was first broadcast there.

Bulgaria banned fracking a year later not because of a documentary or because of wonderful clean air untouched by coal—it has the worst air pollution in Europe[13]—but because of covert meddling from a gas-pushing Russia.[14] Fracking was prohibited in Bulgaria with flair and consequence: a fine of $65 million for each incident. The country would have to catch only 838 frackers in flagrante, and it could double its GDP.[15]

Of course, people chuckled at George Mitchell in 1997 and Harold Hamm a decade later. Technology and trial and error have opened up once condemned reservoirs and made supposedly bad rock unthinkably cheaper to develop. By 2025, Polish shale might still kill in the comedy clubs of Pittsburgh (and Moscow), but some countries—maybe even Poland—will forge the right elements into a credible shale industry. Yet we can't ignore the paltry success to date.

A TOTAL REVERSAL of the direction of its energy economy has happened in America alone. It is still, however, unclear whether the effects of this have durably altered America's course. Change can mean turning from a soft-waisted donut nibbler into a cross-fit addict with a body harder than a yoga-pants mannequin. Change can also mean getting a slightly jazzier haircut.

From the questions directed at me in my job, I sense that people are expecting a whole body change. Indeed, I've heard the same question so often that you'd think I was a ukulele instructor.

How do I play this?

Investors understand that, years into the shale revolution, there are few secrets left in the oil business. Everyone knows that Permian Basin drilling opportunities are better in Martin County than in Sterling, two counties to the east. They have also been reminded that there are no vacations from supply and demand, or cyclicality. They play the long game, become macro thinkers, and want to understand the second-order opportunities. Plastics in Pennsylvania? Nightclubs in North Dakota? Short the Russian ruble and go long the Turkish lira?

The second-order consequences start with jobs. When I rejoined the oil business in 2004, employees of U.S. E&P, oilfield service, and midstream companies—a geologist at an oil company headquarters, a worker making drill bits, a pipeline crew foreman—totaled about 450,000 people. That was only about 4 percent higher than when I started in the business nine years before.[16] But from 2004 to the end of 2014, the number of jobs almost doubled to 850,000. This is particularly impressive in a decade shocked and split by a global recession. The jobs created to get oil and gas out of the ground and move it to the right place represented 6.4 percent of *total* American job growth in that decade even though, in 2004, only 0.35 percent of American workers were employed in the oil and gas upstream and midstream sectors. Had employment in those sectors grown at the same rate as the rest of the country, the shale revolution would have created 23,000 direct jobs, not over 400,000.

Not every job in the oil patch is the well-paid blue-collar job of boosters' fantasies, adding honorably rough hands to our nation of baristas and graphic designers. But even after the drop in oil prices, pumpers in the field make $20 to $30 per hour, plus benefits, bonuses, and overtime pay. Field supervisors make $125,000 per year. Petroleum geologists can make double that. The national average across all upstream and midstream salaries increased to $112,000 per year in the first quarter of 2014, from $71,000 in 2004.[17]

If you are oil and gas worker number 450,001 or 850,000, with a job paying the industry average, the oil and gas boom has been a toweringly important economic phenomenon. In terms of the national impact, however, these jobs should be kept in perspective. Upstream oil and gas workers still account for only 0.6 percent of the total U.S. workforce.[18] Their $100 billion in annual wages, triple the level of ten years ago, sounds country-changing until you are reminded that Americans in total make $7 trillion per year. Investment bankers and securities brokers also earn about $100 billion per year.[19]

Enthusiasts of the boom point out correctly that it has also led to all sorts of indirect jobs. In many cases, such as an unemployed Seattle real estate agent becoming a waiter in a Williston steakhouse, this is obvious. But how many of these indirect and "induced" jobs are attributed to the oil and gas industry or the shale revolution specifically often depends on who is measuring. An American Petroleum Institute brochure, dominated by stock photo collages of hard-hatted men and women of all imaginable races and hard hats, tallies up 9.2 million people "supported" by the oil and gas industry.[20] The API number assumes three indirect jobs for every direct one. (The API also counts 879,000 gas station workers as supported by the oil industry and not, in the era of self-service, by the beef jerky or Marlboro Light industries.)[21]

The famous 2012 Citigroup report speculated broadly how many new American jobs the shale revolution could create by 2020. It forecast "as admittedly the high end" another 550,000 direct jobs in oil and gas extraction and another 3 million or so indirect jobs from machinery, chemicals, and general economic growth.[22] In 2015, these numbers look unlikely. For one, the industry is showing itself capable of doing more with less. In 2014, the United States' two-year production growth of 17 percent was nearly double the rate of growth of related employment.[23] And with the 2014 oil price correction, the rising employment and wage trends reversed. We will probably not know the full wage and job declines for some time, but my guess is that industry employment will settle somewhere between where it was in the first half of 2014 and where it was in the first half of 2009, after the last commodity price correction. At the midpoint of those two employment levels, 109,000 jobs will have been lost.[24]

HIGHER ACTIVITY AND OILFIELD JOBS are part of the shale revolution. Lost jobs are part of it, too, because the boom's oversupply led to lower prices. Isolating higher U.S. oil and gas production, assigning to that production precise impacts on price, and applying those two variables to GDP, trade balances, and currency strength oftentimes feels like trying to determine what Americans as a nation will eat for breakfast in 2023. (Pancakes!) Yet, however difficult to unify statistically, the increase in U.S. oil and gas production is indisputably good for the American economy. In 2014, America's net imports of oil, natural gas, and petroleum products were $195 billion, $211 billion less than they were in 2008.[25] (Almost all of those imports were oil or oil products like gasoline. We are net importers of only about $6 billion per year of natural gas.)[26] America in 2014 imported less oil because we consumed about 2 percent less, because oil averaged 4 percent cheaper over the year,[27] and because of the two-thirds rise in domestic production caused by the shale revolution. Net imports in 2015 will have been much lower still.

In 2008, $416 billion of oil and gas imports were not some minor element on the national balance sheet. It was half of our total trade deficit.[28] Yes, money sent to buy oil and gas from Saudi Arabia, Nigeria, or Canada can have secondary benefits to the American economy if those countries, their oil companies, or their rulers use their hydrocarbon export revenue to buy American products or services: drilling technology from Halliburton, fighter jets from Boeing, mansions in Malibu. But oil-rich countries don't buy all their imports from Americans. After all, there are Mercedes and Prada and concerts by Elton John. They also don't spend all their oil revenue; in many cases, they build up giant national account surpluses when oil prices are high. (Saudi Arabia had $750 billion in cash at the end of 2013.)[29] And so the secondary benefits of importing oil can't compare to $221 billion more spent on domestic oil or gas or—because of lower oil consumption and prices—something else altogether.

How much multiplying does the multiplier effect multiply? What is the national output impact, in a $17 trillion annual economy, of $221 billion in lower imports? What does the tripling—$66 billion more—of direct wages from the boom mean to GDP? Estimates vary. In late 2014, the Congressional Budget Office estimated that by 2020, GDP will be 0.75 percent higher than it would have been had the shale revolution never happened. It will be 1 percent higher by 2040.[30] Citigroup, in 2012, calculated a 1.4 percent economic benefit by 2020.[31] An estimate between those poles of 1 percent growth in six years does not, obviously, add up to a major shift in the American economy or way of life. But the United States' real GDP growth rate for thirty years has been only about 2.8 percent. And 1 percent of U.S. GDP is equivalent to the entire economy of Vietnam or Ukraine.[32]

The industry also highlights the government revenue generated by the shale revolution and the multiplier effect of that revenue in roads built and teachers paid. Texas oil and gas production taxes, for instance, generated $5.7 billion for the state in 2014, 5.5 percent of its total revenue (in a state, as my Houston friends endlessly remind me, with no income tax). That $5.7 billion was $3 billion more than seven years earlier.[33] Nationwide, much oil and gas tax revenue, including oilfield-related property taxes and royalties from state-owned lands, are distributed to local governments, oftentimes local governments in boom-struck communities that need to provide more services. A 2014 Duke University study calculated that, in 2012, Colorado, Texas, and North Dakota alone distributed $6 billion of oil and gas revenue to local governments, three-quarters of which went to school trust funds and individual school districts.[34]

EACH WEEK IN LATE 2014, as oil prices bent even lower under the limbo stick, I would read the newspapers with an irrational, gnawing sense of betrayal. For the same *Wall Street Journal* that for years mainly celebrated the boom, a celebration I accepted graciously on my own behalf, was now marveling over how absolutely wonderful low oil prices were for the economy.

I knew the *Journal* was right. A central irony of the national perspective of the shale revolution is that of all of its benefits for America, the effects that might matter the most are the ones that its cause—we in the oil industry—like the least: lower oil and gas prices. But those lower prices bring many gifts: lower inflation (and equally important, lower expectations for it), higher consumer confidence, better balance of trade, higher profitability at big oil consumers like airlines, and more money for consumers to spend on less imported, more labor-intensive stuff.[35] Lower oil prices also profit our large trading partners. The United States, China, Japan, and the European Union together account for 65 percent of the global economy and 51 percent of oil consumption.[36] Together they import 59 percent of their oil.[37]

In 2013, the average U.S. family spent $2,611 on gasoline and $535 more on home heating oil and natural gas. This was just under half of what they spent on food.[38] If gasoline prices continue to be, as they were in the first half of 2015, 30 percent—$1.09 per gallon—lower than they were in the first half of 2013, the average American family would save nearly $800 each year.[39] That savings would allow the average family to spend nearly twice as much as the $964 they already averagely do on audiovisual equipment,[40] maybe buying such a spectacular 5-D deep-def TV that they would never leave home—or buy gasoline—again.

There is no American Commissar of Consumption who proclaims, We will not spend money on foreign oil; we will spend it on American peas and pears. To the extent that Americans redirect their savings from "discounted" gasoline to other American goods and services, the U.S. economy will experience second-order benefits. But if Americans spend less on gasoline to run errands to buy Heinekens or a Korean TV of the Gods, there would be no net economic benefit. Some import *re*placement seems to be happening, although the data is murky. Oil and gas net imports fell by $221 billion from 2008 to 2014. Total net imports fell by only $94 billion.[41]

Total U.S. net imports were $722 billion in 2014.[42] Will our balance of trade ever become positive again? Can oil and gas alone be the answer, as some oil-goggled optimists predict? Probably not $722 billion, but analyses like the Citigroup report predict that we could dramatically reduce by 2020 our current account deficit, a tally that includes imported and exported goods and services as well as financial investments and receipts.[43] (Eliminating the current account deficit as a hypothetical math exercise should not be confused with the intelligence of doing so, as economic policy. The U.S. current account deficit, $411 billion in 2014,[44] serves a healthy role in encouraging profitable U.S. foreign investment and in allowing the U.S. dollar to be the reserve currency of the world.) The oil and gas business could eat away at the current account deficit in four ways: higher domestic production, higher exports, lower domestic consumption, or lower prices. In the oil business, we call these the good way, the great way, the bad way, and the really bad way.

We still imported on a net basis $196 billion of oil, petroleum products, and gas in 2014, most of that from the 5 million barrels of oil imported each day. And if every barrel imported in 2014 was $25 cheaper, total U.S. net oil imports would be $46 billion less.[45] If Americans continue to consume 1 percent less oil per year, equal to a ten-year trend, we would import $4 to $5 billion less per year.[46] Yet most of the stunning 55 percent net reduction in oil and oil products imports since 2008 has come from increased domestic supply. This can continue. For aren't we, with over 4 million barrels per day of American shale oil production, up from practically nothing seven years ago, just before halftime? So we just have to wait for the second half, right? Analysts forecast that it is possible, at reasonable prices, for shale oil production to double again, as early as 2020.[47] However, eliminating imports would mean that the other half of American oil production, which comes from basins other than the shales (from Alaska,

California, stripper wells, offshore) would need to remain unchanged. That seems unlikely.

But might we be able to export enough natural gas in dollar terms to offset the dollars spent importing oil, even though in a fungible national economy there is no real difference between exporting gas or exporting Reese Witherspoon movies? We already sell via pipeline about $8 billion of gas per year to Mexico and Canada, totally offset now by the $14 billion in gas we import annually from Canada.[48] But we are building massive liquefied natural gas exporting facilities. If we add 10 billion cubic feet of LNG exports per day within five years—a not conservative assumption, equivalent to about 14 percent of U.S. demand—the total revenue for gas producers and liquefaction facilities would be $22 billion or so at today's prices.[49] And LNG exports could double again by 2025.

So the United States could, if not easily, eliminate the $221 billion in net oil and gas imports by cobbling together import displacement, lower consumption, and gas exports. Yet it's hard to imagine the U.S. becoming some Western Hemisphere Russia exporting such massive amounts of hydrocarbons that the oil and gas industry alone eliminates the $200 billion of the current account deficit "left over" after hypothetically erasing the fuel trade deficit. (For instance, $44 billion of LNG exports in 2025 would be about equal to America's annual imports from Italy alone, of which only one-tenth, to the shame of our nation, is food and wine.)[50]

For the shale revolution to erase the other half of the current account deficit, it would need to produce secondary import and export effects. The boom would need to spur the revival of American manufacturing.

A COLLAPSE OF AMERICAN MANUFACTURING is often told as the first chapter of a story, true or not, of American decline. Manufacturing's decline, it goes, led to the decline of high-paying factory work and the decline of a robust middle class and the decline of income equality and the decline of cities that once prospered from thriving factories. (I grew up in the Rust Belt. I still have a proud attachment to the beer and motorcycles and—less macho—industrial control systems Milwaukee makes.) That decline narrative—two stories in fact, one of lost jobs and one of a less material, tangible economy—is so bipartisanly accepted that no opposite, triumphant statistics on American services, Internet colossi, finance, culture, movies, and now oil and gas production seem capable of offsetting the lament that fewer of us make stuff. Manufacturing is America's prodigal son.

But thy brother was dead, and is alive again. (Maybe the president will kill the fatted calf live on NBC.) There is a national buzz about a resurgence in American manufacturing, with companies shifting production back to the United States—insourcing instead of outsourcing, reshoring instead of offshoring—all unthinkable a decade ago. Even without much definitive data, the enthusiasm for American factories makes it feel sometimes like I woke up in 1794, marveling at spindles and industrious child workers.

The early signs of an American manufacturing revival coincided with the shale revolution providing lower energy prices and requiring new drilling rigs, pump trucks, drill bits, and the rest. To some, the cause and effect are obvious, kindling to flame, with much more possible. The 2015 Harvard Business School-Boston Consulting Group report began, "Unconventional gas and oil resources are perhaps the single largest opportunity to improve the trajectory of the U.S. economy, at a time when the prospects for the average American are weaker than we have experienced in generations."[51]

To others, the oil and gas boom and the manufacturing revival are a coincidence—if the revival is happening at all.

BEFORE TRYING TO DETERMINE who's right, it's important to note that the decline in American manufacturing is more about jobs and national comparisons than about the quantity of stuff produced. From 2004 to 2014, the U.S. economy lost 2.1 million manufacturing jobs, even though total jobs rose by 7.3 million in that time.[52] Manufacturing in the United States now accounts for only about 12 percent of the economy, which looks pathetic next to Germany and Japan at about 20 percent, export powerhouses like Korea and China closer to 30 percent, and our own past (we were at 28 percent ourselves fifty years ago).[53] But it's not as if the United

States makes nothing. Taking into account the head-spinning number of ways one can compare national manufacturing levels, America still makes 16 to 19 percent of the world's goods with 4.5 percent of the world's people. While our share of global manufactured goods production has shrunk, the United States in 2012 still produced goods worth 21 percent more than in 2002, accounting for inflation.[54]

The narrative of America's manufacturing decline, the employment data to the side, may simply be the story of the world's largest population, after centuries of imperialist meddling and communist cruelty and inefficiency, seizing on political change and international trade agreements to regain its natural spot in the global economy. As measured by current dollars, the value adding output of United States manufacturing was three times China's in 2002. Ten years later, it was 25 percent *less*.[55] China now produces, by the most cited measures, 20 to 22 percent of the world's goods, about the same number as its 19 percent share of the world's people.[56]

China's manufacturing growth is slowing down. (It would have to: at the 2004–2013 growth rate, the value of Chinese manufacturing by 2025 would expand to equal everything made by every other country in 2013, leaving the rest of the world time to idle at the beach and/or starve.)[57] Some of the manufacturing once done in China and other lower-cost countries is coming back to the United States. Whirlpool has shifted washing machine manufacturing back to Ohio from Mexico.[58] Wham-O is producing Frisbees in California again.[59] Apple is making Mac Pros in Austin, great news for America if annoying news for those of us already at our lifetime fill of Don't Mess with Texas boosterism.[60] Journalists on the manufacturing beat most frequently visit what has become the Disneyland of Reshoring, GE's rejuvenated Appliance Park factory in Kentucky, now making high-end refrigerators and dishwashers for the American market. Appliance Park is an inspiring story of American innovation, management-labor cooperation, and perseverance[61]—a story slightly complicated by GE's attempt to sell its entire appliance division to a company based in Sweden.

Fueled by these big-company moves and a small-scale "maker" movement addressing different issues than what to do with Detroit—such as what to do with Wesleyan grads—Americans crave even more momentum in a manufacturing revival. Of the 229 State of the Union addresses, President Obama, as of 2015, gave three of the five that mentioned manufacturing most frequently.[62] Even environmentalists can join the celebration: the Chinese economy emits 3.5 times more carbon dioxide per dollar of GDP than the United States.[63] Making stuff here is better for the climate than making stuff there.

U.S. manufacturing employment has risen cyclically along with total employment after the global recession. At the end of 2014, there were about 800,000 more manufacturing jobs in the United States than there were at the end of 2009. (At 12.2 million, there are still 15 percent fewer manufacturing jobs than ten years earlier.)[64] But does this revival have anything to do with the American oil and gas renaissance? Like the tortured young suitor picking petals off a daisy—she loves me, she loves me not—each month seems to bring evidence of a greater causal connection between manufacturing and energy renaissances or little connection at all.

THE EASIEST CAUSALITY TO TRACE is the direct manufacturing of products for the shale revolution. As of late 2014, the number of oilfield equipment manufacturing jobs had doubled, by about 40,000, since 2004.[65] In Youngstown, Ohio, a French company opened the first new steel mill in fifty years, with a new oilfield pipe plant employing 350 people.[66] Oilfield manufacturing jobs, however, represent only 0.7 percent of total American manufacturing jobs. Even if we include related factory jobs not counted in these statistics (to make the pipe factory doors and hard hats, forklifts, etc.), the boom's ultimate direct impact on manufacturing is modest—and likely to be even more modest as oilfield manufacturing jobs were among the most vulnerable after the oil price plunge. We were drilling less, and needed fewer new rigs.

The shale revolution's greatest manufacturing impact may not be on the products made to advance it but on its results: cheaper and more ample oil and gas, which can be used as a fuel to make cheaper products and as cheaper extracted molecules that can be converted, as chemicals, into manufactured goods. Hydrocarbons are the raw material of ethylene, propylene, benzene, methane, and from those other building blocks, all sorts of plastics, fibers, fertilizers, fluids, dyes, and inks—the whole wonderful, scary, and mysterious lot without which modern life is unthinkable unless you have figured out how to make a television out of pinecones. The steady whittling down of American gas prices from the shale revolution has given U.S. chemical plants among the cheapest feedstocks in the world, matched only by the Middle East and Western Canada, both farther from large end user markets. (Less expensive petrochemicals, of course, have their own environmental consequences.)

America's chemical cost advantage is never constant; it compresses with lower oil prices or higher U.S. gas prices. But as of April 2015, chemical companies had announced $138 billion of planned investment in over 225 U.S. new factory and factory expansion projects, betting on the durability of America's gas price advantage.[67] Chemical company Methanex is not only moving methanol production from Chile to Louisiana but moving the actual factories.[68] (Whoever advised them to build gas-fed factories in a country with no gas in the first place probably advised another company to open up a yarmulke stand in Kabul.) Most of these chemical expansion projects won't be ready until closer to 2020.[69] They nonetheless represent the most obvious secondary economic impact of the shale revolution—and for gas producers, desperately needed new consumers. The chemical industry in 2015 forecasted 46,000 new direct jobs created by its investments, 485,000 temporary jobs to build the plants and supply equipment to them, and (using definitions of workforce induction that rival the oil business's) over a million more indirect and induced jobs.[70]

A shift of chemical production back to the United States could play a role in the balance of trade. The United States imports and exports about the same amount of chemicals per year, around $200 billion.[71] We could, in theory, eliminate our $411 billion current account deficit by eliminating oil, gas, and chemical imports.

Even if chemicals did not rely on oil and gas as a feedstock, they are in a larger group of energy-ravenous producers that benefit from an American fuel cost advantage. According to Morgan Stanley, energy accounts for 5 to 9 percent of the cost to produce steel, paper, chemicals, glass, aluminum, gasoline—all the bulk industries that make something out of something else.[72] These bulk American industries may not spur many new high-paying manufacturing jobs. For instance, in 2015, iron and steel mills in the United States employed only 90,000 workers, less than half of the number of people who worked in shoe stores.[73] Yet large energy-consuming industries produce about a quarter of U.S. industrial output. Cheaper energy could lead to rising production of lower-cost glass or paper. It could generate greater profit margins or price competitiveness of American windows or get-well cards or books about cheaper energy.

In a fine American tradition, some chemical, aluminum, and steel companies joined several electric utilities to form a lobbying group with an inarguably American and righteous name—America's Energy Advantage—to oppose LNG exports in order to trap more gas in the United States, keeping it cheap.[74] So far, they have had little measurable success; LNG export projects have been steadily approved by the Obama administration, to the dissonant delight of oilmen. But tussles over who should capture the economic benefit of America's shale endowment—oil and gas producers or oil and gas consumers—will continue. They may not be settled wholly by the market.

Analysts at the Boston Consulting Group put cheaper gas as one of the four key factors that rebalanced global manufacturing costs. From 2004 to 2014, according to its research, U.S. natural gas costs fell by 25 percent and electricity costs rose by 30 percent. In the rest of the world's twenty-five largest economies, gas prices doubled and electricity costs rose 75 percent. Of the world's ten largest exporters, only China and Korea still have any cost advantage over the United States—and China, broadly speaking, by only 5 percent.[75]

FOR BOOSTERS OF the shale revolution, there is—she loves me not—dispiriting news late in the Boston Consulting Group report: natural gas accounts for only 2 percent of average manufacturing costs, electricity 1 percent.[76] This fact, in and of itself, is not dispiriting: it comes from impressive leaps of energy efficiency. In 2014, U.S. GDP per barrel of oil and natural gas consumed was 2.5 times higher than forty years earlier.[77] But from data like this, Morgan Stanley in 2013 concluded that the U.S. oil and gas boom and any small U.S. manufacturing revival until then were primarily coincidences, with grand patterns being drawn from a few isolated corporate moves.

In 2010 or 2011, when I talked to investors about the shale revolution, I proudly and proprietarily emphasized its benefit to U.S. manufacturing as much as I did its role in reducing carbon emissions. Both were examples of American ingenuity leaping from renaissance to renaissance. Then, after studying the data, I became the sophisticated realist, forwarding around Morgan Stanley's downbeat news as if I had calculated the competitive advantages of national aluminum industries myself.

But can it really be true that a manufacturing revival has nothing to do with the shales—or me? One can make that argument. America's hope for manufacturing, as mentioned, is twofold: producing more of the stuff we consume ourselves; and reviving more high-paying manufacturing jobs we nostalgically associate with our better days. But what's good for stuff isn't always good for jobs. U.S. manufacturers benefit from commanding labor productivity. For big companies, we may be in a maker culture again, but the makers are often robots. (Labor, for instance, now accounts for only 6 to 7 percent of the total cost of a car.[78]) Indeed, America's improving relative manufacturing costs in some sectors may have less to do with natural gas prices than with U.S. companies' success at keeping American workers' wages down. According to Morgan Stanley, total U.S. manufacturing wages rose only about 4 percent annually from 2006 to 2011. Chinese and Brazilian manufacturing wages, on a U.S. dollar basis, rose 14 to 18 percent per year.[79] In China, labor cost inflation was driven by both Chinese workers being paid more and the Chinese currency strengthening—trends that largely accelerated since 2011.

And any new trendiness of American factories may exist for reasons independent of executives' coldblooded cost comparisons. Just as tween girls drop Justin Bieber for Taylor Swift, companies follow fads. The largest impulse for reshoring may be that offshoring didn't work as well as the outsourcers had hoped. It added complexity to the supply chain, divorced companies from an understanding of their own products, degraded quality, exposed intellectual property to theft, inhibited greater customization of products, slowed time to market, and generated mountains of bad publicity (and likely feelings of guilt) with reports of the conditions, the children, the suicides, the fires in factories overseas. None of these offenses or disappointments will forever stop U.S. companies from building factories elsewhere; the current fashion is to have manufacturing close to customers. But companies now seem less likely to build foreign factories to manufacture goods for the U.S. market. This includes non-U.S. companies too: the Sino-Swedes of Volvo announced in 2015 that they were going to open their first U.S. factory, in South Carolina, by 2018.[80]

Finally, renaissance may be fighting renaissance. That is, the shale revolution may be impeding a manufacturing revival in some ways. One of the benefits of a lower trade deficit, all else being equal—and in economics, all else is never equal—is a stronger dollar, which is bad for American exporters. In early 2015, large companies like Procter & Gamble and GE, excusing quarterly declines in profits, complained that a strong dollar was making their products more expensive in international markets.[81] A stronger dollar also encourages American companies to buy cheaper companies and factories in other places. Also, one of the reasons that outsourcing lost popularity was the high cost of shipping and air travel. After the boom-caused drop in oil prices and transportation costs, outsourcing math improved. And in more American-manufacturing-stunting news, LNG prices in most countries are tied to oil prices. Lower oil prices have led to cheaper non-U.S. gas, eroding some of the United States' cost advantages.[82]

These countervailing factors are real, as are the doubts about the reshoring trend's significance beyond appealing anecdotes. The manufacturing revival is not yet an economy-redefining phenomenon, like Taylor Swift. But part of me is suspicious of doubters who claim that what is not yet will thus never be. This is especially true now. We live in an age open to transformation and wonder; our society and economy have been reshaped by smartphones and shales in seven years, so who can say what the next seven years will hold? The shale revolution itself taught us repeatedly how wrong were the skeptics who missed how "anecdotal" innovations (like the rebirth of slickwater fracking near Fort Worth) or isolated developments (EOG's initial forays in the Eagle Ford Shale) can tip into changes once thought unimaginable. Most of the chemical factories that are the most direct manufacturing effect of the boom haven't been completed. Plastics applications, metal mills, and oilfield manufacturers could yet adjust or explode into new industries with lower gas and electricity prices as a cause—or maybe just an inspiration.

And inspiration comes from other sources—pride, adventure, confidence, love—than just the output of a corporate budget responding to the inputted price of natural gas. Each of us is more than our money. We are also citizens of a country. We look to it for our own sense of possibility and power.

13. AND THE LAND OF THE FREE

FOR TO EVERYONE WHO HAS, MORE WILL BE GIVEN, AND HE WILL HAVE abundance; but from him who does not have, even what he has will be taken away.[1]

It is not a coincidence—nor, okay, foreordained by the Parable of the Talents—that the shale revolution happened in the largest, most responsive economy on earth: the character of the U.S. economy and people caused, in large part, the boom. But it seems, depending on your point of view, suspicious, incredible, annoying, just, or teeth-gnashingly unfair that America, already rich, has through 2014 alone been blessed with 6 billion "extra" barrels of oil production and 28 trillion cubic feet more gas because of the shales. India, Ethiopia, El Salvador, frack-banning Bulgaria could use a windfall like that more.

But fair or not, America now has even more abundance. In 2014, the United States produced 16 percent more oil and gas than Russia, the former champion supplier to the world. A decade earlier, it produced 15 percent less.[2] The primary international effects of this production surge are easy enough to see: lower global fossil fuel prices, and the reduced ability of non-U.S. producers to sell oil and gas to Americans. Those effects have been an earthquake in an ecosystem of alliances, economies, and power structures, which had evolved on the old bedrock that non-U.S. producers would forever—increasingly—sell oil and gas to Americans at high and rising prices. The earthquake has already meant a shrinking fear that events overseas will trip oil shortages, price spikes, and voter ire. In a few cases, the United States has already arrived on new land—and new strength—when dealing with oil producing countries. But the permanence and significance of these changes—with the Middle East, Russia, Mexico, others—depend not just on the volume of oil coming out of North Dakota, but also on how governments of oil and gas importers and exporters *choose* to respond to the U.S. supply increase and lower prices. As with the shale revolution's impacts on the American economy, its consequences for America's vulnerabilities, activities, and strengths are at their dawn. No end is yet fated to be.

BY MY ESTIMATE, the oil and gas exports of the thirty leading exporting nations aggregate to about a trillion dollars in annual revenue at today's prices.[3] The shales have discomforted those countries' sense of the rules, many built—into an economy, as a self-image—on the Resource Triangle physics that their lower-cost, "easy" reserves would get more scarce and valuable by the decade. Despite the stock casting of American movie villains—if you sell oil, you're bad news—not all of these thirty leading exporters are America's adversaries. Indeed, only about 22 percent of the trillion dollars goes to three "enemies" of the United States: Iran, Russia, and Venezuela. (It might be only two. The United States plays an all-explaining, all-malevolent psychological role in the Chavista mind. Venezuela occupies space in the average American's thoughts roughly on par with Mars.) Another 18 percent or so of oil and gas exports is collected by seven countries that are clearly friendly with the United States, as strained as those relationships can sometimes be: Canada, Mexico, Colombia, the U.K., Norway, the Netherlands, and Australia.

The remaining 60 percent of global oil and gas exports is generated by countries hard to categorize by friendliness. Just under half of this balance comes from a grab bag of nations that seem on the fringes of American foreign policy: large, important, and generally allied countries but with varying levels of amicability depending on who is in charge there and here (Brazil, Nigeria, Indonesia); small countries on the fringes of American concerns (sorry, Turkmenistan); a small country that seems to yearn to be on the enemies list (Bolivia); and petrostates that, to Americans, are neither more nor less than that (such as Angola). And then there are our frenemies: six Arab Gulf states—Saudi Arabia, the UAE, Qatar, Kuwait, Iraq, and Oman—states that produce about one-third of global oil and gas exports, Saudi Arabia 14 percent alone.

The U.S. shale revolution has scrambled the economies, national budgets, and influence of all thirty of the major exporters as well as dozens of smaller ones, like South Sudan. The scale of U.S fracking's influence on other countries is partly due to the asymmetry of oil and gas's importance in any nation's welfare. To oil and gas importers, import prices and volumes will influence economic health. Extreme high prices can send countries into recession. But oil and gas import levels over the long term rarely determine importers' existential state. A trillion dollars of oil and gas exports, after all, is equivalent to only 1.3 percent of the global economy.[4]

To oil and gas exporters, however, the revenue from hydrocarbons is sometimes the determining factor of the country's economic health and its rulers' political legitimacy. Oil and gas represented 68 percent of Russia's export revenue in 2013 and 95 percent of Nigeria's.[5] The asymmetrical impact is not just a quirk of economics. It reflects the much discussed resource curse, in which countries able to access easy money from extracting hydrocarbons, or minerals, end up atrophying in other parts of their economies. People's behavior becomes dominated by "rent-seeking"—getting the most for themselves from the resource bounty—instead of being directed to productive economic ends.[6] With easy loot from oil, why start developing new medicines or manufacturing flat screens?

There is another asymmetry. The shale revolution's lower global oil and gas *prices* are unsettling international relations far more than its *volumes*, whether we are buying specific barrels from specific enemies or friends. Crude oil is easy to transport. In a balanced market, it will find a customer, with regional pricing adjusting. The United States in 2014 imported 21 percent less oil from Saudi Arabia than it did in 2007, but Saudi Arabia produced 12 percent more oil than seven years earlier.[7]

Of course, if the United States no longer has a direct commercial relationship with a country, if all Saudi or Venezuelan oil goes to China or

Japan, sentimental ties can fray. Other countries may draw closer as allies over direct trade interests. In late 2014, China became the lender of last resort for Venezuela. The idea of more world-changing impacts, of Chinese troops defending Saudi Arabia from some Emirati Napoleon, seem too odd to dwell on. Or maybe it's just premature. What would an Englishman in 1813 have said to a prediction that the United States would protect his country from Germany one day?

ANY GLOBAL REALIGNMENT OF ALLIANCES, based on trade flows, will take time. The economic impact of the shale revolution's lower oil and gas prices has already exploded. In late 2014, investors and observers started speculating on ever-changing "fiscal breakeven prices": what price oil exporting countries needed to balance their budgets. By mid-2015, estimates ranged from $90 to $100 per barrel for Saudi Arabia, Venezuela, Nigeria, and Iran—double the prices after they crashed.[8] Many rulers of oil exporting countries need, desperately, to achieve that fiscal breakeven: the second infliction of the resource curse is that extraction-oriented economies rarely have well-developed civil societies. Oil and gas revenue is necessary to buy social peace and political legitimacy. Half the oil revenue means half the bread and half of the World Cup circuses.

Twenty years ago, American concern about instability and mayhem in oil producing countries was an economic worry: what overseas instability would do to oil prices and the American economy. Now, as evidenced by the collective yawn of the global oil markets (and, more or less, U.S. foreign policy) to the civil war in Libya, the main worry is what people in unstable oil producing countries will do to each other, to us, and to the world. In 2014 and 2015, two of the primary American foreign policy initiatives were checking Russia's unneighborly aggressiveness and limiting Iran's nuclear capabilities. After the oil price fall came daily speculation on whether lower prices would make Russia and Iran, those siblings in messianic and paranoid self-regard, more conciliatory or more aggressive, leading to peace on earth or tanks on the border of Lithuania and missiles en route to Tel Aviv.

Average Americans are probably less afraid of unrest in Iran and Russia than in countries like Saudi Arabia that have exported their domestic tensions to the United States. (We probably re-exported a few back.) The Gulf Arab states, awash with competing brands of conservative Islam, had a trillion dollars in foreign currency reserves at the end of 2013. A trillion dollars can pay for peace and quiet for some time, even at low oil prices.[9] But the staggering population growth of the big Gulf exporters has led to more underemployed sons and more checked ambitions that can metastasize in the usual, horrible ways—and now in large numbers. In 1970, in the early hours of the modern global oil market, the population of our six Gulf Arab allies was 18 million. As recently as 2000, it was 53 million. It was 81 million in 2013.[10]

And then there is the other half of the oil and gas exporting world: the nations friendly and neutral to the United States. No American worries about tall, handsome Norwegians, but who knows what (even-keeled) pandemonium the Norwegians will cause Swedes if their great gløgg of happiness and wealth, the North Sea, becomes unprofitable in a world of lower energy prices. Indonesia, Brazil, and Nigeria also don't haunt the nightmares of the American people, but these major oil producers have the fourth, fifth, and seventh largest populations in the world—625 million people in total. Colombia and Mexico worry Americans more because of the other exports that will presumably go up (drugs, gang violence, illegal immigrants) if hydrocarbon revenues, and domestic opportunities, decline.

ONE SHOULD BE SKEPTICAL of oilmen telling you that lower oil prices are one of the World's Most Dangerous Threats. (Lower oil prices will also make you fat. You're more likely to drive somewhere than to walk.) The impact of lower prices—and the diminishing threat of spiking prices—is probably more good news than bad. For one, there may be zero connection between oil prices in any period and the threats that scare us, such as terrorism or Middle Eastern instability. September 11 happened when oil was $27 per barrel, up 23 percent in two years. The Arab Spring started in December 2010 when oil was at $91 per barrel, steadily rebounding from lows in 2008.[11]

And there is more than just absence of bad news: lower oil prices are liberating American and European diplomacy with encouraging global consequences. "No blood for oil" always seemed naive to me.[12] The sinister swap in that equation implied that U.S. foreign policy was driven by an imperialist need to own other countries' oil and gas. The aftermath of the 2004 Iraq War demonstrated clearly what American oil and oilfield service companies received in Iraq, at least, for American blood: low margins, difficult operating conditions, and no particular privilege compared to European and Chinese companies. (American oil operations in Iraq often seem less the payment for American foreign policy than the punishment for it.) But antiwar protesters in 2004 could have shouted a less elegant "no blood to prevent oil spikes." Particularly since the 1970s oil crises, U.S. policy has tried to make the United States less vulnerable to energy price shocks. From 1973 to 1985, this policy worked; the country imported less oil due to energy efficiency and stable national production—thanks primarily to the Alaska North Slope. From 1985 to 2007, however, with declining U.S. production, oil imports increased by over two and a half times.[13]

And so before the shales, U.S. policymakers had only three tools to try to prevent oil price shocks. The first, morally messy one—and not without its backdrafts—was to be nice to Saudi Arabia, which if stable itself could, on its own, stabilize global oil prices. Saudi Arabia was happy to serve its role as the global swing producer for its own ends. The Truman administration–initiated de facto policy to promote Middle East oil region stability was formalized with the "Carter Doctrine" in the 1980 State of the Union address: "An attempt by any outside force to gain control of the Persian Gulf region will be regarded as an assault on the vital interests of the United States of America."[14] The Carter Doctrine was the underpinning of the second tool to defend price stability, the American military, used rarely in this function—and primarily against Saddam Hussein.

The final tool to make America less vulnerable to energy price spikes was to encourage (or maybe just to hope for) the American economy to grow faster than its own oil use. That economic inoculation, as mentioned in the last chapter, has been an uncelebrated, immoderate success. In 2014, there were 49 percent more Americans than forty years earlier. The U.S. economy was triple the size. We consumed only 26 percent more oil and gas.[15] If oil prices returned from their prices at the end of 2014 to where they were six months earlier, American consumers would on an annual basis pay 2.2 percent more of national GDP to oil producers. Oil prices doubling, generally speaking, would have had more than double the negative economic consequences in 1974.[16]

The unlocking of the shales has built even higher walls of protection against oil price spikes. And the lower prices that came in 2014 may mean that future spikes, if they do come, will have a smaller total dollar effect as they start from a smaller base. A price spike today would also be less important because American companies and workers, whose production has displaced imports, would benefit from the spikes. (It would be a burden for us in the oil business to accept higher prices, but we would do it for America.) Increased domestic oil volumes could also prevent temporary physical shortages, making a highly unlikely event even more improbable. And the boom has averted, maybe forever, an American dependence on imported gas. We can put away our unused "no blood for natural gas" protest signs.

The ability to extract oil and gas from shale and other tight reservoirs has domesticated, for everyone on earth, the snarling threat of destructive oil and gas prices. In 2015, the U.S. oil industry did not drill in fields that were considered thrilling moneymakers six months earlier because lower oil and gas prices made that drilling unprofitable. If prices rise, oil companies will start drilling again in those U.S. fields—some are close to profitable today—and rebalance the market. This will not prevent higher prices forever. But it does, for a while, change the risks facing the world.

As energy scholar Michael Levi has pointed out, when oil price spikes can't crash the economy, the flexibility of American foreign policy increases.[17] In 2013 and 2014, the United States implemented sanctions against Russia for annexing Crimea, did not intervene in a chaotic civil war in Libya, and led the tightening of global sanctions against Iran. Oil prices barely budged in response to any of these actions—or nonactions—even though those three countries produced one-fifth of the world's oil as recently as 2010.[18] The politically convenient timing of the oil price plunge in 2014, so economically damaging to countries diplomatically sparring with the United States, led to all sorts of conspiracy theories in

Moscow and Tehran. It also led to conspiracy theories in Houston, with Putinesque complaints that Their Royal Highnesses B. Hussein Obama and King Abdullah were colluding in Thanksgiving Day gut-punches to their Russian and Texan enemies alike. However, 2015 tensions between the United States and Saudi Arabia over the best strategy to attempt to halt Iranian nuclear development raised doubts about any collusion. It also gave more evidence of America's freer hand: the United States proceeded ahead with its own Iran strategy, unmoved by Saudi complaints.[19]

The United States' freer hand with Russia and Iran, evident even at $100 per barrel oil, demonstrated a confidence that America was more resilient to oil producer disruptions because the world oil market could tolerate them. U.S.-led sanctions halved Iranian oil exports from 2011 to 2013, removing about 1.3 million barrels per day from the market. This is as if Mexico or Norway stopped exporting oil.[20] It is hard to imagine U.S. elected officials establishing such a tough, supply-reducing policy if it led to one of the most clichéd (and most inaccurate) images of American campaign commercials: grainy shots of a retail gasoline sign and Politician X personally, singlehandedly responsible for $4.50 per gallon gasoline.

Optimists predict that this greater freedom of action could multiply, benefiting other American values and interests. The long American intervention in the Middle East, through major wars and smaller incursions, has cost trillions of dollars and tens of thousands of lives—American and Arab—all the while exhausting American sympathy and creating a tidal wave of anti-American backlash. It stings many Americans that oil revenue in Saudi Arabia, an ally and trading partner, is spent in part on Uzbek or Pakistani madrasas whose curricula don't exactly include America Appreciation Days.[21] Liberal and conservative Americans alike understand the practical facts of foreign policy, but they still have regrets, for likely different reasons, over an alliance with Saudi Arabia whose values on democracy, freedom of expression, religious tolerance, women's rights, gay rights, and minority rights are a negative image of our own. Reduced worries about oil price spikes may allow a period of "benign neglect," to use Pat Moynihan's phrase from another context,[22] in Middle Eastern foreign policy. That neglect could reset and heal American-Arab interdependence. (It could, of course, also hurt efforts to solve the Israeli-Palestinian conflict.)

Outside the Middle East, too, the freer hand could allow the United States to support more sympathetic governments or movements, without having to worry about that support's impact on the oil markets. We could actively or passively encourage democratic progress in places like Kazakhstan, if such things are possible, and new governments in oil-rich dictatorships with other talents besides embezzling their nations' wealth. If lower oil prices persist, the freer hand will also push against oil exporters' weakened hand. Ukraine's parliament voted to work toward joining NATO days after the Russian ruble, following the oil price, plummeted.[23] It might be a coincidence that Cuba and the United States had their most important diplomatic breakthrough in a half century one month after Cuba's sponsor, Venezuela, was in an oil price panic. Then again, the Castro regime might have smelled Venezuela's fear.

Finally, the freer hand might tighten into a stronger grip if the United States becomes a major exporter of natural gas to certain countries. The United States, business-minded as it is, likes to sell products mainly for the sheer greedy fun of it, not to control its customers' foreign policy. ("Abide by our Iranian sanctions, Slovaks, or no Reese Witherspoon for you.") Yet Russia has shown how a psychological hold, and clutches of self-interest, can result from controlling another country's supply of electricity and heat.

It can be disappointing that the national perspective on the shale revolution is not an unobstructed view of a new and improved future. But there are measures of changes' beneficence other than whether America has been transformed for all time. It may be enough to be more liberated from a confining fear of oil price spikes, able to push off for decades worries about secure sources of imported gas, and better positioned to deal with Russia, Iran, and—why not, you too—Venezuela. If you live in Ukraine or Cuba, that might be more than enough. A period of benign neglect of the Arab world might do absolutely nothing for America for years. But it could open up a path at the end of which, in fifty years, Islamic terrorism seems as strange as anarchist terrorism does today. Yes, the world will still be dangerous, and unstable oil and gas prices might make it more dangerous in places. But the intention of the shale revolution, by those who caused it, was simply to make money. Anything else good is good.

For the U.S. economy, too, we may want to moderate our expectations and be thankful for the direct and secondary benefits the boom brings—and not seek a savior in the shales. For the people of Youngstown, Ohio, who lived under decades of evidence that there was little ongoing economic reason for Youngstown to exist, a new drill pipe factory brings not just jobs but an existential endorsement. That can't be measured just by the percentage impact on national GDP.

Sometimes, when bored, I amuse myself by narrating the American oil and gas renaissance's appearance in 2009 in an overwrought movie trailer baritone: in a world without hope, in a country without joy, one industry rose from the ashes . . . For where would America be in our dealings with Iran or ISIS if oil prices had risen $50 per barrel in 2014, instead of fallen by that amount? The economic and cultural optimism that came from "more having been given" to "everyone who has" seems to have spread in other subtle ways. When Apple or Whirlpool executives decided where to locate factories, they weighed loads of variables. If America, in their analyses, was suffering from spiking energy costs, if Ohio or Texas, the states where the factories went, did not have once-a-generation discoveries of hydrocarbons that brought jobs and vigor to those states, would the executives have concluded that new factories made sense there or would they have just inhaled the dead-end odor of a nursing home?

We can never attribute economic growth (or national power) to one factor. There are, always, other variables of policy and cyclicality and relative competitiveness. John Maynard Keynes wrote about one such factor: economic actors' "animal spirits," their urge to action. It seems more than just a coincidence that, seven years after the global financial crisis, the strongest major economy in the world was also the economy with the largest domestic energy boom—a huge unleashing of animal spirits.

Those animal spirits, I believe, did not stop at buying and selling. As imperfect, contentious, and alarming as the world still sometimes is, there has also been an urge to American action to contain threats in ways that were not possible under the world's old oil realities. The shale revolution has not smited all our nation's enemies with one blow. But what were once fights defined by their oil and gas strength and our oil and gas weakness have become a fight redefined, with the weapon now in our hands.

CONCLUSION

THE BOYFRIEND OF A FRIEND ONCE SAT HER DOWN SO HE COULD DELIVER a tearful plea. He needed the stability and emotional support of their relationship. He loved her completely. But—and oh, this was where the tears really started pouring—he also needed to "date" other women. That's just who he was. Babe.

Against the collected wisdom of humanity, my friend agreed to stay with him. She gave him permission to do what he needed to do.

The boyfriend was the U.S. gas producers' reality from 2004 to 2008, during the start of the shale gas revolution. He was the U.S. oil producers' from 2009 to 2014. In those years, American oil and gas companies had the stability and emotional support of high prices. But they drilled everywhere, experimented across basins, and increased production riotously, with no impact on those sweet comforting prices. They were in periods I call, after the boyfriend, Lucky Guy.

But as made clear by the gas and then oil price corrections, Lucky Guy periods are not the only (or even natural) situation for the energy industry. They are only one of the four primary quadrants of the business, if we divide what is possible into a matrix of high or low prices, and into high U.S. shale growth or no growth. Lucky Guy periods of high U.S. supply growth and high prices were possible only because competing global sources of oil and gas unwittingly made room because of geology, economics, politics, bad luck.

However, there have also been periods of high U.S. volume growth and low prices, as began for gas in 2009 and started—in a blink—for oil five years later. I called these Mr. Economics periods, for a bow-tied professor pedantically instructing handsome, immature Lucky Guy on the laws of supply and demand. Mr. Economics would lecture that, *of course*, ridiculously unconstrained volume growth from shale basins had to over-supply the market, crushing prices. You really thought you'd be allowed to "date" whomever you wanted forever?

Mr. Economics and Lucky Guy periods describe situations marked by high U.S. volume growth. The other two possible quadrants in the matrix remind us of the oil industry's cyclicality. A Flashback period would be (for the oil industry) a reprise of years of glum profitability, like when I was first building oil supply-demand tables in the 1990s. It would be an era of no U.S. volume growth and low prices. This dynamic could occur again if the fracking and horizontal drilling techniques developed in the boom either spread globally or become so perfected in the United States that they become too cheap and routine. Flashback could also occur if the world's total demand for fossil fuels continues to stagnate or starts to decline.

The final quadrant of the matrix is also a remembrance of things past. Re-Peak periods, with new predictions of imminent peak oil, would have the worst economic ramifications for America: high prices and no U.S. oil and gas growth. (Re-Peak would be cheered by environmentalists opposed to fossil fuels.) Re-Peak could occur because of an implausible-seeming political event, such as President Andrew Cuomo and Vice President Robert F. Kennedy Jr. banning fracking nationwide on their first day in office. (And on the second day, Texas secedes.) Re-Peak could also return because of what shale skeptic Jeremiahs have been warning about for a decade: that the amount of recoverable oil and gas in shale reservoirs is much smaller than everyone claims.

Even if the skeptics continue to be wrong—and they have been very wrong so far—a Re-Peak period could occur if demand surges with a healthy global economy, as we had a decade ago, and supply growth fails to keep up. Oil supply will peak one day. It's just not clear *what* day that will happen, sometime between now and the end of time.

Market forecasters have, over the decades, put their chips on one of the matrix's four squares, pontificating that Mr. Economics or Flashback is how the future will be. (As is the tendency with all forecasting, many predict trends that most closely resemble the present.) Yet the oil business will not occupy one quadrant for all time, like a Great Pyramid. I've seen the industry in all four quadrants in just two decades. Oil and gas prices and volumes move across situations as the balance of supply and demand responds, overshoots, and remains subject to factors outside the energy industry. Oil and gas can also inhabit separate quadrants, sometimes influencing each other, oftentimes not. There is also no high wall between the squares. Prices and volumes can sometimes hover between them—or move from one to the next. Medium high prices and low volume growth, or okay prices and high volume growth, can coexist, even if they aren't that fun to name.

Predicting the further effects of the American shale revolution, from all the key perspectives of this book, requires us to speculate on the probability of price and volume scenarios. The direct stimulus of the domestic oil and gas business on the American economy is different, for instance, during a Lucky Guy period than in a Flashback period. The local environmental challenges, ensuring that the health and land of those living inside the boom are protected, would be easier to meet in a Lucky Guy period, harder in a Flashback period, and unnecessary in a Re-Peak period. Re-Peak might arrest climate change, but it also may allow Russia to molest its neighbors in ways it could not if oil prices were weak.

I could go on, describing every implication in every scenario, drowning us all in conditions and subtleties and yes-but-consider-this-toos. As we sink, my last dying words would be that everything can happen and will happen (so why worry about anything anyway). A surrender like that would be maddening to people who need to make decisions for the long term: the executive wondering whether to reshore a factory, the diplomat deciding how tough to be with Iran, the chief investment officer determining a foundation's allocation to the oil and gas sector.

Thankfully, not every scenario is equally likely at every moment, or this one. Re-Peak seems improbable. Lucky Guy, for the oil business, as for my friend's boyfriend—she eventually dumped him—seems possible only for contained periods.

When speculating on America's path through the quadrants, I base my understanding on the conviction that the *potential* for high U.S. volume growth is not likely to disappear. Technically, geologically, industrially, the U.S. oil and gas renaissance has chapters left. From an industrial perspective, American oil and gas companies are still optimizing well length, spacing, proppants, and fluids. They are upgrading where they are drilling, within the cores of the shales. New technologies are still being developed to improve shale well production and drive down unit costs. Oilfield service prices also declined swiftly in 2015, making shale oil and gas around 30 percent less expensive to develop.

Researchers at ITG examined tens of thousands of wells across hundreds of North American basins. They forecast that onshore U.S. crude oil production from the Lower 48 states alone could rise from 8 million barrels per day now to nearly 12 million barrels per day in 2020, as long as oil prices remain above $90 per barrel.[1] (U.S. shale oil production in these types of scenarios will grow faster than the United States overall, as nonshale U.S. production is almost certain to decline.) That oil price prerequisite may seem improbable when oil ended 2014 at $53 per barrel, but prices and drilling and completion costs can quickly change. For natural gas, where new sources of demand are needed to induce faster growing supply, ITG notes that as of late 2014, there had been only 6,000 wells drilled in the Marcellus Shale. It calculated 110,000 locations in the shale that the industry could theoretically drill, with 500 trillion cubic feet of gas in them—enough gas in one play to supply the entire United States for twenty years.[2]

If someone waved a magic wand to make oil $90 per barrel and gas $4.00 per thousand cubic feet forever, the U.S. oil and gas industry would yip with delight. At those prices, the industry would be able to steadily increase U.S. production. But no one has that magic wand. And no matter how often I look to the sky, no space aliens are coming down to buy all of America's excess oil and gas to ship back to Alpha Centauri, to use as condiments. Hydrocarbon prices will continue to be fluid. Whatever the factors influencing them, fluid prices will determine how quickly shale reserves are developed. That *pace* will set which of the four quadrants is the industry's temporary home.

Predicting the long-term price of oil and gas, to me, feels less like predicting which college your teenage son will attend than guessing who will be his favorite singer his senior year there. It requires projecting dynamics that we can barely understand or observe today: non-U.S. supply sources if prices are high, non-U.S. supply sources after prices have crashed, Saudi market share strategy, global economic growth, Chinese economic growth, Middle Eastern domestic consumption, politics of every country in the world, technological breakthroughs from renewable energies, scaling limits to renewable energies, discrete decisions made by a factory owner in Vietnam or a car buyer in Phoenix on what to do tomorrow in a confusing world.

Yet the difficulties in predicting the pace of U.S. oil and gas supply growth, as set by the accelerator and break of prices, should not disguise the historical lunacy of even asking the question. Ten years ago, forecasters argued only about the pace of U.S. decline.

IN THIS BOOK, I have avoided the phrase "energy independence," one well-worn almost my entire life. Richard Nixon used it in a speech in 1973, a few months after I was born.[3] For many years, for us in the oil business, using the phrase was a sign that you were a) deeply unsophisticated or b) running for office. It was a bipartisan cliché. "I want to bring Americans together, fight for the middle class, and achieve energy independence" meant that you were a Republican, a Democrat, or a robot with software not updated since 1982.

American energy self-reliance is less of a punch line today, thanks to a long history of demand success and a short history of supply success. Since Nixon's call for energy independence, American fossil fuel consumption has increased because our population has grown by half. But in 2014, despite decades of economic growth, despite the electrification of every aspect of American life (even, unholy smokes, our cigarettes), the average

American consumed about 1,955 gallons of energy on an oil-equivalent basis. That was 621 gallons less than each of us consumed in 1973.[4]

Nonetheless, for decades energy self-reliance slipped further away as American oil and gas supply declined even faster than per capita consumption. Then came the shales. We now have a domestic oversupply of gas and natural gas liquids to join a long-standing abundance of coal. Oil is the last remaining imported fossil fuel. Can we fully displace all imports? A doubling of U.S. shale production, as ITG forecasts, would get us close. And Goldman Sachs in 2015 hypothesized that if the U.S. oil shales could experience continuing efficiency improvements, production could triple by 2026, leading to a clear need to export U.S. oil.[5] Even if that doesn't happen, in a high-but-not-crazy $90 per barrel price environment, there are projects beyond the shales—in Alaska, in the Gulf of Mexico, in recovery techniques from older fields—that the U.S. industry might be able to profitably tap.

We may not yet be energy self-reliant, but we are no longer doomed to be reliant forever. This is good for America. Extracting oil and gas from shale rock, thought of as a desperate and eccentric quest two decades ago and still considered a local business phenomenon ten years later, has sparked an American energy revolution that has created jobs and wealth. It has aided our balance of trade and economic growth. It is playing a role in a still ongoing revival of American manufacturing. Is has lowered American carbon dioxide emissions, at a world-beating pace. It has freed us to pursue foreign policy objectives by adjusting international relationships that once felt in permanent chains. And for the world, American shales are spreading cheaper energy everywhere and improving the lives of those who urgently need more of it.

But the boom hasn't been all good, all simple, or ever constant. The shale revolution will make a shift away from oil harder. Our global fight against climate change, even as we've lowered American emissions by astonishing amounts, just got more difficult. From a national perspective, if your nation isn't the United States, the boom has given even more power to a country not exactly suffering from its lack. From a local perspective, the boom has disrupted communities, increased polluting accidents, and asked people—some compensated, some not—to tolerate spills, exhaust, noise, and occasional small earthquakes for the good of their neighbors and the country. Even from a financial perspective, the shale revolution hasn't benefited everyone. ExxonMobil probably wishes it never happened.

How do you reconcile the good and the bad? For some of the green and the black, environmentalists and oilmen, the solution seems to be to say that the shale revolution is all good or all bad and say that forcefully enough to seize the national conversation and the levers of power. But for those of us who sympathize to some degree with both the green and the black (and almost all of us care about the world and also enjoy what fossil fuels can do), reconciling the boom's credits and debits on the moral and practical ledgers of the world can overwhelm.

Whenever my own headaches from attempting some grand synthesis overwhelms, I remind myself that there is no one-sentence answer to our energy challenges any more than there is a one-sentence answer to life. There is, as in everything, only compromises and imperfect solutions and best available decisions based on data, probabilities, and hope.

And so we ask the unsolved questions. Can the United States really extract itself from the Middle East? What would the world look like if the Chinese consumed less energy? Can U.S. or Chinese shale gas shrink Chinese coal consumption? Will that accomplish anything if oil is cheaper for us all? What if methane leakage really is a problem?

Questions like these can't be wished away. I don't like the phrase energy independence because of its platitudinous past. But I really don't like it because it seems to emerge from a dream that one day we will be free from thinking about oil and gas, its volatility, its dirtiness, and its global complications. And one day, energy—who gave it the right?—will stop influencing our foreign policy, our economy, our pocketbooks, our neighborhoods.

I hope that the opposite is true: that one day, we think more about our energy use and become more mindful of its costs and perils and intriguing possibilities, to allow us to get as close as we can to the most precise, best available solutions. This is the prize: Isaiah Berlin's "uneasy equilibrium," promoted and repaired.

This has been a book about the American shale revolution, a single improbable energy phenomenon. But it has also been a book about energy *dependence*. Looking at the boom clear-eyed, from all five perspectives, reminds us how totally dependent we are, in our production and use of oil and gas, on technology, industry, our modern needs, other countries, our shared climate, and an economy to support 7 billion people. It also reminds us that that dependence travels in both directions. By the dollars we invest, the protests we join, the factories we build, the policies we advocate, the things we buy, and the candidates we elect, we will continue to guide the direction of the shale revolution, our energy challenges, life.

To dream of being independent of that story, to me, seems like a dream of being independent of some of today's most captivating instances of individual striving, to be free of some of humanity's most urgent physical and economic and moral challenges. But to look hard at our dependence on energy allows us to see the world at its most interconnected, its most fragile, and its most hopeful. For this, too, the boom taught us: the power of the past will not always decide our future.

ACKNOWLEDGMENTS

I could not have written this book without the knowledge, hard work, research, patience, advice, and support of many friends, colleagues, and experts.

I am indebted to the research and pioneering thoughts of three excellent precedents on the shale revolution: Seamus McGraw's *The End of Country*, Gregory Zuckerman's *The Frackers*, and Russell Gold's *The Boom*. I have also learned much from the tireless reporting on the revolution from many journalists, particularly the work of Clifford Krauss and Christopher Hellman.

I am continually awed by the resources available today to writers on energy, and I relied on several sources again and again—and the people behind them. These include the databases and research of the BP Statistical Review of World Energy, Bureau of Labor Statistics, International Energy Agency, World Bank, Global Carbon Atlas, Environmental Defense Fund, IHS, Energy in Depth, Environmental Protection Agency, ITG, Tudor Pickering Holt, Simmons & Company, Morgan Stanley, Credit Suisse, Barclays, and Goldman Sachs. I would especially like to thank the people at the U.S. Energy Information Administration, whose incredibly thorough research and data have been invaluable to me for two decades.

Many friends, colleagues, and acquaintances took time to respond thoughtfully to requests for data, clarity, and perspective. My gratitude, for specific answers and general lessons, begins with a listing of their names and ends well beyond this book: J McLane, Townes Pressler, Eric Mullins, Lawrence Ross, Tim Miller, Chris Butta, Trevor Burgess, Tim Dunn, Suzanne West, Mike Minarovic, Todd Stone, Frank Motycka, Steve Boyle, Stan Bishop, Eric McClusky, Spencer Cox, David Gibson, Morrow Evans, Hossam Elbadawy, Rob Willings, James Wallis, Lynn Calder, Ben Smith, Blair Barlow, Oliver Phillips, Andrew Gautier, Will Todd, Anu Metha, Kris Agarwal, Sue Oswald, Jonathan Hickman, Elizabeth Burton, Kevin Kindrick, Debra Sandefer, Janet Kruse, Patrick Lauria, Mike Loudermilk, Alex Krulic, Ben Heller, David Wesson, Manuj Nihkanj, Carter Ward, Nick Reiland, Ben Conner, Chris Veeder, and—at the beginning—Alessandra Zortea, Don Textor, and especially Todd L. Bergman.

Four friends read the entire manuscript, provided encouragement and feedback, and heroically saved me from embarrassment: Jeff Scofield, Mark McCall, Greg Highberger, and Charlie Adcock. Allie Stone was a tireless colleague and critical ally, sending data and thoughts at all hours of the day. And Lisa Lopez's support for the book, and for much more, was essential every day.

John Reynolds and Jonathan Farber have been immensely supportive in their friendship and continually thoughtful in a twenty-year discussion on the oil and gas industry. They have created a uniquely open-minded, creative, and caring firm in which I've always felt encouraged as a writer and colleague, even when my thoughts were heterodox or inconvenient. I owe them both incalculable gratitude.

I also want to thank dear friends who helped me navigate the practical and aesthetic choices of the book: Tom Bissell, Andrew Miller, Diana Miller, Will Lippincott, Jeff Alexander, Michelle Orange, Adelle Waldman, Evan Hughes, Carlin Flora, Giovanni Escalera, Kate Bolick, Ruth Altchek, Jana Prikryl, Colin Gee, Chris Parris-Lamb, Whitney Parris-Lamb, Colby Hall, Louisa Hall, Ian Parker, Sam Douglas, Jim Rutman, Rick Greenberg, Jessica Greenberg, Ted Westhelle, Pontus Willfors, and Brian Niles.

And once the book was written, I relied on the help of many generous professionals: John Bennett for his fantastic work above and beyond fact-checking; Claire Lampen for keeping the entire project moving forward, with wit; Laura Clark, Kathryn Hough, and Alistair Hayes for helping the book reach readers; and Henry Kaufman, Rebecca Smeyne, Alison

Devereux, Pete McCarthy, and Jess Johns. I am grateful to Keith Gessen, Mark Papa, and Jim Hackett for their generosity in reading and commenting on the book after it was complete.

I am immensely thankful to my agent, Gillian MacKenzie, for her perseverance, passionate partisanship, and acute counsel through success and struggle, and to my editor, Tim Bartlett, for understanding the project and its purpose immediately and providing incisive edits, sage advice, and even-keeled good humor on a compressed timetable.

I want to express love and thanks to my family for their support throughout this project: Jim Sernovitz, Millie Sernovitz, Arnold Pulda, Pat Pulda, Andy Sernovitz, Julie Grisham, and the spirit of the late Theodore Sernovitz.

And for being awoken by my typing during the small hours, for reading every word multiple times, for saving me from bad jokes, and for proving that even if I'm not Henry James, it all might be okay, my wife and inspiration, Molly Pulda, is owed thanks beyond measure.

NOTES

Introduction

1. Based on data from Energy Information Administration database, accessed April 2015, www.eia.gov.
2. Ibid.
3. Based on data from BP Statistical Review of World Energy 2015 database, accessed June 2015, http://www.bp.com/en/global/corporate/about-bp/energy-economics/statistical-review-of-world-energy.html; and International Energy Agency, "Oil Market Report," March 13, 2015.
4. Based on data from International Energy Agency, "Oil Market Report," March 13, 2015; World Bank database, www.data.worldbank.org, accessed April 2015; United States Census Bureau database, http://quickfacts.census.gov, accessed April 2015; and Energy Information Administration database, accessed April 2015.
5. Based on data from International Trade Administration TradeStats Express database, accessed April 2015, http://tse.export.gov/TSE/TSEhome.aspx.
6. American Chemistry Council, "Shale Gas and New U.S. Chemical Industry Investment: $138 Billion and Counting," accessed May 2015, http://www.americanchemistry.com/Policy/Energy/Shale-Gas/Shale-Investment-Infographic.pdf.
7. Based on data from Bureau of Labor Statistics Quarterly Census of Employment and Wages database, accessed April 2015, http://www.bls.gov/cew/.
8. Based on data from Energy Information Administration database, accessed April 2015.
9. Based on data from Global Carbon Atlas database, accessed March 2015, http://www.globalcarbonatlas.org.
10. Based on data from BP Statistical Review of World Energy 2015 database, accessed June 2015.
11. Lawrence Ulrich, "With Gas Prices Less of a Worry, Buyers Pass Hybrid Cars By," *New York Times,* May 14, 2015.
12. Based on data from Global Carbon Atlas database, accessed April 2015.
13. Isaiah Berlin, *The Proper Study of Mankind*, ed. Henry Hardy and Roger Hausheer (New York: Farrar, Straus & Giroux, 1998), 10.

14. Ipton Sinclair, *I, Candidate for Governor: And How I Got Licked,* quoted in Goodreads .com, http://www.goodreads.com/author/quotes/23510.Upton_Sinclair.

15. "Yoko Ono, Sean Lennon Put Anti-Fracking Message on New York Billboard," *Rolling Stone,* November 8, 2012.

Part I: The Industrial Perspective

1. Robbing the Mint

1. ITG, "Diamonds are Forever, $60 Oil Probably Not," September 23, 2015; Thomas A. Petrie, *Following Oil: Four Decades of Cycle-Testing Experiences and What They Foretell About U.S. Energy Independence* (Norman: University of Oklahoma Press, 2014), 125; and Daniel Yergin, *The Quest: Energy, Security, and the Remaking of the Modern World,* rev. ed., (New York: Penguin, 2012), 230.

2. Based on data from BP Statistical Review of World Energy 2015 database, accessed June 2015.

3. John Kemp, "Is Bakken Set to Rival Ghawar?," Reuters, November 9, 2012.

4. Based on data from International Energy Agency, "Oil Market Report," March 13, 2015.

5. Matt Simmons, "The World's Giant Oil Fields," Simmons & Company International, July 2011, http://www.firstenercastfinancial.com/pdfs/3221.pdf.

6. Selina Williams, Géraldine Amiel, and Justin Scheck, "How a Giant Kazakh Oil Project Went Awry," *Wall Street Journal,* March 31, 2014.

7. Based on data from BP Statistical Review of World Energy 2015 database, accessed June 2015.

8. Gregory Zuckerman, *The Frackers: The Outrageous Inside Story of the New Billionaire Wildcatters* (New York: Portfolio/Penguin, 2013), 74.

9. Ibid.

10. Ibid., 19.

11. Ibid., 30.

12. Russell Gold, *The Boom: How Fracking Ignited the American Energy Revolution and Changed the World* (New York: Simon & Schuster, 2014), 80.

13. Ibid., 82.

14. Zuckerman, *The Frackers,* 29.

15. Ibid., 78.

16. Ibid., 80.

17. Chris Veeder, e-mail to author.

2. Peakers, Bunkers, Imports, and Yurts

1. Devon Energy, "Devon Energy Completes Acquisition of Mitchell Energy," January 24, 2011.

2. Based on data from Energy Information Administration database, accessed April 2015; and Texas Railroad Commission, "Texas Barnett Shale Total Natural Gas Production," April 20, 2015, http://www.rrc.state.tx.us/media/22204/barnettshale_totalnaturalgas _day.pdf.

3. Zuckerman, *The Frackers,* 63.

4. Based on ibid.

5. Based on data from BP Statistical Review of World Energy 2015 database, accessed June 2015.

6. Yergin, *The Quest*, 318.

7. Based on data from Jeff Hayden and Dave Pursell, "The Barnett Shale: Visitors Guide to the Hottest Play in the US," Pickering Energy Partners, Inc., October 2005, http://www.tphco.com/Websites/tudorpickering/Images/Reportspercent20Archives/TheBarnettShaleReport.pdf; and Texas Railroad Commission, "Texas Barnett Shale Total Natural Gas Production."

8. Based on data from BP Statistical Review of World Energy 2015 database, accessed June 2015.

9. Based on data from Baker Hughes Rig Count database, accessed April 2015, http://www.bakerhughes.com/rig-count.

10. Yergin, *The Quest*, 163.

11. Based on data from BP Statistical Review of World Energy 2015 database, accessed June 2015.

12. Yergin, *The Quest*, 223.

13. Based on data from BP Statistical Review of World Energy 2015 database, accessed June 2015.

14. Ibid.

15. Based on data from Bloomberg database, accessed April 2015.

16. Yergin, *The Quest*, 236.

17. Benjamin Kunkel, "World Without Oil, Amen," *GQ*, July 2008.

18. Based on data from Energy Information Administration database, accessed April 2015.

19. Based on data from Bloomberg database, accessed April 2015.

20. Steve Gelsi, "New 'Super-Spike Might Mean $200 a Barrel Oil," Marketwatch, March 7, 2008.

21. Based on data from Energy Information Administration database, accessed April 2015.

22. Ibid.

23. Based on data from Baker Hughes Rig Count database, accessed April 2015.

24. Based on data from Energy Information Administration database, accessed April 2015.

3. Shalemania and Science Experiments

1. Based on data from Bloomberg database, accessed June 2015.

2. Based on data from Chesapeake Energy Corporation, 2003 10-K, March 15, 2014.

3. Zuckerman, *The Frackers*, 193.

4. Ibid., 223.

5. Based on Chesapeake Energy Corporation, 2008 10-K, March 2, 2008, 40.

6. Zuckerman, *The Frackers*, 200.

7. Trefis Team, "A Look at Chevron's Key Deepwater Projects," *Forbes*, March 26, 2014.

8. Ben Casselman, "Chesapeake, Plains Set to Tap Gas Field," *Wall Street Journal*, July 3, 2008.

9. Ibid.

10. Adam Nossiter, "Gas Rush Is On, and Louisianans Cash In," *New York Times*, July 29, 2008.

11. Based on data from Bloomberg database, accessed April 2015.

12. Mark J. Kaiser and Yunke Yu, "Haynesville Update—1: North Louisiana Gas Shale's Drilling Decline Precipitous," *Oil and Gas Journal*, December 2, 2013.

13. Based on data from Energy Information Administration database, accessed April 2015.

14. Hayden and Pursell, "The Barnett Shale."

15. Associated Press, "Shell Abandons Oil-Shale Project in Colorado After Pumping Millions into Exploration," September 25, 2013.

16. Based on data from Energy Information Administration database, accessed April 2015.

17. Based on data from Baker Hughes Rig Count database, accessed April 2015.

18. Zuckerman, *The Frackers,* 147–49.

19. Arun Jayaram, "EOG Resources (EOG): The Harvard of Shale Drills a Prolific East Texas Well," Credit Suisse, May 14, 2014.

20. C. Mark Pearson, "Hydraulic Fracturing of Horizontal Wells," Society of Petroleum Engineers, March 2013, http://www.spealaska.org/wp-content/uploads/2013/05/2012-13-DLS-Presentation-on-Horizontal-Well-Fracturing-03-13.pdf.

21. PacWest Consulting, e-mail to author.

22. Based on data from BP Statistical Review of World Energy 2015 database, accessed June 2015; and Energy Information Administration database, accessed April 2015.

23. Zuckerman, *The Frackers*, 271.

24. Ibid., 284.

25. Gold, *The Boom*, 201.

26. Joshua Schneyer and Jeanine Prezioso, "After McClendon's Trades, Chesapeake Board Gave Blessing," Reuters, May 5, 2012.

27. Zuckerman, *The Frackers*, 300.

4. How the Oil Business Reversed Gravity

1. Based on data from Energy Information Administration database, accessed April 2015.

2. Ibid.

3. Based on data from Edmunds database, accessed April 2015, http://www.edmunds.com/industry-center/data/market-share-by-manufacturer.html.

4. Based on data from Baker Hughes Rig Count database, accessed April 2015.

5. Arun Jayaram and Jan Stuart, "U.S. Natural Gas: Update on Fundamentals," Credit Suisse, February 2015.

6. ITG, "No More Guessing," May 2015, 40.

7. Based on data from World Bank database, accessed April 2015; BP Statistical Review of World Energy 2015 database, accessed June 2015; Energy Information Administration database, accessed April 2015; and United States Census Bureau database, accessed April 2015.

8. Author interview with Manuj Nikhanj; and ITG, "No More Guessing," 39.

9. Based on data from Bloomberg database, accessed April 2015.

10. Henry Tarr et al., "420 Projects to Change the World: Executive Summary," Goldman Sachs, May 15, 2015.

11. Based on data from International Energy Agency, "Oil Market Report," March 13, 2015.

12. Russell Gold, "Fracking Gives U.S. Energy Boom Plenty of Room to Run," *Wall Street Journal*, September 14, 2014.

13. Ana Campoy, Mark Peters, and Erica E. Phillips, "Oil States' Budgets Face Crude Awakening," *Wall Street Journal*, January 12, 2015.

14. Based on data from BP Statistical Review of World Energy 2015 database, accessed June 2015.

15. Joe Carroll, "Exxon Confounds XTO Deal Critics by Swelling Oil Holdings," *BloombergBusiness*, February 27, 2014.

16. Based on data from Energy Information Administration database, accessed April 2015.

17. Based on data from BP Statistical Review of World Energy 2015 database, accessed June 2015.

18. Yergin, *The Quest*, 371.

Part II: The Local Perspective

5. The Fox in the Frack House

1. Mike Soraghan, "Groundtruthing Academy Award Nominee 'Gasland,'" *New York Times*, February 24, 2011.

2. Energy in Depth, "Debunking Gasland," November 2011, http://energyindepth.org/wp-content/uploads/2011/11/Debunking-Gasland.pdf.

3. Josh Fox, *Gasland,* quoted in Soraghan, "Groundtruthing Academy Award Nominee 'Gasland.'"

4. Vincent Carroll, "'Gasland' Versus Colorado," *Denver Post,* January 31, 2011.

5. Steve Everley, "From Flaming Faucet to Flaming Hose: The Continuing Fraud of Gasland," Energy in Depth, July 7, 2013, http://energyindepth.org/national/the-continuing-fraud-of-gasland/.

6. Seamus McGraw, *The End of Country* (New York: Random House, 2011), 215.

7. Laura Legere, "DEP Cites Persistent Flaws in Cabot Wells and Keeps Drilling on Hold in Parts of Dimock," *Times Tribune* (Scranton), May 7, 2011.

8. "Halliburton Cements Wells," American Oil and Gas Historical Society, accessed May 2015, http://aoghs.org/technology/cementing-oil-wells/.

9. Based on data from Pennsylvania Department of Environmental Protection Database, accessed April 2015, http://www.depreportingservices.state.pa.us/ReportServer/Pages/ReportViewer.aspx?/Oil_Gas/Wells_Drilled_By_County.

10. Based on data from Pennsylvania Department of Environmental Protection, "Water Supply Determination Letters," accessed May 2015, http://files.dep.state.pa.us/OilGas/BOGM/BOGMPortalFiles/OilGasReports/Determination_Letters/Regional_Determination_Letters.pdf.

11. McGraw, *End of Country*, 155, 204.

12. Laura Legere, "DEP Lets Cabot Resume Dimock Fracking," *Times Tribune* (Scranton), August 22, 2012.

13. Laura Legere, "DEP Drops Dimock Waterline Plans; Cabot Agrees to Pay $4.1M to Residents," *Times Tribune* (Scranton), December 16, 2010.

14. McGraw, *End of Country*, 215.

15. Ian Urbina, "A Tainted Water Well, and Concern There May Be More," *New York*

Times, August 3, 2011; and Steve Early, "EID Statement on (Latest) Joint Effort by NYT/ Environmental Working Group Aimed at Attacking Natural Gas," Energy in Depth, August 3, 2011, http://energyindepth.org/national/eid-statement-on-latest-joint-effort -by-nytenvironmental-working-group-aimed-at-attacking-natural-gas/.

16. Environmental Protection Agency, "Assessment of the Potential Impacts of Hydraulic Fracturing for Oil and Gas on Drinking Water Resources," June 2015, ES-6, http:// cfpub.epa.gov/ncea/hfstudy/recordisplay.cfm?deid=244651.

17. Ibid., 10–20.

18. Ibid., 6–57.

19. Jennifer Hiller, "Players in Eagle Ford Shale Work on Upping Their Games," *San Antonio Express-News*, September 17, 2014.

20. "§ 78.83. Surface and Coal Protective Casing and Cementing Procedures," The Pennsylvania Code, http://www.pacode.com/secure/data/025/chapter78/s78.83.html; and Oklahoma Corporation Commission, "Oklahoma Hydraulic Fracturing State Review," January 2011, http://www.occeweb.com/STRONGER%20REVIEW-OK -201-19-2011.pdf.

21. "Groundwater Advisory Unit," Texas Railroad Commission, accessed April 2015, http://www.rrc.state.tx.us/oil-gas/applications-and-permits/groundwater-advisory -unit/.

22. "HT-400™ Pump," Halliburton, http://www.halliburton.com/public/cem/contents /Data_Sheets/web/H/H04798.pdf.

23. Simmons & Company, "Perspectives on the U.S. Pressure Pumping Market," August 6, 2014.

24. PacWest Consulting, e-mail to author.

25. Manuj Nikhanj, e-mail to author.

26. Based on data from Frac Focus database, accessed May 2015, www.fracfocus.org; and Monika Freyman, "Hydraulic Fracturing & Water Stress: Water Demand by the Numbers," Ceres, February 2014, http://www.ceres.org/resources/reports/hydraulic -fracturing-water-stress-water-demand-by-the-numbers.

27. Environmental Protection Agency, "Potential Impacts of Hydraulic Fracturing," ES-6.

28. Ibid., 4–8.

29. Ibid., 4–4.

30. Based on data from U.S. Geological Survey Water Use Data for the Nation database, accessed June 2015, www.waterdata.usgs.gov; Energy Information Administration database, accessed April 2015; and Environmental Protection Agency, "Outdoor Water Use in the United States," August 2008, http://www.epa.gov/WaterSense/docs/ws _outdoor508.pdf.

31. Alison Sider, "Demand for Sand Takes Off Thanks to Fracking," *Wall Street Journal*, August 4, 2014.

32. "Chemical Use in Hydraulic Fracturing," FracFocus, accessed May 2015, https:// fracfocus.org/water-protection/drilling-usage.

33. McGraw, *End of Country*, 101.

34. Cole Mellino, "EPA Report Finds Nearly 700 Chemicals Used in Fracking," Eco-Watch, April 1, 2015, http://ecowatch.com/2015/04/01/epa-700-chemicals-fracking/.

35. Mellino, "EPA Report Finds Nearly 700 Chemicals Used in Fracking"; and Environmental Protection Agency, "Potential Impacts of Hydraulic Fracturing," ES-11.

36. "What Chemicals Are Used," FracFocus, accessed April 2015, http://www.fracfocus .org/chemical-use/what-chemicals-are-used.

37. Catherine Tsai, "Halliburton Executive Drinks Fracking Fluid at Conference," Associated Press, August 22, 2011.

38. Environmental Protection Agency, "Potential Impacts of Hydraulic Fracturing," 3–12; and "The Basics: What Is Groundwater," Groundwater.org, accessed May 2015, http://www.groundwater.org/get-informed/basics/groundwater.html.

39. "NWISWeb: New Site for the Nation's Water Data," U.S. Geological Survey, accessed June 2015, http://waterdata.usgs.gov/nwis/si; and "The Basics: What Is a Well," Groundwater.org, accessed May 2015, http://www.groundwater.org/get-informed /basics/wells.html.

40. Environmental Protection Agency, "Potential Impacts of Hydraulic Fracturing," 6–33.

41. Ibid., 6–47.

42. "Hydraulic Fracturing: The Process," FracFocus, accessed April 2014, https://fracfocus .org/hydraulic-fracturing-how-it-works/hydraulic-fracturing-process.

43. PacWest Consulting, e-mail to author.

44. Shawn C. Maxwell, "Hydraulic Fracture Height Growth," *Recorder* (Canadian Society of Exploration Geophysicists), November 2011, http://csegrecorder.com/articles/view /hydraulic-fracture-height-growth.

45. Based on "Water Usage Chart," Washington Suburban Sanitation Commission, accessed April 2015, http://www.wsscwater.com/home/jsp/content/water-usagechart .faces.

46. Michael Dale and Sally Benson, "Energy Balance of the Global Photovoltaic (PV) Industry—Is the PV Industry a Net Electricity Producer?," *Environmental Science and Technology*, February 26, 2013, http://pubs.acs.org/doi/abs/10.1021/es3038824.

47. Environmental Protection Agency, "Potential Impacts of Hydraulic Fracturing," ES-6.

48. Jon Entine, "Gas Heat," *Philanthropy*, Summer 2014.

49. Scott Waldman, "State to Make Fracking Ban Official, Not Permanent," Capital New York, April 29, 2015.

50. See, for example, Nicholas St. Fleur, "Fracking Chemicals Detected in Pennsylvania Drinking Water," *New York Times,* May 4, 2015.

51. "The Water in You," U.S. Geological Survey, accessed May 2015, http://water.usgs .gov/edu/propertyyou.html.

52. ITG, "Energy Market Wrap," December 17, 2014.

6. When Fracking Doesn't Mean Fracking Anymore

1. Based on Energy Information Administration database, accessed May 2015.

2. Environmental Protection Agency, "Potential Impacts of Hydraulic Fracturing," ES-6.

3. McGraw, *End of Country*, 102; and "Oil and Gas Production Waste," Environmental Protection Agency, accessed April 2015, http://www.epa.gov/radiation/tenorm /oilandgas.html#howmuchradiation.

4. Environmental Protection Agency, "Potential Impacts of Hydraulic Fracturing," ES-13.

5. Norimitsu Onish, "A California Oil Field Yields Another Prized Commodity," *New York Times*, July 7, 2014.

6. John Veil, "U.S. Produced Water Volumes and Management Practices in 2012," Groundwater Protection Council, April 2014, http://www.gwpc.org/sites/default /files/Produced%20Water%20Report%202014-GWPC_0.pdf.

7. Based on data from Energy Information Administration database, accessed April 2015.

8. Jim Efstathiou Jr., "Radiation in Pennsylvania Creek Seen as Legacy of Frackin [*sic*]," *BloombergBusiness*, October 2, 2013.

9. Environmental Protection Agency, "Potential Impacts of Hydraulic Fracturing," 8–33.

10. Based on data from Energy Information Administration database, accessed April 2015.

11. "Indoor Water Use in the United States," Environmental Protection Agency, accessed May 2015, http://www.epa.gov/WaterSense/pubs/indoor.html; and John Veil, "U.S. Produced Water Volumes and Management Practices in 2012."

12. ITG, "Induced Seismicity: Disposing of Some Earthquake Myths," April 22, 2015.

13. Rivka Galchen, "Weather Underground," *New Yorker*, April 13, 2015.

14. Based on data from Energy Information Administration database, accessed April 2015.

15. Galchen, "Weather Underground."

16. Oklahoma Corporation Commission, "Media Advisory—Ongoing OCC Earthquake Response," March 25, 2015, http://www.occeweb.com/News/2015/03-25 -15%20Media%20Advisory%20-%20TL%20and%20related%20documents.pdf.

17. "What We Are Doing," Oklahoma Corporation Commission, accessed May 2015, http://earthquakes.ok.gov/what-we-are-doing/.

18. Jennifer Reeger, "Man Pleads Guilty to Dumping Millions of Gallons of Waste," *Pittsburgh Tribune-Review*, February 11, 2012.

19. Based on data from Spears & Associates.

20. Thomas Darrah et al., "Noble Gases Identify the Mechanisms of Fugitive Gas Contamination in Drinking-Water Wells Overlying the Marcellus and Barnett Shales," *Proceedings of the National Academy of Sciences of the United States of America*, September 9, 2014, http://www.pnas.org/content/early/2014/09/12/1322107111.full.pdf+html.

21. Environmental Protection Agency, "Potential Impacts of Hydraulic Fracturing," 8–23; and "Class II Wells—Oil and Gas Related Injection Wells (Class II)," Environmental Protection Agency, accessed June 2015, http://water.epa.gov/type/groundwater/uic /class2/.

22. Environmental Protection Agency, "Potential Impacts of Hydraulic Fracturing," 5–75.

23. Amy Mall, "Incidents Where Hydraulic Fracturing Is a Suspected Cause of Drinking Water Contamination," Natural Resources Defense Council, accessed April 2015, http://switchboard.nrdc.org/blogs/amall/incidents_where_hydraulic_frac.html.

24. Based on data from Pennsylvania Department of Environmental Protection, "Water Supply Determination Letters," accessed May 2015; and Pennsylvania Department of Environmental Protection database, accessed May 2015.

25. Bruce Finley, "Oil and Gas Spills Surge, Two a Day, Residents Often Not Notified," *Denver Post*, July 29, 2014; and Colorado Oil and Gas Conservation Commission,

"Spill Analysis by Year 1999–4thQtr 2014," accessed June 2015, http://cogcc.state
.co.us/documents/data/downloads/environmental/SpillAnalysisByYear.pdf.

26. Colorado Oil and Gas Conservation Commission, "Spill Analysis by Year 1999–4thQtr
2014."

27. Deborah Sontag and Robert Gebeloff, "The Downside of the Boom," *New York
Times*, November 22, 2014.

28. Based on data from Energy Information Administration database, accessed June 2015.

29. Based on data from Energy Information Administration database, accessed April
2015; and BP Statistical Review of World Energy 2015 database, accessed June 2015.

30. Anthony Cotton, "Oil Spill from Tank Dumps 7,500 Gallons into Poudre River Near
Windsor," *Denver Post*, June 20, 2014.

31. Encana, "Truck Traffic During the Stages of a Well," accessed June 2015, https://
www.encana.com/pdf/communities/usa/truck-traffic.pdf.

32. Jason Morris, "Texas Family Plagued with Ailments Gets $3M in 1st-of-Its-Kind
Fracking Judgment," CNN, April 26, 2014.

33. Energy Information Administration, "North Dakota Aims to Reduce Natural Flaring," October 20, 2014, http://www.eia.gov/todayinenergy/detail.cfm?id=18451.

34. Based on data from Bureau of Labor Statistics database, accessed April 2015, http://
www.bls.gov/iif/.

35. Based on data from City-Data.com database, accessed April 2015, http://www.city
-data.com.

36. Ibid.

37. Richard Heinberg, *Snake Oil: How Fracking's False Promise of Plenty Imperils Our Future*
(Santa Rosa, California: Post Carbon Institute, 2013), 88.

38. McGraw, *End of Country*, 10.

39. Ibid., 75

40. See, for instance, Peter M. Rabinowitz et al., "Proximity to Natural Gas Wells and Reported Health Status: Results of a Household Survey in Washington County, Pennsylvania," *Environmental Health Perspectives*, September 14, 2014, http://ehp.niehs.nih.gov/wp
-content/uploads/advpub/2014/9/ehp.1307732.pdf; and Katie Brown, "Yale Health
Study Misses the Mark on Fracking," Energy in Depth, September 11, 2014, http://
energyindepth.org/national/yale-health-study-misses-the-mark-on-fracking/.

41. Soraghan, "Groundtruthing Academy Award Nominee 'Gasland.'"

42. Kate Sinding, "Adding Injury to Insult: Cabot Wants Dimock Residents to Drink Polluted Water," Natural Resources Defense Council, accessed April 2005, http://
switchboard.nrdc.org/blogs/ksinding/adding_injury_to_insult_cabot.html.

43. Based on data from Bureau of Labor Statistics Quarterly Census of Employment and
Wages database, accessed April 2015.

44. St. Fleur, "Fracking Chemicals Detected in Pennsylvania Drinking Water."

45. Shale Gas Subcommittee of the Secretary of Energy Advisory Board, "Ninety-Day
Report," Department of Energy, August 11, 2011, http://www.shalegas.energy.gov
/resources/081111_90_day_report.pdf.

46. Lisa Song, "In Rare Effort, Ohio Scientist to Test Water Before Fracking Soars," Inside Climate News, July 8, 2014, http://insideclimatenews.org/news/20140708
/rare-effort-ohio-scientist-test-water-fracking-soars.

47. Environmental Protection Agency, "Potential Impacts of Hydraulic Fracturing," 8–18 and 8–31.

48. Reuters, "France's Hollande Rules Out Shale Gas Exploration," July 14, 2013.

49. Sontag and Gebeloff, "The Downside of the Boom."

50. "Act 13 Frequently Asked Questions," Pennsylvania Department of Environmental Protection, accessed April 2015, http://www.portal.state.pa.us/portal/server.pt /community/act_13/20789/act_13_faq/1127392.

51. Sontag and Gebeloff, "The Downside of the Boom."

52. Michael E. Porter, David S. Gee, and Gregory J. Pope, "America's Unconventional Energy Opportunity," Harvard Business School and The Boston Consulting Group, June 2015.

53. "Tracking and Reporting Foodborne Disease Outbreaks," Centers for Disease Control and Prevention, accessed March 2015, http://www.cdc.gov/features/dsfoodborneoutbreaks/.

54. New York State Department of Health, "A Public Review of High Volume Hydraulic Fracturing for Shale Gas Development," December 2014, http://www.health.ny .gov/press/reports/docs/high_volume_hydraulic_fracturing.pdf.

55. Based on data from Baker Hughes Rig Count database, accessed April 2015.

56. Paraphrased by Allan Bloom, *The Closing of the American Mind* (New York: Simon & Schuster, 1985), 85.

Part III: The Financial Perspective

7. The Two Trillion–Dollar Revolution

1. Brian Singer et al., "Dear E&P CEO," Goldman Sachs, March 6, 2015.

2. Based on data from Energy Information Administration database, accessed April 2015.

3. Based on data from Energy Information Administration database, accessed April 2015; and Simmons & Company.

4. Yergin, *The Quest*, 230.

5. Based on data from BP Statistical Review of World Energy 2015 database, accessed June 2015.

6. Ibid.

7. Based on data from ITG, "No More Guessing: Hardcore"; and Energy Information Administration database, accessed May 2015.

8. Manuj Nikhanj, e-mail to author.

9. Tom Fowler and Ben Lefebvre, "Oil Boom Spurs New Investment," *Wall Street Journal,* December 27, 2012.

10. Adam Nossiter, "Gas Rush Is On, and Louisianians Cash In," *New York Times,* July 29, 2008.

11. Author interview with Manuj Nikhanj.

12. Christopher Helman, "The Two Sides of Aubrey McClendon, America's Most Reckless Billionaire," *Forbes,* October 5, 2011.

13. National Association of Royalty Owners, "National Association of Royalty Owners— Rockies Chapter Asks Colorado's Oil and Gas Task Force to Not 'Unduly Burden Mineral Owners,'" September 25, 2014.

14. Based on data from Pioneer Natural Resources, 2014 10-K and Annual Report, February 19, 2015, 110.

8. The Internet of Oil

1. Justin Fox, "The Disruption Myth," *Atlantic,* October 2014.
2. Based on data from BP Statistical Review of World Energy 2015 database, accessed June 2015.
3. "The World's Billionaires," *Forbes,* accessed April 2015, http://www.forbes.com /billionaires/list/3/#version:static.
4. Robert Wood, "Harold Hamm's $975 Million Divorce Check: First Rejected, Then Cashed, Now Taxed," *Forbes,* accessed May 2015.
5. Zuckerman, *The Frackers,* 146.
6. Based on Oklahoma Christian University, "Harold Hamm—Oklahoma Christian Q&A," accessed May 2015, https://www.youtube.com/watch?v=bcQyLr4wLhM.
7. Zuckerman, *The Frackers,* 156, 167.
8. Ibid., 154.
9. Caroline Preston, "10 Families Add Their Names to Giving Pledge," Philanthropy .com, April 28, 2011, https://philanthropy.com/article/10-Families-Add-Their -Names-to/158521.
10. Zuckerman, *The Frackers,* 171.
11. Ibid., 166.
12. Ibid.
13. Ibid., 294.
14. Ibid., 253.
15. Based on data from Energy Information Administration database, accessed April 2015.
16. Based on data from Continental Resources, Inc., 2008 10-K, February 27, 2009, 2.
17. John Kuehner, "Ohio Was Once Oil King, but Production Peaked in 1896," Resilience .org, accessed May 2015, http://www.resilience.org/stories/2005-07-30/ohio-was-once -oil-king-production-peaked-1896.
18. Singer et al., "Dear E&P CEO."
19. Jill Lepore, "The Disruption Machine," *New Yorker,* July 23, 2014.
20. Based on data from Bloomberg database, accessed April 2015.
21. Soraya Permatasari, "BHP Agrees to Buy Petrohawk for $12.1 Billion to Secure Gas," *BloombergBusiness,* July 15, 2011; and Christopher Helman, "Shale Gas Mania: BHP Pays Up in $15 Billion Deal for Petrohawk," *Forbes,* July 15, 2011.
22. Alexis Flynn, "BHP Puts Fayetteville Shale Gas Assets Up for Sale," *Wall Street Journal,* October 27, 2014.
23. Based on data from Bloomberg database, accessed May 2015.

9. *Guar and Lease,* or Another Side of Disruption

1. Leo Tolstoy, *War and Peace,* trans. Richard Pevear and Larissa Volokhonsky (New York: Vintage, 2008), 754.
2. Ibid., 785.
3. Ibid., 605.
4. Zuckerman, *The Frackers,* 165.
5. Ibid., 10.

6. Ibid., 76.

7. Gold, *The Boom*, 108.

8. Rebecca Leung, "Why Is America So Fat," *60 Minutes,* July 12, 2004; and Malcolm Gladwell, "The Pima Paradox," *New Yorker,* February 2, 1998.

9. David Einhorn, Sohn Investment Conference Presentation, Greenlight Capital, May 4, 2014, https://www.greenlightcapital.com/926698.pdf.

10. Zuckerman, *The Frackers*, 142.

11. Based on data from Bloomberg database, accessed April 2015.

12. Based in part on Zuckerman, *The Frackers*, 129.

13. Based on data from Bloomberg database, accessed April 2015.

14. East Resources, "East Resources, Inc. to Expand Natural Gas Operations in Appalachian Basin's Marcellus Shale Region," June 9, 2009.

15. Kohlberg Kravis Roberts & Co., 2010 Annual Report, accessed June 2015, http://www.kkr.com/ar/power_of_partnership/east_resources.html.

16. "The World's Billionaires," *Forbes*, accessed April 2015.

17. "Terry Pegula," *Forbes*, accessed April 2015, http://www.forbes.com/profile/terrence -pegula/.

18. "'You Didn't Build That,' Uncut and Unedited," FactCheck.org, July 23, 2012, http://www.factcheck.org/2012/07/you-didnt-build-that-uncut-and-unedited/.

19. Ryan Dezember, "Energy Investor Bets on Aubrey McClendon's Second Act," *Wall Street Journal*, November 24, 2014.

Part IV: The Global Perspective

10. When Rachel Carson Meets Al Gore

1. Based on data from National Centers for Environmental Information database, accessed April 2015, http://www.ncdc.noaa.gov/cag/time-series/global.

2. Intergovernmental Panel on Climate Change, "2014: Climate Change 2014: Synthesis Report. Contribution of Working Groups I, II, and III to the Fifth Assessment Report of the Intergovernmental Panel on Climate Change [Core Writing Team: R. K. Pachauri and L. A. Meyer, eds.]," 2015, http://www.ipcc.ch/report/ar5/syr/.

3. Based on data from BP Statistical Review of World Energy 2015 database, accessed June 2015.

4. Based on data from World Bank database, accessed June 2015.

5. William Nordhaus, *The Climate Casino: Risk, Uncertainty, and Economics for a Warming World* (New Haven: Yale University Press, 2013), 40.

6. "Addressing Ocean Pollution and Climate Change," Oceana.org, accessed March 2015, http://oceana.org/en/our-work/climate-energy/climate-change/learn -act/the-greenhouse-effect.

7. Steven Graham, "Svante Arrhenius," NASA Earth Observatory, January 28, 2000, http://earthobservatory.nasa.gov/Features/Arrhenius/.

8. David Wogan, "Why We Know About the Greenhouse Gas Effect," *Scientific American*, May 16, 2013.

9. Denise Robbins, "Myths and Facts About the Koch Brothers," Media Matters, August 27, 2014, http://mediamatters.org/research/2014/08/27/myths-and-facts-about -the-koch-brothers/200570; and Suzanne Goldberg, "Exxon Knew of Climate

Change in 1981, Email Says—but It Funded Deniers for 27 More Years," *Guardian*, July 8, 2015.

10. Lee Raymond, "Energy—Key to Growth and a Better Environment for Asia-Pacific Nations," Presentation at World Petroleum Congress, October 13,1997, https://www.heartland.org/sites/all/modules/custom/heartland_migration/files/pdfs/2957.pdf.

11. "Poverty Overview," World Bank, accessed March 2015, http://www.worldbank.org/en/topic/poverty/overview#1.

12. "Energy Poverty," International Energy Agency, accessed March 2015, http://www.iea.org/topics/energypoverty/.

13. Based on data from World Bank database, accessed April 2015.

14. Ben Casselman, "Sierra Club's Pro-Gas Dilemma," *Wall Street Journal*, December 22, 2009.

15. Gold, *The Boom*, 249.

16. Ibid., 259.

17. Ibid., 240.

18. Ibid., 249.

19. Based on data from International Energy Agency, "Oil Market Report," March 13, 2015.

20. Based on data from Energy Information Administration database, accessed April 2015.

21. "How Much Carbon Dioxide Is Produced When Different Fuels Are Burned?," Energy Information Administration, accessed March 2015, http://www.eia.gov/tools/faqs/faq.cfm?id=73&t=11.

22. Based on data from Energy Information Administration database, accessed April 2015.

23. Michael Grunwald, "Inside the War on Coal," Politico, May 2015.

24. Based on data from Energy Information Administration database, accessed April 2015.

25. Based on data from Energy Information Administration database, accessed April 2015; and United States Census Bureau database, accessed April 2015.

26. Based on data from Global Carbon Atlas database, accessed March 2015.

27. Based on data from Energy Information Administration database, accessed April 2015.

28. Based on data from Global Carbon Atlas database, accessed March 2015.

29. Ibid.

30. Based on data from Bureau of Economic Affairs database, accessed March 2015, http://www.bea.gov/national/xls/gdplev.xls.

31. Based on data from Google Public Data database, accessed March 2015, http://www.google.com/publicdata/explore.

32. Robert F. Kennedy Jr., "How to End America's Deadly Coal Addiction," *Financial Times*, July 19, 2009.

33. Kenneth P. Vogel, "John Kerry, Swift Boat Backer Meet," Politico, March 3, 2010.

34. "The Plan," Pickens Plan, accessed May 2015, http://www.pickensplan.com/the-plan/.

35. "Time for Lansing to Catch, Not Ignore, the New-Tech Energy Wave," 5 Lakes Energy, accessed July 2015, http://5lakesenergy.com/time-for-lansing-to-catch-not-ignore-the-new-tech-energy-wave/.

36. "About," American Clean Skies Foundation, accessed March 2014, http://www.cleanskies.org/about/.

37. Marie Cusick, "Robert F. Kennedy Jr. Calls Natural Gas a 'Catastrophe,'" NPR, October 3, 2013, http://stateimpact.npr.org/pennsylvania/2013/10/03/robert-f-kennedy -jr-calls-natural-gas-a-catastrophe/.

38. Bill Steele, "Ben Nichols, Professor Emeritus, Former Mayor of Ithaca and Lifelong Activist, Dies at 87," *Cornell Chronicle*, November 26, 2007.

39. Entine, "Gas Heat."

40. Shale Gas Subcommittee, "Ninety-Day Report," 19.

41. "Overview of Greenhouse Gases," Environmental Protection Agency, accessed April 2015, http://www.epa.gov/climatechange/ghgemissions/gases.htm and http://epa .gov/climatechange/ghgemissions/gases/ch4.html.

42. Based on data from Environmental Protection Agency, "Inventory of U.S. Greenhouse Gas Emissions and Sinks: 1990–2013," April 15, 2015, http://www.epa.gov /climatechange/Downloads/ghgemissions/US-GHG-Inventory-2015-Main-Text.pdf.

43. "Frequently Asked Questions: UT Methane Study," Environmental Defense Fund, accessed May 2015, http://www.edf.org/climate/methane-studies/UT-study-faq.

44. Robert W. Howarth, Renee Santoro, and Anthony Ingraffea, "Methane and the Greenhouse-Gas Footprint of Natural Gas from Shale Formations: A Letter," Cornell University, March 31, 2011, //www.acsf.cornell.edu/Assets/ACSF/docs/attachments /Howarth-EtAl-2011.pdf.

45. Dana R. Caulton et. al,. "Toward a Better Understanding and Quantification of Methane Emissions from Shale Gas Development," *Proceedings of the National Academy of Sciences,* April 29, 2014.

46. David T. Allen, et. al, "Measurements of Methane Emissions at Natural Gas Production Sites in the United States," *Proceedings of the National Academy of Sciences of the United States,* October 19, 2013, http://www.pnas.org/content/110/44/17768.full.pdf.

47. "Frequently Asked Questions: UT Methane Study," Environmental Defense Fund.

48. Bobby Magill, "Fracking May Emit Less Methane than Previous Estimates," Climate Central, September 16, 2013, http://www.climatecentral.org/news/study-fracking -emits-less-methane-than-estimated-16483.

49. Ibid.

50. Rebecca Leber, "Why Cow Farts and Belches Are Obama's Next Big Targets on Climate Change," *New Republic,* July 31, 2014.

51. Andrew C. Revkin, "Two Climate Analysts Fault Gas Leaks, but Not as a Big Warming Threat," *New York Times,* August 1, 2013.

52. Based on data from Environmental Protection Agency database, accessed April 2015, http://epa.gov/climatechange/ghgemissions/usinventoryreport.html.

53. Based on data from Environmental Protection Agency database, accessed April 2015; and data from Energy Information Administration database, accessed May 2015.

54. The White House, "Climate Action Plan: Strategy to Reduce Methane Emissions," March 28, 2014.

55. Robert Pear, "In Final Spending Bill, Salty Food and Belching Cows Are Winners," *New York Times*, December 14, 2014.

56. Jennifer A. Dlouhy, "Energy Department: U.S. Must Act Now on Methane Emissions," Fuel Fix, October 20, 2014, http://fuelfix.com/blog/2014/10/20/energy -department-u-s-must-act-now-on-methane-emissions/.

57. Based on data from Global Carbon Atlas database, accessed March 2015.

58. "Green in the Barnett Shale," Devon Energy, accessed May 2015, http://www .devonenergy.com/featured-stories/green-completions-the-standard-in-barnett-shale.

59. Rachael Bunzey, "Natural Gas and Green Completion in a Nut Shell," Energy in Depth, November 26, 2012, http://energyindepth.org/marcellus/natural-gas-and -green-completion-in-a-nut-shell/.

60. Charles Mann, "How to Talk About Climate Change So People Will Listen," *Atlantic*, September 2014.

61. "Frequently Asked Questions: UT Methane Study," Environmental Defense Fund.

62. Environmental Defense Fund, "Methane Research: The 16 Study Series," accessed May 2015, https://www.edf.org/sites/default/files/methane_studies_fact_sheet.pdf.

63. Based on data from Energy Information Administration database, accessed April 2015.

64. Based on data from Bloomberg database, accessed July 2015.

65. Based on data from Energy Information Administration database, accessed April 2015.

11. On to All of the Above

1. Based on data from Baker Hughes Rig Count database, accessed April 2015.

2. Based on data from Energy Information Administration database, accessed April 2015; and BP Statistical Review of World Energy 2015 database, accessed June 2015.

3. "How Much Carbon Dioxide Is Produced," Energy Information Administration.

4. Based on data from World Bank database, accessed June 2015.

5. Based on data from and BP Statistical Review of World Energy 2015 database, accessed June 2015.

6. Based on data from Michael Cohen et al., "The Blue Drum: Everybody Hurts," Barclays, January 28, 2015, 18, 22.

7. Based on data from International Energy Agency, "Oil Market Report," June 11, 2015.

8. Based on data from Global Carbon Atlas database, accessed March 2015.

9. Pavel Molchanov and Carlos Newall, "Energy Stat: How Many Electric Vehicles Can the U.S. Power Grid Handle?," Raymond James, March 2, 2015.

10. Edmunds.com, "Hybrid and Electric Vehicles Struggle to Maintain Owner Loyalty, Reports Edmunds.com," April 21, 2015.

11. James Hansen, "Game Over for the Climate," *New York Times*, May 9, 2012.

12. Based on data from and BP Statistical Review of World Energy 2015 database, accessed June 2015; and Canadian Association of Petroleum Producers, "Crude Oil Forecast, Markets & Transportation," June 2015, ii, http://www.capp.ca/publications -and-statistics/publications/264673.

13. IHS CERA, "Oil Sands, Greenhouse Gases, and US Oil Supply," November 2012, http://www.api.org/~/media/Files/%20Oil-and-Natural-Gas/Oil_Sands/CERA _Oil_Sands_GHGs_US_Oil_Supply.pdf.

14. Coral Davenport, "Keystone Pipeline Pros, Cons and Steps to a Final Decision," *New York Times*, November 18, 2014.

15. Canadian Association of Petroleum Producers, "Crude Oil Forecast, Markets & Transportation," 7.

16. Peter Tertzakian, "It's 'Business Not As Usual' in Alberta," *Financial Post,* May 4, 2015.

17. Bill McKibben, *Oil and Honey: The Education of an Unlikely Activist* (New York: St. Martin's Griffin, 2014), 65.

18. Ibid.

19. Bill McKibben, "Global Warming's Terrifying New Math," *Rolling Stone,* July 19, 2012.

20. Raymond T. Pierrehumbert, "A Real Deal," Slate, November 17, 2014.

21. Bill McKibben, *Oil and Honey*, 228.

22. "Divestment Commitments," Fossil Free, accessed June 2015, http://gofossilfree.org /commitments/

23. "S&P 500," S&P Dow Jones Indices, accessed July 2015, http://us.spindices.com /indices/equity/sp-500.

24. Drew Faust, "Fossil Fuel Divestment Statement," Harvard University, accessed March 2015, http://www.harvard.edu/president/fossil-fuels.

25. Benjamin M. Friedman, "Industrial Evolution," *New York Times,* December 9, 2007.

26. "The End of the Oil Age," *Economist*, October 23, 2003.

27. Based on data from Energy Information Administration database, accessed April 2015.

28. Justin Gillis, "Sun and Wind Alter Global Landscape, Leaving Utilities Behind," *New York Times*, September 13, 2014.

29. Ehren Goosens, "Wind Power Rivals Coal with $1 Billion Order from Buffett," *BloombergBusiness*, December 17, 2013.

30. Based on data from Global Carbon Atlas database, accessed March 2015.

31. Based on data from World Bank database, accessed June 2015.

32. Based on data from BP Statistical Review of World Energy 2015 database, accessed June 2015.

33. Yergin, *The Quest*, 223.

34. Based on data from Global Carbon Atlas database, accessed March 2015.

35. Bill McKibben, *Oil and Honey*, 18

36. Based on data from BP Statistical Review of World Energy 2015 database, accessed June 2015; and Canadian Association of Petroleum Producers database, accessed April 2015, http://www.capp.ca/library/statistics/basic/Pages/default.aspx.

37. Based on data from BP Statistical Review of World Energy 2015 database, accessed June 2015.

38. "Mercury and Air Toxics Standards (MATS) Basic Information," Environmental Protection Agency, accessed April 2015, http://www.epa.gov/mats/basic.html.

39. Brian Chin, et. al, "Supreme Court Emissions Ruling Not an Inflection Point," Bank of America Merrill Lynch, June 29, 2015, 1.

40. United States General Accountability Office, "Update on Agencies' Monitoring Efforts and Coal-Fueled Generating Unit Retirements," August 2014, http://www.gao.gov /assets/670/665325.pdf.

41. Based on data from Bloomberg database, accessed July 2015.

42. Based on data from Bureau of Labor Statistics Quarterly Census of Employment and Wages database, accessed April 2015; and Scott Wartman, "Fact Checking the 'War on Coal,'" *Cincinnati Enquirer*, October 18, 2014.

43. Based on data from Energy Information Administration database, accessed April 2015; and Grunwald, "Inside the War on Coal."

44. Based on data from Baker Hughes Rig Count database, accessed April 2015.

45. Edward Wong, "In Step to Lower Carbon Emissions, China Will Place a Limit on Coal Use in 2020," *New York Times*, November 20, 2014.

46. Jacob Gronholt-Pedersen and David Stanway, "China's Coal Use Falling Faster Than Expected," Reuters, March 26, 2015.

47. Energy Information Administration, "Shale Oil and Shale Gas Resources Are Globally Abundant," January 2, 2014, http://www.eia.gov/todayinenergy/detail.cfm?id=14431.

48. Charles C. Mann, "Renewables Aren't Enough. Clean Coal Is the Future," *Wired*, March 2014.

49. The White House, Office of the Press Secretary, "Obama Administration Finalizes Historic 54.5 MPG Fuel Efficiency Standards," August 28, 2012.

50. Coral Davenport, "Obama to Take Action to Slash Coal Pollution," *New York Times*, June 1, 2014.

51. Mark Landler, "U.S. and China Reach Climate Accord After Months of Talks," *New York Times*, November 11, 2014.

52. Erik Voeten, "How the Lima Accord May Nudge Countries to Do Better on Climate Change (but Won't Solve the Problem)," *Washington Post,* December 14, 2014.

53. Coral Davenport, "Obama Builds Environmental Legacy with 1970 Law," *New York Times,* November 26, 2014.

54. The White House, Office of the Press Secretary, "President Barack Obama's State of the Union Address," January 28, 2014.

55. Pierrehumbert, "A Real Deal."

Part V: The National Perspective

12. Renaissance After Renaissance?

1. Based on data from Energy Information Administration database, accessed June 2015.

2. *The Simpsons,* https://www.youtube.com/watch?v=hUVwR0rw5fk.

3. Edward L. Morse et al., "Energy 2020: North America, the New Middle East," Citigroup, March 20, 2012, 3.

4. "Shale Oil and Shale Gas Resources Are Globally Abundant," Energy Information Administration, January 2, 2014.

5. Based on data from Canadian Association of Petroleum Producers database, accessed May 2015.

6. Based on distances from Toronto to Edmonton, Alberta and Toronto to Waynesburg, Pennsylvania, according to Google Maps database, accessed March 2015.

7. Tarr et al., "420 Projects to Change the World," 35.

8. Christina Larson, "Water Shortages Will Limit Global Shale Gas Development, Especially in China," *BloombergBusiness*, September 2, 2014.

9. Based on data from Energy Information Administration database, accessed April 2015; "China's 2014 Shale Gas Output at 1.3 Bcm," Natural Gas Asia, accessed June 2015, http://www.naturalgasasia.com/chinas-2014-shale-gas-output-at-1.3-bcm-14498; and Tarr et al., "420 Projects to Change the World" 20.

10. Emily Gosden, "Fracking Plans Rejected: Lancashire Council Throws Out Cuadrilla Proposal—Live," *The Telegraph,* June 29, 2015.

11. Based on data from BP Statistical Review of World Energy 2015 database, accessed June 2015.

12. Henry Chu, "Pressure Builds Against France's Ban on Fracking," *Los Angeles Times,* June 22, 2014.

13. Danny Hakim, "Bulgaria's Air Is Dirtiest in Europe, Study Finds, Followed by Poland," *New York Times,* October 15, 2013.

14. Andrew Higgins, "Russian Money Suspected Behind Fracking Protests," *New York Times,* November 30, 2014; and Jim Yardley and Jo Becker, "How Putin Forged a Pipeline Deal That Derailed," *New York Times,* December 30, 2014.

15. Based on data from World Bank database, accessed April 2015; and Elizabeth Konstantinova and Joe Carroll, "Bulgaria Bans Gas Fracking, Thwarting Chevron Drilling Plan," *BloombergBusiness,* January 19, 2012.

16. Based on data from Bureau of Labor Statistics Quarterly Census of Employment and Wages database, accessed April 2015.

17. Ibid.

18. Ibid.

19. Ibid.

20. American Petroleum Institute, "State of American Energy 2013," http://www.api.org/~/media/Files/Policy/SOAE-2013/SOAE-Report-2013.pdf.

21. American Petroleum Institute, "Economic Impacts of the Oil and Natural Gas Industry in 2011," July 2013, http://www.api.org/~/media/Files/Policy/Jobs/Economic_impacts_Ong_2011.pdf.

22. Morse et al., "Energy 2020," 80.

23. Based on data from Energy Information Administration database, accessed April 2015.

24. Based on data from Bureau of Labor Statistics Quarterly Census of Employment and Wages database, accessed April 2015.

25. Based on data from International Trade Administration TradeStats Express database, accessed April 2015.

26. Based on data from Energy Information Administration database, accessed April 2015.

27. Based on data from Bloomberg database, accessed April 2015.

28. Based on data from International Trade Administration TradeStats Express database, accessed April 2015.

29. Based on data from World Bank database, accessed April 2015.

30. Congressional Budget Office, "The Economic and Budgetary Effects of Producing Oil and Natural Gas from Shale," December 9, 2014, https://www.cbo.gov/publication/49815.

31. Morse et al., "Energy 2020," 78.

32. Based on data from World Bank database, accessed June 2015.

33. Based on data from Texas Comptroller of Public Accounts, accessed July 2015, http://www.texastransparency.org/State_Finance/Revenue/Revenue_Watch/.

34. Daniel Raimi and Richard G. Newel, "Oil and Gas Revenue Allocation to Local Governments in Eight States," Duke University Energy Initiative, October 2014,

http://energy.duke.edu/sites/energy.duke.edu/files/files/Oil%20Gas%20Revenue%20Allocation%20to%20Local%20Government%20FINAL.pdf.

35. Kathleen Madigan, "5 Ways Falling Oil Prices Are Helping the Economic Numbers," *Wall Street Journal*, October 24, 2014.

36. Based on data from World Bank database, accessed April 2015; and International Energy Agency, "Oil Market Report," March 13, 2015.

37. Based on data from International Energy Agency, "Oil Market Report," March 13, 2015.

38. Based on data from Bureau of Labor Statistics Consumer Expenditure Survey database, accessed April 2015, http://www.bls.gov/cex/2013/combined/quintile.pdf.

39. Based on data from Energy Information Administration database, accessed July 2015.

40. Based on data from Bureau of Labor Statistics Consumer Expenditure Survey database, accessed April 2015.

41. Based on data from International Trade Administration TradeStats Express database, accessed April 2015.

42. Ibid.

43. Morse et al., "Energy 2020," 81.

44. U.S. Department of Commerce Bureau of Economic Analysis, "U.S. International Transactions: Fourth Quarter and Year 2014," March 19, 2015, http://www.bea.gov/newsreleases/international/transactions/transnewsrelease.htm.

45. Based on data from Energy Information Administration database, accessed April 2015.

46. Based on data from BP Statistical Review of World Energy 2015 database, accessed June 2015.

47. ITG, "No More Guessing: Hardcore," 39.

48. Based on data from Energy Information Administration database, accessed April 2015.

49. Ibid.

50. Based on data from International Trade Administration TradeStats Express database, accessed April 2015.

51. Porter, Gee, and Pope, "America's Unconventional Energy Opportunity," 2.

52. Based on data from Bureau of Labor Statistics Quarterly Census of Employment and Wages database, accessed April 2015.

53. Nigel Coe et al., "Manufacturing Renaissance: Is It a Masterpiece or a (Head) Fake?," Morgan Stanley, April 29, 2013, 11.

54. Based on data from World Bank database, accessed April 2015.

55. Ibid.

56. Ibid.

57. Ibid.

58. James Hagerty, "Whirlpool Shifts Some Production to U.S. from Mexico," *Wall Street Journal*, December 19, 2013.

59. Charles Fishman, "The Insourcing Boom," *Atlantic,* December 2012.

60. Sam Oliver, "Tim Cook Lauds 'American Manufacturing Expertise' During Visit to Texas Mac Pro Factory," Apple Insider, June 6, 2014.

61. Fishman, "The Insourcing Boom."

62. Based on data from State of the Union Project of Onetwothree.net database, accessed May 2015, http://stateoftheunion.onetwothree.net/.

63. Based on data from World Bank Database, accesssed April 2015.

64. Based on data from Bureau of Labor Statistics Quarterly Census of Employment and Wages database, accessed April 2015.

65. Ibid.

66. Nelson D. Schwartz, "Boom in Energy Spurs Industry in the Rust Belt," *New York Times*, September 9, 2014.

67. American Chemistry Council, "Shale Gas and New U.S. Chemical Industry Investment."

68. Associated Press, "Methanex Moving 2nd Plant from Chile to Louisiana," April 26, 2013.

69. Based on data from Bentek database, accessed April 2015.

70. American Chemistry Council, "New US Chemical Industry Investment: An Analysis Based on Announced Projects," May 2013, http://chemistrytoenergy.com/sites/chemistrytoenergy.com/files/shale-gas-full-study.pdf.

71. Based on data from International Trade Administration TradeStats Express database, accessed April 2015.

72. Coe et al., "Manufacturing Renaissance," 29.

73. Based on data from Bureau of Labor Statistics Quarterly Census of Employment and Wages database, accessed April 2015.

74. Ben Geman, "Manufacturers Go to War with Oil Industry Over Gas Exports," *The Hill,* January 10, 2013.

75. Harold L. Sirkin, Michael Zinser, and Justin R. Rose, "The Shifting Economics of Global Manufacturing," Boston Consulting Group, August 2014.

76. Ibid., 18.

77. Based on data from Energy Information Administration database, accessed May 2015; and World Bank database, accessed April 2015.

78. Coe et al., "Manufacturing Renaissance," 16.

79. Ibid., 15.

80. Jeff Bennett and Cameron McWhirter, "Volvo Car to Build First U.S. Car Plant in South Carolina," *Wall Street Journal*, May 11, 2015.

81. Neil Irwin, "In Battle Between Strong Dollar and Cheap Gas, the Strong Dollar Is Winning," *New York Times*, April 23, 2015.

82. Eric Yep, "Price for LNG in Asia Falls to Lowest Level in Nearly Four Years," *Wall Street Journal*, December 9, 2014.

13. And the Land of the Free

1. Matthew 25:30 (New King James Version).

2. Based on data from BP Statistical Review of World Energy 2015 database, accessed June 2015.

3. Based on data from CIA World Factbook database, accessed April 2015, https://www.cia.gov/library/publications/the-world-factbook/rankorder/2242rank.html.

4. Based on data from World Bank database, accessed April 2015.

5. Energy Information Administration, "Oil and Natural Gas Sales Accounted for 68%

of Russia's Total Export Revenues in 2013," July 23, 2014, http://www.eia.gov /todayinenergy/detail.cfm?id=17231; and "Nigeria," Energy Information Administration, accessed May 2015, http://www.eia.gov/countries/cab.cfm?fips=NI.

6. Yergin, *The Quest*, 110.

7. Based on data from Energy Information Administration database, accessed April 2015; and BP Statistical Review of World Energy 2015 database, accessed June 2015.

8. Elliot Bentley, Pat Minczeski, and Jovi Juan, "Which Oil Producers Are Breaking Even?" *Wall Street Journal*, May 20, 2015 update.

9. Based on data from World Bank database, accessed April 2015.

10. Ibid.

11. Based on data from Bloomberg database, accessed April 2015.

12. See also Yergin, *The Quest*, 149.

13. Based on data from Energy Information Administration database, accessed April 2015.

14. James Earl Carter, "The State of the Union Address Delivered Before a Joint Session of the Congress," American Presidency Project, January 23, 1980, http://www .presidency.ucsb.edu/ws/?pid=33079.

15. Based on data from World Bank database, accessed April 2015; and BP Statistical Review of World Energy 2015 database, accessed June 2015.

16. Based on data from World Bank database, accessed April 2015; and Energy Information Administration database, accessed April 2015.

17. Michael Levi, *The Power Surge: Energy, Opportunity, and the Battle for America's Future* (New York: Oxford University Press, 2013).

18. Based on data from BP Statistical Review of World Energy 2015 database, accessed June 2015.

19. Ben Hubbard, "Despite Displeasure with U.S., Saudis Face Long Dependency," *New York Times*, May 11, 2015.

20. Organization of the Petroleum Exporting Countries, "OPEC Annual Statistical Bulletin 2014," http://www.opec.org/opec_web/static_files_project/media/downloads /publications/ASB2014.pdf.

21. "Analysis Madrassas," *Frontline*, accessed April 2015, http://www.pbs.org/wgbh/pages /frontline/shows/saudi/analyses/madrassas.html.

22. George F. Will, "The Wisdom of Pat Moynihan," *Washington Post*, October 1, 2010.

23. BBC, "Ukraine Votes to Drop Non-Aligned Status," December 23, 2014.

Conclusion

1. Based on data from ITG, "No More Guessing: Hardcore."

2. Ibid.

3. Yergin, *The Quest*, 269.

4. Based on data from Energy Information Administration database, accessed April 2015.

5. Tarr et al., "420 Projects to Change the World," 31.

INDEX